Handouts for Psychotherapy

Tools for Helping People Change

Elsbeth Martindale, PsyD

Portland, Oregon

To all the clients
who have shaped, honed, and challenged me
to be effective in my work.

Contents

Acknowledgments vii

Introduction ix

Therapist's Directions and PDFs xi

Part I. BASIC TRAINING

Goals for Therapy 3-5
    Client's View 3
    Therapist's View 5
Session Goals 7
Session Summary 9
Self-Observation 11
Mood Chart 13
Feelings List 15
Needs List 17
Getting Needs Met 19
Strengths List 21
Higher Self Qualities 23
Higher Self Practice 25
Self-Compassion Break 27
Self-Compassion Exercises 29-31
Self-Soothing Statements 33
Self-Empathy Practice 35
ROLF Filter 37
Retroactive Learning 39
Why Questions 41
Five States of Being 43
Four Versions of the Self 45
Therapy Summary Sheet 47

Part II. SYMPTOM CARE

Stress Boulders 51
Crisis Management 53
Depression Pit 55
Critic Catcher 57
Hold Yourself in a Positive Light 59

Elsbeth Martindale
CLINICAL PSYCHOLOGIST

Anger Balloon 61

Anger Continuum 63

Distress Tolerance Activities 65-67

Letters to Myself When I'm Depressed 69

Grief and Loss 71

Grief and Loss Ritual 73

Goodbye Letter 75

Part III. SELF-CARE

Assess Your Support 79

Restoration and Rejuvenation 81

Resilience Building 83

Resiliency Factors 85

Self-Encouragement 87

Self-Care 101 89

Selfishness Defined 91-94

Give Yourself a Hand 95

Gratitude Homework 97

Making Life Sweeter 99

Savoring the Moment 101

Stages of Change 103

Motivation to Change 105

Self-Reinforcement 107

Landing Pads 109

Journal Protector 111-113

Caregiving Assessment 115-123

Commitments to Better Self-Care 125

Gems of Wisdom 127

Part IV. HEALTHY CONNECTION

RELATIONSHIPS

Differentiation vs. Fusion 131

Ladder of Differentiation 133

Managing Self in Conflict 135

Conflict in Relationships 137

I'm Sorry vs. What I Wish I Would Have Done Differently 139

COMMUNICATION

Hidden Feelings and Needs 141

Five-Finger Communication 143

Reflective Listening 145

Elsbeth Martindale
CLINICAL PSYCHOLOGIST

Reflective Listening Practice 147
Who Owns the Problem? 149
Five Ways to Say It..51
Reflective Shield..153-155
Content-to-Process Shift..157

BOUNDARIES
Boundary Fences..159
Characteristics of Healthy Boundaries 161

MAKING CONNECTION
Encouragement...163
Twenty-Second Hug 165
Kudos Catcher 167
Phone Nap Pad...169

Part V. ENHANCEMENT AND GROWTH

DEEPER EXPLORATION
Existential Givens...173
Questions About Existential Givens 175
Contentment Defined..177-179
The Person I Want to Become 181
Playing Angels 183
Qualities of Wisdom 185
Imagine Outrageous Success 187
Values in Action - Strength Inventory...189
Identifying Core Values 191
Common Values 193
Meta-Perspective..195
Meta-Perspective Expanders 197
Trigger Fingers...199-201
    Noticing Automatic Reactions 199
    Managing Automatic Reactions 201

GROUP THERAPY
Group Therapy Invitation..203-205
Group Therapy Cheat Sheet...207
Group Therapy Contract..209

HEALING WORK
Aggress Energy...211
Making Space for Healing Work..213
Collecting Stories of Injury 215

Elsbeth Martindale
CLINICAL PSYCHOLOGIST

Healing Old Wounds...217-219

Part VI. PROFESSIONAL ENHANCEMENT

Stress Symptoms for Therapists.. 223
Trauma Exposure Response.. 2135
Professional Self-Care Assessment...227-231
Professional Self-Care Solutions..233-235
Buoyancy Factors for Therapists..237
Super Hard Questions..239-241
Healing Salves...243-247
Creating Handouts and Tools.. 249

Index.. 251

Elsbeth Martindale
CLINICAL PSYCHOLOGIST

Elsbeth Martindale
CLINICAL PSYCHOLOGIST

Elsbeth Martindale
CLINICAL PSYCHOLOGIST

Acknowledgments

I have been honed, taught, and transformed by the clients who have shown me their challenges, who have been vulnerable with their woundedness, and who have allowed me entrance into their inner worlds. These individuals have trusted my intention and attention to help identify the missing ingredients they needed to create and sustain a meaningful life. I have been honored, humbled and enriched by my experiences with each of their contributions. It is through this journey with my clients that I have identified the essential psycho-educational tools and high level skills which, when implemented, lead to a life of greater contentment and ease.

Outside the office I have been supported by colleagues who have encouraged and believed in my mission. Paul Elmore, Colleen Moloney, Julianna Waters, Susan Wilmoth, TJ Christenson, and countless others have been beside me throughout this process of identification, distillation, and dissemination of effective tools and strategies for successful psychotherapy. Special thanks to Ruthie Matinko-Wald, whose editing talent made this manuscript sing. My sweet husband, Gerry, has been my biggest champion, encouraging me to do what I do "because it is art." I am blessed to be so surrounded by the kindness and generosity of such excellent mentors and friends.

Introduction

I've been a practicing therapist for over thirty years. I am a trained expert in offering a safe and comfortable environment where my clients can get curious about their lives. In this environment they can begin to explore what stands in the way of their health, comfort, or success. Beyond a healing and nonjudgmental setting, my work is enhanced by taking on the role of psycho-educator, teacher, and coach. There are many basic tenets of psychology, personal growth, and wisdom which individuals benefit from exploring, understanding, and integrating into their day-to-day lives. My role is to provide them this information in a manner that is accessible and easily digested. I want my clients to catch these concepts readily and implement these ideas with deftness. In the service of these goals, I love making handouts for my clients.

You have before you a compilation of my most useful handouts. These are the tools I use over and over again in my work. When talking with clients about a skill they could develop, a concept which could bring clarity to their struggle, or a method for change which could benefit from practice, I will pull out an explanatory handout as a way to assist their understanding. The handouts are not designed to be a substitute for deep and personalized conversation, but rather a summary of a useful concept that needs integration specific to their concern. Often clients benefit by seeing the universality of their issues, helping them not feel so alone in their suffering. Clients gain comfort by seeing how common human challenges have been studied and useful tools and strategies have been developed for managing them. This can be quite a relief. My job is to bring these ideas into view and explore with my clients how this wisdom can be used and skillfully applied to their own unique circumstances.

I often give a handout to a client with instructions to go home and share the concept with another, maybe a spouse or a friend. By explaining the concept to another solidifies the client's own understanding. Teaching others is often the best way to deeply integrate new learning. Others in the client's life may also benefit from learning what the client is gaining during therapy sessions. Sometimes I ask clients to teach the concept to me, in a following session, so I can assess their understanding and integration of the material. In using handouts, as with all other therapeutic interventions, it is important to assess a client's readiness and openness to an educative experience. Certainly not all clients will be receptive or find value in being taught something new. The therapist must be able to read a client's openness before placing a teaching handout in the client's lap. Within my practice, a majority of my clients love receiving these handouts. Some keep a notebook of the tools they acquire so they can remind themselves of these important psychological principles long after therapy is over.

I welcome you to make copies of these pages to offer to your clients. Use these handouts as inspiration for your own creation of useful tools specific to your therapy style and interests. I hope this collection of psycho-educational teaching handouts will build both your confidence and your effectiveness.

Elsbeth

Elsbeth Martindale
CLINICAL PSYCHOLOGIST

Therapist's Directions and PDFs

Each handout comes with a set of directions for therapists on the page opposite the handout. These directions provide a description of the handout, how I use it, and, often, an example from my practice.

Included in the directions, below the title of the handout, is a PDF link to the handout on my website. This will allow you to send an electronic copy of any of the handouts in this book to clients. I ask that you only use the handouts for the purpose of enhancing your work with your clients. Please do not post any handouts on the Internet without explicit consent from me.

Elsbeth Martindale
CLINICAL PSYCHOLOGIST

PART I

Basic Training

The Basic Training handouts offer the foundational tools, attitudes, and skills upon which effective therapy is built. Herein are tools for setting goals and reviewing accomplishments, tools for discussing the importance of objective observation—necessary for directing change—and tools for productive exploration of the inner world. Several handouts speak to the importance of holding an attitude of kindness toward self when pursuing introspection and change. When clients understand the concepts made visible in these handouts, they are set up to be empowered and successful in their therapy.

Goals for Therapy......3-5
    Client's View 3
    Therapist's View......5
Session Goals 7
Session Summary......9
Self-Observation......11
Mood Chart......13
Feelings List......15
Needs List 17
Getting Needs Met......19
Strengths List......21
Higher Self Qualities......23
Higher Self Practice......25
Self-Compassion Break......27
Self-Compassion Exercises 29-31
Self-Soothing Statements 33
Self-Empathy Practice......35
ROLF Filter 37
Retroactive Learning 39
Why Questions 41
Five States of Being......43
Four Versions of the Self......45
Therapy Summary Sheet......47

Goals for Therapy - Client's View

elsbethmartindale.com/goal-sheets-clients-view

Setting goals is a HUGE part of what makes psycho-educational therapy so effective. Right from the start, I encourage my clients to think in a solution-focused rather than problem-focused manner. I find it helpful to steer early therapy discussions away from what's wrong to a discussion of how clients want things to be. This future-focused view privileges solutions over problems. I want to know what my clients desire and how strongly they're willing to fight to bring about change. I want to activate a visioning of what's possible. I want to quickly make an alliance with the parts of the client that are motivated to make adjustments. Looking at goals in the first session allows these things to come into clear view.

How I use this:

In the first session, as part of my informed consent, I talk about the value and benefit of being goal driven in our work together. I say, *"You are here (pointing to the client sitting on the couch), you want to go there (pointing to the other side of the room), and you are hiring me to help you get there. Since I want to know what my job is, I need you to describe the outcome as clearly as possible. What do you want to get out of our work together? How do you want things to be different?"* This explanation is sufficient for clients to shift to a solution-driven focus for our work.

I then give the *Goals for Therapy - Client's View* to my clients, asking them to fill out the handout and bring it to their next session. I show them the *Goals for Therapy - Therapist's View* and explain that this is *my* homework to do before we meet again. I tell them we will look together at our individual goal sheets at the beginning of our next session and compare notes. I say, *"By the end of our second session together, you will know whether I get you or not. You will see that I have strategies for you to consider in moving toward your goals. If I don't get you or you don't like my strategies, then you might want to ask for a referral to a therapist more in alignment with your needs."* By this second session, they are usually completely bought-in to the process of effective therapy. They see they have a therapist that gets them, takes seriously their desire to make things better, and has clear ideas of how to make changes and progress toward their self-defined goals. They also hear loud and clear that change is going to come about by the actions *they* take and not through some magic created by talking about their problems.

Elsbeth Martindale
CLINICAL PSYCHOLOGIST

Goals for Therapy
- Client's View

Name _____ Date _____

When therapy is complete, I hope to:

1 _____

_____

2 _____

_____

3 _____

_____

The steps or methods I will use to achieve these goals might include:

1 _____

_____

2 _____

_____

3 _____

_____

How will we both know when therapy is done? How will you be different? What will we both see?

_____

_____

What you get by achieving your goals is not as important as what you become by achieving your goals.
- Henry David Thoreau

Goals for Therapy - Therapist's View

elsbethmartindale.com/goal-sheets-therapist-view

The Therapist's View of goals includes three sections: the hopes, steps, and methods. These three areas allow me to develop a plan for change. I take the role of an architect by designing a structure or plan for shifting my clients from where they are to where they want to be. I want the plan to be attainable with clear steps and strategies. I want to instill hope in the attainment of their desires, and I want to demonstrate competence as an effective guide for this process—something like, *"Trust me. I know the way."*

In the first section, I clarify the three goals I heard the client identify in the first session. I want to list the goals in an action-oriented manner which focuses on the client's agency for change (e.g., "Get along better with mom," or "Have more meaningful interactions" rather than "Not have mom be so upset with me all the time."). The focus should be on what to do rather than on what needs to stop.

In the Steps section, I want to identify the broader-picture actions (e.g., "Create more peaceful and joyous interactions with mom, less conflict and arguing."). I include here what will need to occur to help the clients reach their goals (e.g., "Learn or review effective communication skills, both sending and listening skills.").

In the Methods section, I want to list the specific strategies the clients will need to implement in order to achieve their goals (e.g., Read *Non-Violent Communication*. Role-play difficult conversations in therapy. Learn to listen for and speak about needs effectively.)

When the plan for treatment is spelled out like this, clients have clear reason to trust. They see their therapist listened well and understands them. They can lean in to the process because the therapist has identified a specific plan of action based on their desired outcome. The clients can feel assured they are in good hands and can trust the therapist knows what they are doing. The journey can begin on a strong foundation.

The goals for therapy can be reviewed anytime during the course of treatment. If the therapy is not progressing as desired, the goals can be brought out to see how therapy may have gone off course or if new goals need to be identified. When therapy is complete, reflecting on the original goals that are now partially or fully accomplished can be very rewarding, for both client and therapist!

Elsbeth Martindale
CLINICAL PSYCHOLOGIST

Goals for Therapy
- Therapist's View

Name _____ Date _____

When therapy is complete, my client hopes to:

1 _____

_____

2 _____

_____

3 _____

_____

The steps on the way to achieving these goals include:

1 _____

_____

2 _____

_____

3 _____

_____

The methods that will be used to achieve these goals include:

1 _____

_____

2 _____

_____

3 _____

_____

Elsbeth Martindale
CLINICAL PSYCHOLOGIST

Session Goals

elsbethmartindale.com/session-goals-and-summary

Some clients really find it valuable to think through what they need or want to talk about in their sessions. These *Session Goals* sheets are ideal for helping create a structure for the content of their session. The *Session Summary* sheets give a chance to capture the things learned in the session so they don't evaporate immediately after leaving the office.

How I use this:

I leave a stack of these in the waiting area for clients to pick up before they come into my office. I tell my clients, *"Some people really like having a way to structure their thoughts before they come into their sessions. These sheets are available to fill out before our meetings, either at home or in the waiting room. Stay after your session, if you want, and capture some of the ideas we discussed today. This is not at all a requirement, but, if it helps you, use it."*

Example from practice:

Aiko wanted to get the most out of her therapy. She only had eight weeks before she returned to college. She set up weekly appointments to address the conflicts she was experiencing with her father while home on summer break. Aiko was serious, conscientious, and driven. She absolutely loved the idea of being organized for each of her therapy sessions. The Session Goal sheet gave her a place to outline the concerns she wished to address, and what she hoped to achieve, in each session. This format helped direct Aiko from a simple discussion of her frustration to a focus on her hopes and desires for change. Bringing awareness to her needs helped lead to a clarification of the strategies she could use in addressing her concerns.

Elsbeth Martindale
CLINICAL PSYCHOLOGIST

Session Goals

Date _____

Important topics to cover today:

1)

2)

3)

4)

5)

What I hope to get out of today's session is:

The needs most prominent for me today include:

Elsbeth Martindale
CLINICAL PSYCHOLOGIST

Session Summary

elsbethmartindale.com/session-goals-and-summary

It is often helpful for clients to capture the essence of what they discover during a session. It may be a key concept, new insight, acquisition of a new skill, an affirmation to hold for the week to come, or a homework idea. All these seem to benefit by being captured in writing. I often think of therapy as sort of a dream state wherein, once clients walks out the door, all the content of the session seems to evaporate when met with the realities of everyday life. I provide paper and pen in my office for clients to take notes during sessions. Some prefer to capture content on their phones. This Session Summary sheet is another way to encourage clients to hold tight to what they are learning and the changes they are attempting to implement in their lives.

How I use this:
See *Session Goals* description.

Example from practice:
Aiko was delighted to have a place to record what she learned in each session. She was serious about making changes in her relationship with her father. Each week she left therapy with a plan for how to respond differently to the conflicts she was experiencing at home. She particularly appreciated the value of coming up with a script for what she could say to herself to help her remain steadfast in her plan. Aiko would stay ten minutes after each session and write up her session summary in the waiting room before leaving my building. She was absolutely serious about doing what she could to make things better at home. The *Session Summary* sheet helped her anchor her intentions, remind her of her strategies, and identify ways to support herself in following through.

Elsbeth Martindale
CLINICAL PSYCHOLOGIST

Session Summary

What will I take away from today's session?

What is the most important thing for me to tell myself this week?

What actions do I intend to take this week?

Self-Observation

elsbethmartindale.com/self-observation

I was shown a similar image many years ago in a workshop—a picture of an eye watching a human walking on the planet. I loved this image of a "self-observer." I believe this is what a good therapist teaches their clients to do: watch themselves from an objective place. I often ask my clients about their "relationship with themselves." It is a great way to help them think of how they support themselves, talk to themselves, and protect themselves. This handout helps set an image of this idea of being a witness to self.

How I use this:

This is a laminated handout in a holder of other laminated handouts within reach of my office chair. I reach over and show it to clients at least once a week. I show them the image and say, *"This is what we are creating in therapy: the eye that watches you walk on the planet."* I then explain the difference between the eye of compassion and the eye of the critic (as explained on the handout).

Self-observation is necessary for bringing about self-directed change. I often tell my clients, *"If you can't see it, you can't steer it."* By compassionately observing one's actions, attitudes, thoughts, and feelings, a sense of agency and authorship can emerge. When new skills are learned, in the ongoing process of therapy, an observing eye can see the effect of these new actions. Observing allows for the collection of data, information about what works and what doesn't. All science is founded on observation and data collection. I help my clients see they are able to use the scientific method (observe, gather data, hypothesize, experiment, repeat) in making desired changes.

I've made post-it notes with this image as well and will sometimes offer a sticky note to clients who need to have this image in front of them more often in order to remember to take an objective and guiding position in their own life. I suggest they post it on their dash board, computer screen, or bathroom mirror.

Example from practice:

Mateo wanted to be more mindful of his driving. He was in the habit of seeing traffic as a competitive game in which he strove to win. Recognizing this wasn't helping his anxiety, he chose to practice slowing down and removing himself from the game. He took a post-it note, with this watching eye, and put it on his dash board to help him remember his intention. This helped Mateo become more self-observant in other situations as well.

Elsbeth Martindale
CLINICAL PSYCHOLOGIST

Self-Observation

Self-observation is the first step in making changes. You must be able to see what's going on in order to be clear about what you want to be different. Therapy helps build self-observation from the place of compassion and guidance. It creates a dynamic relationship between the observer self and the actor self. Building a compassionate connection between the observer and the actor allows for guidance and direction, an invitation to move forward in a particular way. The critic, "the other eye," is also an observer, but it stands behind, not in front, kicking you in the backend when you get it wrong. Most people don't need help in developing a critic but appreciate assistance in beginning to see self from a guiding and compassionate position.

Elsbeth Martindale
CLINICAL PSYCHOLOGIST

Mood Chart

elsbethmartindale.com/mood-chart

Here is another tool for creating self-observation. This simple form is easy for clients to fill out each day to get a sense of the patterns of their moods and the things which alter their moods.

Many Mood Tracking Apps exist these days so this paper-and-pencil version is not necessary, although some people prefer it. Whatever the means, it is valuable to give clients some structure for what, and how, to observe themselves in their lives.

How I use this:

When I give this to clients I might say, ***"Here's a means for getting some data about how your mood varies and what might bring about mood shifts."*** I tell them to track the items listed and, if they want, add something on the blank lines they are interested in watching as well. I explain how the chart is designed so that things that are generally negative are marked in a way to fully fill the square, so they get a visual sense of when things are heavy and what excesses or absences might have led to the darker periods. This chart also offers women a way to see how their menstrual cycle impacts their mood and their behavior choices.

Example from practice:

It was challenging for Rayne to understand her shifting mood. She said, "One day I feel great and the next, just terrible." On the terrible days she had body pain, fatigue, and severe irritation. We pondered what could cause such a drastic shift from one day to the next. She hadn't recognized any patterns and couldn't give explanations for her "terrible days." We discussed keeping a mood chart to see if she could notice any contributing factors to these bad days. Although she struggled with daily recordings, she was able to stick with tracking her mood for several months and, as a result, began to notice a pattern. She discovered several important things. She found her mood didn't actually switch from one day to the next, as she had thought. She noticed she actually had many good days, in fact most days were good. And most significantly, Rayne noticed her "terrible days" came most frequently in the weeks preceding her menstrual cycle. With this new data, Rayne was able to predict her "terrible days," manage them with greater self-care, and begin treatment for PMDD through her medical doctor.

Elsbeth Martindale
CLINICAL PSYCHOLOGIST

Mood Chart

Mood Chart

Month _____ Year _____

Legend: □ None ● Mild ◨ Moderate ■ Severe

	1 2 3 4 5 6 7 8 9 10 11 12 13 14 15 16 17 18 19 20 21 22 23 24 25 26 27 28 29 30 31
Emotional	
Irritability	
Anxiety	
Depression	
Mood Swings	
Physical	
Headaches	
Over Eating	
No Exercise	
Poor Sleep	
Environmental	
Caffeine	
Chocolate	
Alcohol	
Stress	
Rel. Conflict	
Menstrual Cycle	

Elsbeth Martindale
CLINICAL PSYCHOLOGIST

Feelings List

elsbethmartindale.com/feelings-list

A feelings list is an important part of your therapist tool kit. Feeling words are the way humans explain their inner experiences. Some folks have a large emotional vocabulary, whereas others get stumped going beyond "good, bad, upset, and pissed."

I love that this list is organized in categories. This helps clients look at the nuances of a common feeling category to find a word that might most specifically capture their emotional world.

How I use this:

This is also a handout I laminate and have ready to pull out to present to clients. When they seem stuck for language to explain a current or past emotional experience, I can grab the list and ask them if they want a "cheat sheet" to help them identify the words that represent their experience most accurately. I might ask, *"Can you find a word on here that might closely match what's happening on the inside?"*

Example from practice:

Raji grew up in a home where feelings weren't commonly discussed nor expressed directly. This didn't pose a problem for him until he started dating. The young women he was attracted to seemed so much more capable of talking about themselves and their feelings, and this was both intriguing and perplexing to Raji. When the girl he was dating became aghast that he couldn't describe his reaction to being invited by her parents to their beach home, Raji decided it was time to visit my office. His sweet naiveté and innocence was coupled with a sincere desire to learn. He earnestly wanted to know how to become skillful at identifying his inner experience. When I showed Raji this *Feelings List,* he was shocked at the number of names for emotions.

We started by looking at the large categories of feelings and identifying times when he knew the experience of this emotion in his body. He soon realized he had known feelings without having language to describe them. We then looked at the nuanced differences between specific feeling words. Raji was delighted to broaden his vocabulary for his inner experience. He enjoyed the challenge of finding the words to represent what was happening on the inside. This, as you can imagine, brought a greater depth of connection with his girlfriend.

Feelings List

HURT
injured
isolated*
offended*
distressed
pained
afflicted
worried
crushed
heartbroken
tortured*
lonely
cold
unwanted*
criticized*

SAD
sorrowful
unhappy
depressed
melancholy
gloomy
dismal
heavy-hearted
quiet
mournful
dreadful
dreary
invisible*
flat
blah
dull
in the dumps
sullen
moody
sulky
out of sorts
low
discontented
worthless*
discouraged
disappointed
concerned
sympathetic
compassionate
choked up
embarrassed
shameful
inadequate*
ashamed
useless
worthless
ill-at-ease
despair
neglected*

ANGRY
resentful*
irritated
enraged
furious
annoyed
provoked*
infuriated
offended*
sullen
indignant
irate
wrathful
cross
sulky
bitter
frustrated
grumpy
boiling
fuming
stubborn
rejected*
belligerent
confused
awkward
bewildered

AFRAID
fearful
frightened
timid
wishy-washy
shaky
apprehensive
fidgety
terrified
panicky
tragic
hysterical
alarmed
cautious
shocked
horrified
insecure
impatient
nervous
dependent
anxious
pressured*
worried
doubtful
suspicious
hesitant
dismayed
scared

threatened*
appalled
petrified
gutless
jealous
distant

DOUBTFUL
bored
unbelieving
skeptical
distrustful
suspicious
dubious
questioning
evasive
wavering
hesitant
perplexed
indecisive
hopeless
powerless
helpless
defeated
pessimistic

EAGER
keen
earnest
intent
zealous
ardent
anxious
enthusiastic
desirous
excited
proud
aggressive

LOVING
close
sexy
tender
seductive
passionate
affectionate
appealing
warm
fond
devoted
caring
amorous
adoring
invested
appreciated*

INTERESTED
concerned
fascinated
engrossed
intrigued
absorbed
excited
curious
inquisitive
creative
cooperative
focused

HAPPY
festive
contented
relaxed
calm
complacent
serene
comfortable
peaceful
joyous
ecstatic
enthusiastic
inspired
glad
pleased
grateful
cheerful
excited
lighthearted
buoyant
carefree
surprised
optimistic
spirited
vivacious
brisk
sparkling
merry
generous
exhilarated
jolly
playful
elated
jubilant
thrilled

FEARLESS
encouraged
courageous
confident
secure
independent

reassured
bold
brave
daring
heroic
hardy
determined
loyal
proud
impulsive

PHYSICAL
taut
uptight
immobilized
paralyzed
tense
stretched
hollow
empty
strong
weak
sweaty
breathless
nauseated
sluggish
weary
repulsed
tired
alive
feisty

MISC.
humble
torn
mixed-up
phony
upset (too broad, find a
more specific word)

*Feelings mixed with
evaluation/judgment

Elsbeth Martindale
CLINICAL PSYCHOLOGIST

Needs List
elsbethmartindale.com/needs-list

We aren't often trained to think about our needs as things to consider but, my gosh, it is so helpful to understand the language of needs. I found the importance of understanding needs by reading *Non-Violent Communication* and studying with the author, Marshall Rosenberg. This material is invaluable in my work with clients.

Needs are the drivers of behavior. Being aware of what is compelling your action, or the actions of others, really helps you understand behaviors. Needs are often hidden from view and aren't identified or owned. When you get indirect and sneaky about getting your needs met, this can bring about a lot of confusion. I teach my clients to be clear about their needs and to listen for the underlying needs in others. Learning to be explicit about needs solves a lot of problems.

How I use this:
I often explain that needs are in four categories: **Foundational** needs for safety, security, and dependability; **Growth** needs for advancement, expansion, and creativity; **Relational** needs for connection and belonging; and **Independence** needs for autonomy and personal freedom.

When teaching clients about needs, I will often ask, ***"So, at this very moment you have needs and I have needs. I have a need to educate, connect, support, and encourage. You have a need for connection, growth, and enhancement."*** I explain how underlying needs are often hidden from view but can be found if we get curious. I explain how strategies differ from needs but often get confused when we speak. (See *Getting Needs Met.)* I explain that language in the form of a request (e.g., "Would you be willing to...") is often an effective means to getting needs met in relationship with others. (See *Five-Finger Communication.)*

Example from practice:
Naming a need seems simple enough, but James had a difficult time because he often mixed needs with strategies. When he would say, "I need *(you) to*...," we were headed straight for a strategy. I suggested he start his sentence with, "I have a need *for*...," and follow this with one of the words on the *Needs List*. This shift in framing allowed James to identify and name his core need from which he could then request adherence to a strategy. This slight change helped him be much clearer in communication.

Elsbeth Martindale
CLINICAL PSYCHOLOGIST

Needs List

Underlying all human behavior are sets of needs or drivers. These are the values that lead to action. Having language for these important drivers helps communicate to others the motivation for actions. When speaking about needs, it is best to start by saying, "I have a need for..."

FOUNDATIONAL

PHYSICAL BODY
air (clean)
cleanliness
clothing
exercise, movement food
health
protection
relaxation, rest
safety
sexual expression
shelter (warm, cold)
touch
water (clean)
well-being

SAFETY
communication
confidentiality
honesty, trust
protection, security
reliability
sincerity

DEPENDABILITY
communication
congruence
efficiency, planning
honesty
integrity
order, documentation
reliability
security
stability
trust

GROWTH

CREATIVITY
alone time
beauty, joy
focus, discipline
inspiration
originality
productivity
reassurance
seclusion
self-expression
sense of aliveness

INTEGRITY
authenticity
completeness
honesty
realness
sincerity
stability
straightforwardness
wholeness

PLAY
celebration
child-likeness
exercise
exuberance
free time
joy, delight
laughter, tears
light-heartedness
playfulness

CONTRIBUTION
freedom
fulfillment
joy
hope
meaning
productivity
progress

RELATIONAL

APPRECIATION
acknowledgment
admiration
adoration
celebration
mourning
self-esteem
reassurance
recognition
validation

COOPERATION
agreement
brainstorming
feedback
negotiation
openness, fairness
peace, harmony

planning
relationship
respect
trust

TEAMWORK
clarity, honesty
communication
connection
consideration
cooperation
flexibility
harmony
inclusion
realistic goals
reliability

COMMUNICATION
celebration
clarity, feedback
closeness, intimacy
confidentiality
connection
diplomacy
grieving
reassurance
requests
respect
safety, trust
sharing, honesty
to be heard, empathy
together time
understanding

INTERDEPENDENCE
belonging
brother/sisterhood
community
companionship
connection
cooperation
friendship
harmony
inclusion
intimacy
kindred spirit
relationship
reassurance
respect, trust
spiritual connection

NURTURING
companionship
connection
consideration
empathy
gentleness
softness
grieving
kindness, comfort
love, affection
support, compassion
tenderness
to be cherished
touch
warmth

INDEPENDENCE

TIME FOR SELF
balance, wholeness
downtime
empowerment
free time, quiet time
freedom, autonomy
laughter, tears
personal space
self-nurturance
spiritual communion
tranquility

AUTONOMY
acceptance, respect
authenticity
choice, freedom
confidence
consideration
dreams, goals, values
independence
self-governance

Elsbeth Martindale
CLINICAL PSYCHOLOGIST

Getting Needs Met

elsbethmartindale.com/getting-needs-met

This handout was developed after a week-long training in *Non-Violent Communication*. I created this diagram to explain the difference between needs and strategies. Strategies are the means by which we attempt to get our needs met. If the strategy is a good one, our needs are generally met. If our needs do not get met, it is often the result of picking a poor strategy.

How I use this:

I give this handout to my clients and say something like, *"We all have needs. They put pressure on our inner world in an attempt to be recognized and resolved. We form strategies, usually requests or actions, in an attempt to get our needs met. If our strategies are effective, happiness tends to naturally bubble up from our beings. An ineffective strategy often causes feelings of annoyance, sadness, or anger to surface."* The needs don't need to be changed, but our strategies can be shifted to see if we can find a way for our needs to be heard and met. I heard in my training that we should, "hold our needs tightly but our strategies lightly." The most effective strategy for asking others to support our needs is explained in the *Five-Finger Communication* handout.

Example from practice:

Christine really wanted her partner to be more engaged in parenting. She told me, "I need him to step up and do his part in being a dad." I affirmed her struggle and asked if she might want to clarify her needs to her partner to increase the odds of having her needs met. She explained how she has told him, time and again, how she needs him to do more discipline, help with care, and get on the floor to play with their son. I suggested she might get more cooperation if she explained her underlying needs, instead of naming the strategies for getting her needs met. This was a new concept for Christine, as she had not seen the distinction between needs and strategies. I pulled out this handout so I could explain how needs are universal and how they push us to form strategies for getting our needs met. I suggested her partner might be more open to hearing her deeper longing than hearing her directions for how he should behave. Christine was able to identify her underlying needs for cooperation, ease, and connection. She formed a request to address these needs, "I have a need for more cooperation and ease in parenting. Would you be willing to play on the floor with the baby so I can make dinner tonight?" This clarity helped Christine get out of nagging and directing, allowing her to be more expressive and known to her partner.

Elsbeth Martindale
CLINICAL PSYCHOLOGIST

Getting Needs Met

Getting your needs met is an essential part of life. You will be most successful in having your needs heard and addressed if you choose effective strategies. Effective strategies create the likelihood of joy and contentment. Hold your needs tightly and your strategies lightly!

Generally Ineffective Strategies:
- Labeling "You are _____."
- Punishment "If You _____ , I'm Gonna _____."
- Denial of Choice "Must, Should, Have to..."
  Demands
- Blame or Withdrawal
- Mix Feeling Words with Judgment

Generally Effective Strategies:
- State an Observation
- State Your Feelings and Needs
- Make a Clear Request
- Ask About the Other's Response
  to Your Request
- Offer Choice

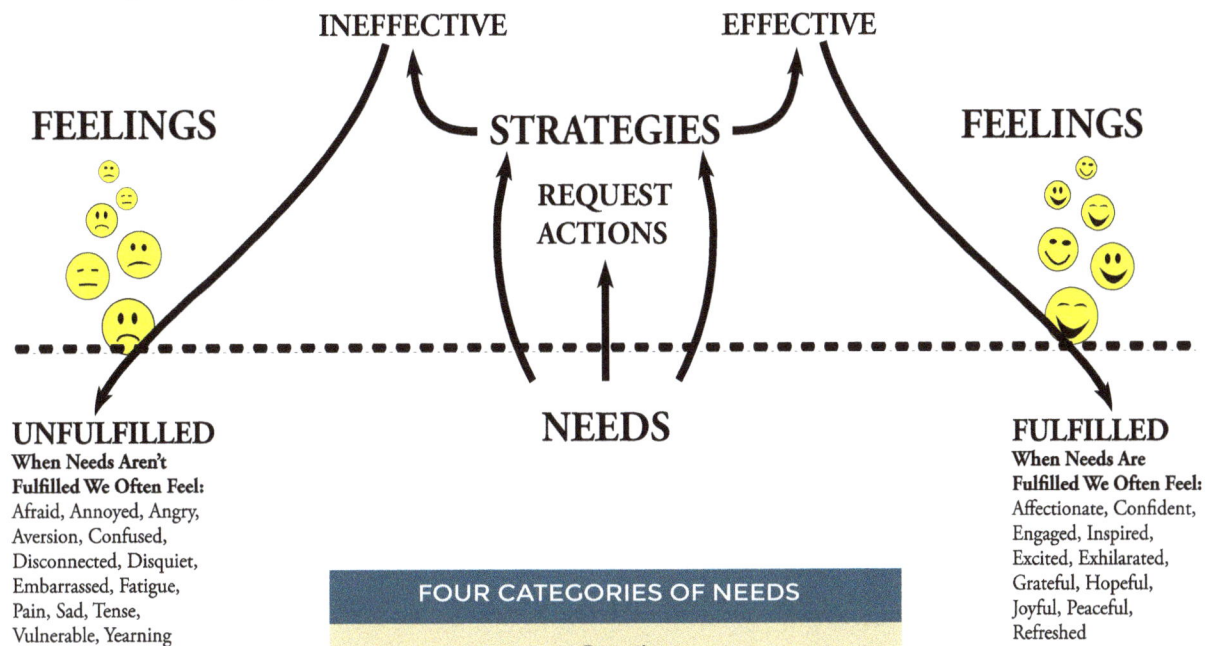

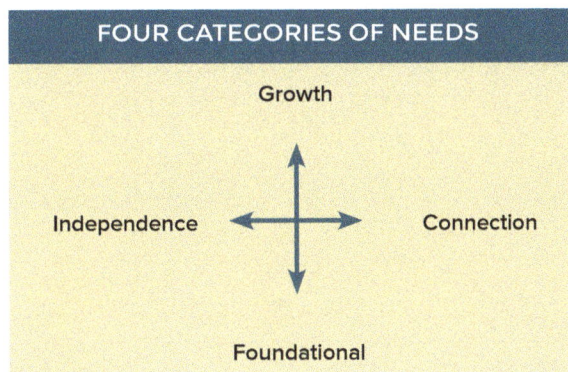

INEFFECTIVE   EFFECTIVE

FEELINGS   STRATEGIES   FEELINGS

REQUEST
ACTIONS

NEEDS

UNFULFILLED
When Needs Aren't
Fulfilled We Often Feel:
Afraid, Annoyed, Angry,
Aversion, Confused,
Disconnected, Disquiet,
Embarrassed, Fatigue,
Pain, Sad, Tense,
Vulnerable, Yearning

FULFILLED
When Needs Are
Fulfilled We Often Feel:
Affectionate, Confident,
Engaged, Inspired,
Excited, Exhilarated,
Grateful, Hopeful,
Joyful, Peaceful,
Refreshed

FOUR CATEGORIES OF NEEDS

Growth

Independence   Connection

Foundational

Elsbeth Martindale
CLINICAL PSYCHOLOGIST

Strengths List

elsbethmartindale.com/strengths-list

It is good to have a list of words that identify internal and interpersonal strengths. Seeing the words helps to find a label for a felt experience known in oneself or in relationship with another.

How I use this:

I find this Strength List helpful when I want to help clients with identifying the strengths they see in others or in themselves. When clients wish to demonstrate more support in an important relationship, this list can help them speak to another's strength as a way to bring a positive vibe to an interaction.

I occasionally use this list with clients at the end of therapy. I will pull out the list and identify several strengths clients demonstrated during therapy. I often will make a set of cards (business-card size) with the strengths I've seen a client use, review these with a client during the last session, and hand the cards to the client as a reminder of the strengths I've witnessed that could be used again and again. Giving clients a tangible positive "gift" is a very sweet way to end the process of therapy.

Example from practice:

Cliff was done with therapy. He had worked through family of origin issues as well as struggles to have meaningful relationships with others. He had gained a great deal in therapy. In the last session, I pulled out the Strength List and asked him to identify the areas of newfound strength resulting from his work in therapy. Cliff was able to circle a handful of strengths he had not previously identified within himself. This helped him recognize and celebrate his achievements.

Elsbeth Martindale
CLINICAL PSYCHOLOGIST

Strengths List

Accepting
Accuracy
Action-oriented
Activating
Adaptive
Adventurous
Ambitious
Analytical
Appreciation of beauty
Appreciative
Artistic
Athleticism
Attracting
Authenticity
Bravery
Calm
Caring
Citizenship
Cleverness
Compassionate
Connecting
Charming
Comfortable
Communicative
Confident
Considerate
Courageous
Creativity
Critical thinking
Curiosity
Dedication
Determination
Disciplined
Empathetic
Energetic
Entertaining
Enthusiastic
Fairness
Flexible
Focused

Forceful
Forgiveness
Friendly
Generosity
Gratitude
Helping
Honesty
Hopefulness
Humility
Humorous
Idealism
Independence
Ingenuity
Industriousness
Inspiring
Integrity
Intelligence
Kindness
Knowledgeable
Leadership
Learning
Liveliness
Logical
Loving
Love of learning
Mercifulness
Modesty
Motivated
Nurturing
Observant
Optimistic
Open-hearted
Open-minded
Orderly
Originality
Organization
Outgoing
Patience
Peacefulness
Perseverance

Persistence
Persuasiveness
Playful
Practicality
Precision
Problem-solving
Protective
Prudence
Quickness
Reservation
Respectful
Responsibility
Seriousness
Self-assured
Self-control
Speaking up
Spirituality
Spontaneous
Social intelligence
Social skillfulness
Straightforward
Strategic thinking
Tactful
Team-oriented
Thoughtful
Thrifty
Tolerant
Trustworthy
Truthful
Versatility
Visionary
Vitality
Warmth
Willpower
Wisdom

Higher Self Qualities

elsbethmartindale.com/higher-self-qualities

Richard Schwartz, PhD, the developer of Internal Family Systems, identified these eight qualities of the self. I like to call them Higher Self Qualities because these attitudes represent the best qualities for self-observation. When you look at yourself through this lens, you can see what is going on and what needs to shift in order to bring you into alignment with your potential and your wise mind. These more spiritual attitudes are often challenging to practice in a consistent fashion, but, as aspirations, they allow you to reach for the very best. I believe it is wise to teach our clients about these attitudes as a choiceful lens through which they can observe and guide themselves.

How I use this:

Sometimes, when teaching about important tools, it is helpful to use an object lesson that is unforgettable. Often the more outrageous, the more memorable. I made a set of Higher Self Glasses which fit this description—outrageous and unforgettable. The glasses, large glow-in-the-dark frames with the eight attitudes written on the lenses, represent the idea that we can choose the frame from which to view our circumstances. When judgment covers a lens, it is difficult to see anything but the smudges. When judgment is set aside (the lens wiped), the view can be more clear and revealing. As silly as this is, my clients don't tend to forget this lesson.

With an understanding of these aspirational attitudes, I can have discussions with my clients about how they can view and respond to themselves from this position; how this perspective makes a difference in their ability to guide themselves; and how challenging it is to remember to wipe off the judgment. This handout is the tool which my clients most often say is placed on their refrigerator at home for easy reference.

Elsbeth Martindale
CLINICAL PSYCHOLOGIST

Higher Self Qualities

"Higher Self Qualities" are derived from the work of Richard Schwartz, PhD, the developer of Internal Family Systems. He identified eight qualities of Self Leadership.

By looking through the eyes of your Higher Self, you approach life with a wise and open mind. Judgment often clouds your view and distorts perception. Judgment is based on stories and already-held conclusions rather than impartial data. Just like the smudges that cloud your vision when wearing eyeglasses, judgment distorts your perception when it attaches itself to your vision of yourself and the world. Clearing judgment from your lens requires both awareness and choice. When you notice yourself speaking or thinking judgmentally, you can ask judgment to step aside. Don't judge the judgment. Just clear the lens and look again. It is an ongoing and choiceful process, resulting in clarity and graciousness.

Connectedness
Calm
Courage
Curiosity

Compassion
Confidence
Clarity
Creativity

ASK JUDGMENT
TO
STEP ASIDE

Elsbeth Martindale
CLINICAL PSYCHOLOGIST

Higher Self Practice

elsbethmartindale.com/higher-self-practice

I offer my clients a Higher Self Practice sheet with examples of imagined situations when judgment could easily arise. I ask them to imagine a particular situation as their own and practice setting judgment aside in an attempt to hold higher self attitudes. It is through practice that this often new and powerful way of relating to self and others can be learned.

How I use this:

Understanding theory is so very different than embodying a skill. I will either pull out this handout in session or give it to a client as homework. After practicing responding from the point of view of the Higher Self for situations which aren't personal, I then suggest taking on some actual situations from the client's own life. Again, the practice is what makes this perspective a known and repeatable possibility.

Example from practice:

Kathleen understands the concept of viewing herself from a supportive place but lacks the actual practice. I pulled out this handout and said, *"Let's take it out of the theoretical and into the practical. How about we imagine these scenarios were real to your life? How might you respond using the attitudes of the Higher Self if these situations were true to your life?"* Practicing them directly helped her understand how challenging it was for her to hold judgment aside. With practice, however, she was able to see the value of seeing things clearly from a place of support and assistance rather than from a place of criticism.

Elsbeth Martindale
CLINICAL PSYCHOLOGIST

Higher Self Practice

Read the scenarios below. Retell each story to include as many Higher Self attitudes as possible. Remember, you can't change the facts of the story, only your response to the story.

Higher Self Attitudes include:

CONNECTION	COMPASSION	CLARITY	CALM
CURIOUSITY	COURAGE	CREATIVITY	CONFIDENCE

PRACTICE HIGHER SELF QUALITIES TOWARD YOURSELF IF THESE SITUATIONS WERE TRUE:

1. You have too much to drink at the office party and make a fool of yourself by flirting openly with your colleague. You are angry with yourself the next day. You call yourself a fool and stupid.

2. You tell your friend that you are too sick to go out for the evening as an excuse. You go out with a different friend and happen to run into the friend with whom you canceled. You are mad at yourself and know your friend is rather upset.

3. Your brother borrows $500 and seems to have forgotten to pay it back. You are mad at yourself for not having the courage to confront him.

4. You borrowed your neighbor's punch bowl for a party. While cleaning up, you accidentlaly chipped the punch bowl and now you feel terrible about having to tell your neighbor.

5. You take your new car out for a drive. You want to get a feel for its power, so you push it beyond the speed iimit. Just as you reach 90 mph, you notice the flashing lights behind you.

PRACTICE HIGHER SELF QUALITIES TOWARD OTHERS IN THESE SCENARIOS:

1. Your coworker confronts you at work, saying you made a fool of yourself at the party. She tells you she believes you have a problem with alcohol and should get some help.

2. You run into a friend while out one night. This friend canceled plans with you earlier that night, claiming she was not feeling well. Your friend looked fine when you saw her laughing with another friend over dinner. You are mad and disappointed but would like to keep the friendship healthy.

3. You decide you want to confront your brother about the $500 he owes you but hasn't mentioned since taking the loan three months ago. You like your brother and wish to not have resentment build up in your relationship.

4. Your partner comes home late on a night you had planned a nice dinner without calling or providing a reason for being late. You are irritated and want to understand the delay.

Elsbeth Martindale
CLINICAL PSYCHOLOGIST

Self-Compassion Break

elsbethmartindale.com/self-compassion-break

Kristin Neff has given us all the gift of researching and creating tools for helping people treat themselves with more compassion. Her book, *Self Compassion*, is my most recommended self-help book for clients. This handout summarizes some of the nitty-gritty of responding to self with self-compassion.

How I use this:

I will pull out this handout in the middle of a session to give clients a script for how to offer compassion to themselves in the midst of their struggle. I took a Mindful Self-Compassion training with Kristin Neff during which she playfully told us, "Self-compassion starts with 'Oh.'" In the spirit of Kristen's teaching, I tell my clients the following is a great place to start: "Oh, Elsbeth, this is really hard." We then practice this tone and attitude for the suffering the client is currently experiencing. The actual words are very helpful for clients to see as they experiment with holding a space of compassion.

Example from practice:

Kelly is worried about her son. He is struggling with depression and has been refusing to go to school. She has tried everything and is broken-hearted to see him in such pain. She looks for blame in herself or her husband. I ask her, "What would self-compassion sound like if you offered it to yourself?" Kelly stops and reflects. She knows about self-compassion and has practiced it. "Right," she says. "I could meet myself in my pain and be kind to myself as I struggle." She drops down into her heart, sees the enormity of her struggle, and, moving her hand to her heart, offers herself some compassion. "I'm really suffering," she says. "Oh, this is really hard."

From this place of connectedness with self, rather than from a place of blame, Kelly can begin to look for the support and care she needs, beginning with herself. Then she can find the requesting words to use with others in an attempt to get them to witness and be present with her in this struggle.

Elsbeth Martindale
CLINICAL PSYCHOLOGIST

Self-Compassion Break

Whenever you find yourself suffering, in pain, confused, or not feeling in balance, take a self-compasison break. Step into the position of your own Wise Inner Guide and follow the steps below.

1 Start with simply acknowledging your pain or sense of suffering. Say words like;
"Oh, _____, this is really hard."
"Ouch!"
"That must hurt."
"This is painful."
"I'm sorry to see you struggling. I care."

2 Offer yourself a soothing touch, a gesture of kindness and care.
Put your hand on your heart,
Touch your cheek, or
Rub the back of your neck.
Touch releases oxytocin, an antidote to stress hormones, and allows this "bonding hormone" to secure your attachment to
your Wise Inner Guide and voice of compassion.

3 Demonstrate a bit of kindness toward yourself by saying;
"May I be kind to myself in this moment."
"May I accept this moment exactly as it is."
"May I accept myself exactly as I am in this moment."
"May I give myself all the compassion I need to respond to this moment wisely."

RECOMMENDATION

Practice in small and frequent doses.
The brain learns new patterns with repetition of experience. Increase your brain's expectation of compassion by practicing compassion breaks often. You don't need a compassion marathon to learn these skills. Offer yourself several 3 - 5-minute experiences throughout the day and your brain will develop the pathways to expect a more gentle self-supporting option for managing suffering and pain.

The Self-Compassion Break was adapted from the work of Kristin Neff, PhD, and Christopher Germer, PhD.

Self-Compassion Exercises

elsbethmartindale.com/self-compassion-exercises

This is a summary of valuable tools for teaching self-compassion to your clients.

How I use this:

When I'm looking for a creative or playful way to help clients integrate the notion of self-compassion, I will look at the ideas presented in this handout to find a fitting option. Having a variety of research-based options allows me to tailor the lessons of self-compassion to the individual preferences and needs of a particular client.

Example from practice:

It was difficult for Malia to be kind to herself, especially when she was physically ill. She was scolded frequently, by her parents, when, as a child, her chronic medical condition flared up. Malia adopted this same harsh management style for herself each time she became sick. She would be angry with herself and tell herself to "get over it."

When members of her therapy group suggested she could use a little self-compassion, in response to a recent flare-up of symptoms, Malia immediately became defensive and guarded. She rejected this idea, calling it silly and not something she would ever be comfortable doing. One group member shared how speaking the Loving-Kindness Meditation was helpful for her and wondered if Malia might find this useful as well. Again, Malia balked, saying that parts of herself would reject those words outright. Another group member spoke up and told how she often used a simple Comfort Gesture, placing a hand on her heart as a sign of tenderness toward herself. Malia was not immediately dismissive of this option but still didn't think it would be very helpful.

This story illustrates the need for a variety of methods for exploring self-compassion with clients. Each client must move at him/fer/their own pace with interventions that allow comfort for experimentation. Malia was able to move a bit further in her self-care after being offered a pillow from yet another group member, who suggested it was okay for Malia to have some protection around something so tender within herself. Malia hugged the pillow and felt safer. The group honored her need to remain safe while hearing about the validity of being tender and compassionate with herself. This was a small but significant first step for Malia.

Elsbeth Martindale
CLINICAL PSYCHOLOGIST

Self-Compassion Exercises

When teaching your clients about how to take good care of themselves emotionally, directing them to the current research and self-help material on self-compassion can be helpful. Kristin Neff's book, ***Self-Compassion: The Proven Power of Being Kind to Yourself*** (2011), is one of my most recommended self-help books on the market. Her website, www.self-compassion.org, offers a variety of guided meditations that can be shared with your clients.

CRITIC/COMFORT CARDS

- Ask clients to talk about how they usually treat themselves when having a difficult time.
- Explore the role of their self-critical voice by having them write down their most common self-critical thoughts, each on a separate brown card.
- Ask clients to think about what they would need in order to feel comforted and understood in times of distress. Ask them to imagine a comment, thought, or action that would be soothing and helpful when they are in the midst of a difficult time.
- Have clients write each comforting thought or action on new cards of more beautiful colors.
- Suggest that clients carry these cards in their pockets or purses throughout the week. They might put a check mark on the back of the card each time the critic or comfort message is used.

INTERVENTION BRACELET

- Suggest your clients make or purchase an easily removed "intervention bracelet" (a simple rubber band will do the job).
- Instruct the clients to move the bracelet from one arm to the other every time they address themselves in a harsh way or felt upset about something.
- This is simply a consciousness-raising tool. It can be used in combination with the cards (above) or on its own. Clients are simply to notice they are in the midst of a challenging situation and they have awareness, and therefore choice, in how they respond.

LOVING-KINDNESS MEDITATION

- Teach your clients a very simple loving-kindness meditation.
- Silently repeat three loving-kindness phrases every night before going to bed:
  May I be at peace
  May I be kind to myself
  May I be free from suffering
- Repeat this process, this time focusing attention on another person:
  May you be at peace
  May you be kind to yourself
  May you be free from suffering

SELF-COMPASSION PHRASES

- Help clients design three personalized self-compassion phrases that correspond with the key elements of self-compassion:
  Mindfulness (e.g., "This is a moment of suffering")
  Common Humanity (e.g., "Suffering is something we all share")
  Self-Kindness (e.g., "I can be kind to myself")
- Encourage clients to use these phrases when encountering difficulties in daily life and to adapt these sentences according to the situation.

COMFORT GESTURE

- Tell clients how a kind physical gesture can activate the soothing parasympathetic body system. Gestures alone can help get us out of storytelling and drop us into physical presence.
- A self-soothing gesture can even produce oxytocin, allowing a bonding experience between distress and self-kindness.
- Find a gesture your clients can use to bring themselves comfort and signify the intention to soothe. Such gestures might be:
  Putting your hand over your heart
  Gently rubbing your arm
  Gently pulling/massaging your ear lobe
  Any gesture that feels comforting will do
- Encourage clients to practice this gesture whenever they feel distressed or upset.

COMPASSION JOURNAL

- Suggest your clients keep a "self-compassion journal."
- In the journal, they can write what they have learned about reprocessing difficult experiences with a sense of kindness, common humanity, and mindfulness.
- They can record their "turn arounds" when they are successful at shifting their negative reactions into a self-compassionate response.
- Recording success reinforces success and stores these accomplishments for review at a later time.

PERSONAL APPRECIATIONS

- Ask clients to tell you five things they appreciate about themselves; write them down, if desired.
- Discuss the experience of relating to oneself in a positive way.
- If these are spoken of with a tone of doubt and dismissal, encourage clients to experiment with holding a posture and tone that is fully supportive of these self-appreciations. Practice this tone and posture to try it on. Discuss the difference they experience by shifting tone.

SELF-COMPASSION LETTER

- As a homework assignment, ask clients to write a compassionate letter to themselves about a difficult issue for them, or for when they notice negative self-talk.
- Instruct them to write the letter from the perspective of an imaginary friend who is unconditionally kind, accepting, and compassionate.
- Invite your clients to read this letter aloud on three separate occasions throughout the coming week.
- Discuss their experiences in the next session.

SOURCE

These exercises were adapted from the writings of Kristin Neff and research presented in the article, "Meeting Suffering With Kindness: Effects of a Brief Self-Compassion Intervention for Female College Students," by Elke Smeets, Kristin Neff, Hugo Alberts, and Madelon Peters, 2014.

Self-Soothing Statements

elsbethmartindale.com/self-soothing-statements

Self-soothing is necessary for self-regulation, and it is one of the "qualities of differentiation" described by David Schnarch, PhD, author of *Passionate Marriage*. For many clients, this is a new concept. Most have previously assumed all comfort and soothing was only accessible from others. This handout gives clients language to understand what self-soothing sounds like. These examples can be helpful as clients find their own words for comforting themselves in times of distress.

How I use this:

I often will read through these sentences with clients, identifying which ones sound like statements they could actually say to themselves and find comforting. Once they have a set of supportive statements, I suggest they pick one message for the week and write this on a post-it or two to place strategically where they might see it when they need it (bathroom mirror, dashboard, inside a journal, and so on). I also suggest they read the statement aloud each time they encounter it. I suggest they repeat it until they can say it like they mean it. Someone told me once, "The unconscious mind believes anything it is told long enough or strong enough." Saying these sort of affirming messages aloud gives the inner emotional world a strong way to hear a reparative message.

Example from practice:

Alana was working through some painful memories of childhood abuse. As she uncovered her experiences and told her stories, she often found herself dis-regulated. I assisted her with ideas for building a "recovery kit" for herself when she recognized she was feeling overwhelmed. The kit included a variety of tools for managing her distress (see the *Distress Tolerance* handout). In addition, Alana built a deck of cards, with each card containing a self-soothing message which she could read as needed to help comfort herself with words. She was quite creative in her deck design and brought the cards to show me. She used these affirmations for many years during her therapy work, changing up the message as needed to support herself in healing.

Elsbeth Martindale
CLINICAL PSYCHOLOGIST

Self-Soothing Statements

Life gets really hard sometimes. When you need to step into the role of comforting and soothing yourself, here are some suggested statements you can make to yourself. Go through the list, fill in the blanks when you are not hurting, then highlight all the statements you would love to hear when you are in need of inner comfort. Keep this list close at hand so the wisest part of yourself can speak to your struggling parts in an effort to own your power to soothe and ease your suffering. You deserve it.

- I want to take healthy and loving care of myself, even when it's hard.
- I am willing to view this challenge as an opportunity to move one step closer to the person I want to be.
- I can trust I'm okay even if I'm mad, sad, lonely, or hurt.
- I accept that it's my job to take good care of myself.
- I can accept myself, just as I am, in this moment.
- I won't do anything to make the situation worse.
- I can separate myself from the conflict in order to restore myself.
- I don't have to be perfect. Neither do others.
- I can accept that there are things in life that I simply won't like.
- I am willing to figure out how I can be a _____ (peaceful, loving, calm) woman/man in the midst of this.
- I can consider what the best of me wants of me in this moment.
- My feelings are okay and I am willing to choose actions with intention.
- I can soothe my body in moments of distress by _____ and _____.
- I can have my thoughts and see that I am more than my thoughts.
- I can have my feelings and know that I am more than just my feelings.
- I can call on my sense of the Divine to be with me in this moment.
- I can stay present in my body and bring myself comfort.
- I can be wise in the way I care for myself in this moment.
- Although parts of me feel _____, that is not all I am.
- Although I may feel strongly negative toward someone in this moment, it is not the whole of my feelings toward this person.
- I can reach out to others for support, like _____.
- I choose to be kind to myself in this moment.
- I can steer my thoughts away from my hurtful thoughts, feelings, and impulses.

- I can release the tension in my body in positive ways by _____.
- A place I can go to feel safe and comforted is _____.
- My strengths that will help me endure this situation include _____ and _____.
- I can filter my beliefs to see if they are realistic, owned, life-enhancing, and flexible.
- I know that my pain and discomfort will pass.
- I can take good care of myself.
- I can manage my life effectively even though my situation is challenging.
- I can care for myself like a good parent cares for a hurting child.
- Right here and right now I can be at peace, even for just a moment.
- I can care lovingly for my needs and feelings.
- My pain is mine to heal.
- I am response-able.
- I'm free to create my life the way I want.
- I can declare my limits and set clear and healthy boundaries.
- I can assess if I like how I am acting at any moment.
- I am my own authority.
- I can keep my long-term goals in mind. I don't need to act on impulse.
- Others are not in this world to take care of my needs.
- I can be okay, even if others do not meet my expectations or I fail to meet theirs.
- I can give others permission to live their lives the way they choose.
- My well-being need not be tied to the behaviors of others.
- I trust my own knowing.
- I can remain non-anxious even if others are tense.
- I can validate my own preferences, thoughts, and desires.
- I can gently hold the place where my hurt lives in my body.
- I can inhale strength and courage, and exhale fear and doubt.

Elsbeth Martindale
CLINICAL PSYCHOLOGIST

Self-Empathy Practice

elsbethmartindale.com/self-empathy-practice

Similar to self-compassion is the notion of self-empathy, responding with tenderness and emotional resonance toward self. When dealing with emotional content, it is important to start engagement from a place of empathy. This non-threatening tone softens things and makes connection possible, whether that connection is with others or with hurt parts of self. Clients aren't always aware of their inner climate—how they respond and react to themselves. Empathy is an important concept to teach. It is a way to create a caring and respectful inner world. This handout offers practice situations. Self-empathy cannot be learned theoretically. It must be practiced.

How I use this:

When clients aren't skilled at self-empathy, this handout offers great opportunities to practice. In therapy we go through the situations one by one, exploring, demonstrating and practicing holding an empathic tone using the scenarios. After expertise is shown using the examples, then we pick a situation from the client's life and practice with real-life challenges.

I have business-sized cards I give to my clients which say, "Always start with empathy." The back of the card has the reflective listening suggestion, "Are you feeling _____ because _____?" I give these to my clients as reminders of how to respond empathically to both self and others.

Example from practice:

Clare had a conflictual dinner with her partner. She got reactive in a manner she has been attempting to avoid. In session, she was expressing a great deal of frustration and anger toward herself. After a bit of venting, I asked her if she might find it helpful to speak to herself with a touch of empathy. She smiled. She'd heard this before. ***"What might empathy toward yourself sound like in this situation?"*** I asked. She slowed, turned inward, and said, "Right, I could say to myself, 'Are you feeling disappointed that you reacted so angrily at dinner?'" This softened her stance toward herself, which allowed her to remind herself of the skills she prefers to demonstrate when she feels annoyed with her partner. From this softened place, she was able to offer some retroactive learning (see *Retroactive Learning* handout) with a non-scolding tone, allowing absorption of the lesson learned.

Elsbeth Martindale
CLINICAL PSYCHOLOGIST

Self-Empathy Practice

Sometimes you will skip right over empathy and jump into solutions, scolding, or reactivity. As you build a more loving relationship with yourself, you will want to have expertise in empathic resonance. Here's a chance to demonstrate self-empathy by imagining encountering one of the following situations. Reflective listening is generally a good place to start because it brings focus to emotion. (e.g., "You're feeling _____ because _____.") Watch the impulse to fix or otherwise distract yourself until you have provided a good dose of self-empathy.

1. You get to work and notice you have a big stain on your shirt.

2. A client tells you he/she/they want to take their business elsewhere because, he/she/they "aren't getting much out of your services anymore."

3. You received a call from the IRS saying you're being audited.

4. Your professional organization called to say you are going to be the recipient of an award for excellence.

5. Your neighbors sold their property to a developer who is building a high-rise right outside your office window.

6. Your client brings a large and aggressive pit bull into your office saying, "You're okay that I brought my dog today, right?"

7. Your partner tells you he/she/they won't be able to attend an upcoming event because of a work commitment.

ROLF Filter

elsbethmartindale.com/rolf-filter

Cognitive awareness is extremely helpful. Many ideas and thoughts pass through our brains. Because a great deal of these are nonsense and sometimes even harmful, it is important to help clients turn up the volume of their inner dialogue and filter the content. The ROLF filter is a tool for learning to filter beliefs. The filter is like a screen which eliminates things that can be harmful if allowed in. If a belief is not realistic, then injury can occur when reality hammers home the truth. If a belief is not owned, given to us by someone else without our choosing, then it may not suit our values and understanding. If a belief isn't life-enhancing, then one should question its utility. Finally, if a belief isn't flexible, then no wiggle-room exists when circumstances are benefited by adjustment.

This idea that we can question and adjust our beliefs is sometimes a new and often uncomfortable concept for some clients. Understanding the power of *choosing* beliefs can be quite empowering for people.

How I use this:

When clients are holding limiting beliefs (e.g., "I can't speak up because Dad will get mad," "I'll never be successful," "I can't question my family's political views," or "I'll just die if I have to give the presentation to the whole committee."), it is valuable to help them hear what they are saying and scrutinize their own conclusions or beliefs. I often suggest the metaphor that beliefs are like a pair of pants. If they don't fit, you can exchange them for something more comfortable and fitting.

Example from practice:

Justin had a disabled sister and had grown up feeling responsible to assist in her care. He stated he knew his mother would disapprove if he took a job in another state. He said, "We have to stay together as a family. My mother would just die if I left her to deal with things all by herself." We looked at his belief that his mother would "die," and it became clear this was an exaggeration. He saw beneath the stated conclusion that he felt a great deal of obligation to support his mother. He also acknowledged wanting to be of assistance to his sister. After examining his beliefs, Justin shifted his story to something like, "I'd love to exercise the freedom to move where I want to, and I realize I value being of service to my family's needs. I will need to weigh the options for work and for the support of my family, because both are important to me." His beliefs now support him and are no longer directed by the unrealistic, unowned, life-limiting, and rigid beliefs he had been holding.

Elsbeth Martindale
CLINICAL PSYCHOLOGIST

ROLF Filter

If a belief passes through the ROLF filter, it is probably healthy, supportive, and valuable to hold. If a belief does not pass the filter, it will be uncomfortable to hold and possibly harmful. Redesign your beliefs to pass a ROLF filter and your beliefs will give you solid support.

Listen to what you are saying to yourself and examine if your beliefs are:

REALISTIC - It's realistic if it is reasonable, logical, and leads to positive consequences.
OWNED - It is owned if you choose it, and it makes sense to you.
LIFE-ENHANCING - It is life-enhancing if it allows you to pursue your needs without undue restriction.
FLEXIBLE - It is flexible if it allows for exceptions when situations warrant.

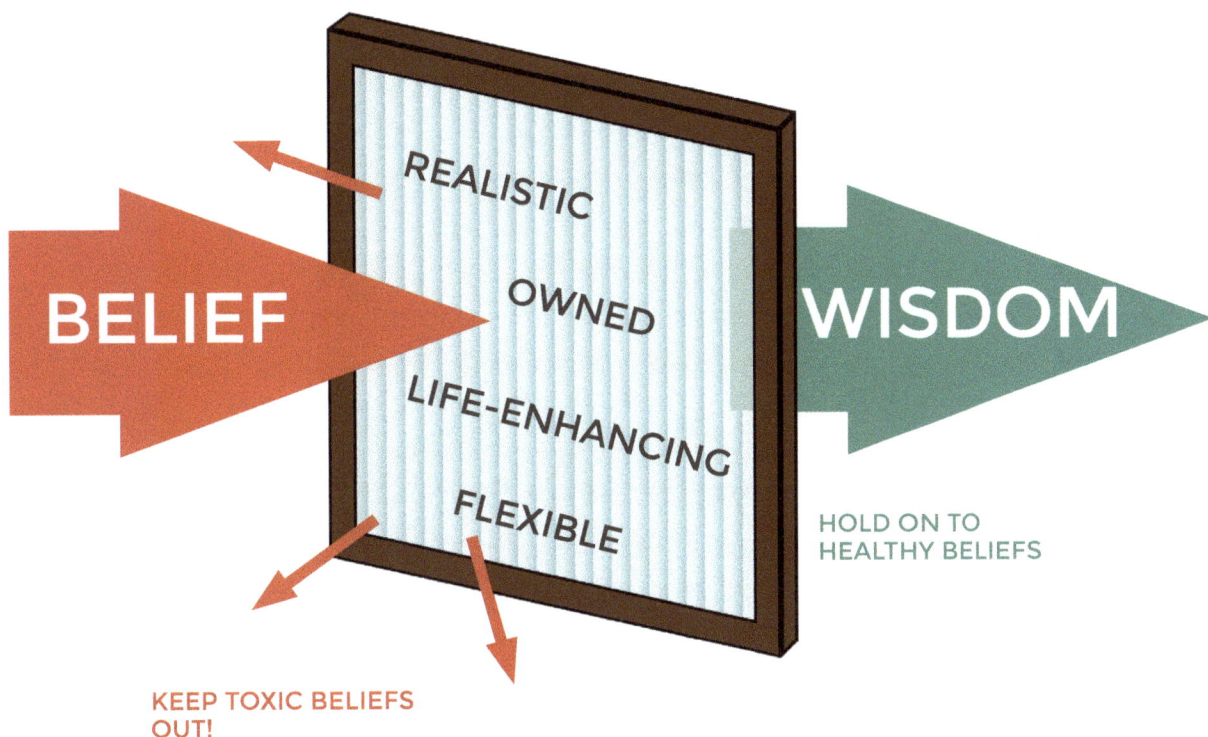

Don't believe everything you think. You may be holding harmful beliefs and not even know it.

Retroactive Learning

elsbethmartindale.com/retroactive-learning

How do we help clients learn from their mistakes? This handout offers a step-by-step approach for finding the path that would have led to a more desired outcome. Mistakes are great teachers if we don't waste time using the mistake as a weapon for self-denigration.

How I use this:

When clients recognize they took a path which led them to the swamp instead of the meadow, I help them see this is a great opportunity to learn. It is a chance to map out a new path, put up some road signs, and get off the paved road to discomfort. I might point out how pain is a fantastic teacher about what doesn't work. Looking back and reviewing what clients wish they would have done differently is an excellent way to design an experiment to avoid a repeat of the discomfort. I might say, *"Let's take your pain or mistake as an opportunity to find a more pleasing outcome. Let's do some retroactive learning."* Once I have buy-in for the learning, I use this handout to point out the steps.

Example from practice:

Charles came into his session and began telling how he and his partner got into a huge fight over his phone again. Charles is self-employed and believes he needs to check his calls and emails frequently so as to not miss a sale. His partner complains the phone interferes with their time together. This is not the first time they've had this argument. Charles defends himself and can't understand why his partner doesn't appreciate he is "just trying to help out the family by making money." Although Charles feels justified in his position, he doesn't like the fights and regrets how he reacts with anger. I suggested we look at the events surrounding the most recent fight in the order in which they unfolded so we could look for the exits off the highway to the familiar battle. We started at the beginning, when he walked in the door after work. We looked for all the choice options along the way. He realized he could have told his partner he was expecting an important call and would like to check his phone several times while having dinner. He realizes this might have helped his partner expect and understand his need to keep his phone nearby. If he had missed that offramp, he realized he could have practiced his reflective listening skills, instead of defending himself, when his partner showed frustration at the presence of his phone at dinner. Similarly, we went through additional steps on the path to the fight and figured out what skills he could have used to prevent the battle he didn't really want to have. I had to help him not judge himself during this process because that would interfere with his ability to observe and learn.

Elsbeth Martindale
CLINICAL PSYCHOLOGIST

Retroactive Learning

When you act in a way with which you aren't pleased, you have several options for how to respond. You could focus on others and how they feel, or you could scold, berate, belittle, or judge yourself. None of these options leads to wisdom and growth. Without conscious awareness, you are likely going to respond the way your parents responded to you when you did something "wrong." This, afterall, is your early learning. There is another path—the path of growth, skill-building, and self-authorship. You can use the event as an opportunity to learn about the person you want to be. You could ask, "How do I wish I would have acted in order to avoid my own displeasure?" If it matters to *you* to behave differently, then take the following steps to learn from your missteps.

STEP 1 - PAUSE

Make some time for reviewing your actions.

STEP 2 - BACK UP

Back up to the moment just before you reacted. Feel into that moment again. Notice your thoughts, feelings, and body sensations. Apply a good dose of self-compassion here. Remember, "It cannot teach us that which we look at with shame" (Lalita Tademy). You don't want to damage the relationship between the observer and the observed, or wisdom will not be transmitted.

STEP 3 - FIND A NEW PATH

Describe, aloud or in a journal, how you wish you would have responded in that situation. Explain to yourself why this is a better choice for *you*. Ground this alternative response in your values. Because your reactive pattern will be difficult to change, you will need a good rationale for creating and choosing a different path. By imagining how you wish you would have responded, you lay down the first layer of a new neural pathway. The more you vision this path, the more detail you include and the more sturdy and clear the path will become. Remember, this won't be easy. It is not the paved path. It will be more like bushwhacking.

STEP 4 - REINFORCE THE NEW PATH

Figure out exactly what you'd have to have said to yourself in order to get off the paved "reactive route" that you were on. Mark the exit off the paved path by identifying what you'd have to remember in order to steer yourself into a new direction. Write this down: "I would have to tell myself _____." It might help to identify the tone you'd prefer to use in this reminder. Again, scolding and belittling only make you resistant to listening to the messenger.

REMEMBER

Habit patterns are hard to change. Repetition is the solution. Each "mistake" is an opportunity to imagine your new preferred response. There is a saying, "Once through the field and the grass bends; three times through the field and the grass lays down." You'll need to imagine this preferred response path many times before it becomes your automatic response. Be patient with yourself. Becoming who you want to be takes time and commitment.

Why Questions

elsbethmartindale.com/why-questions

It seems that one way to stay stuck is to focus on **why** things are the way they are. Many of my clients come to therapy thinking that understanding **why** things are troubled in their lives is the path to the solution to the troubles. Over and over again, it appears to me that an excessive focus on "why" is a prescription for rumination and tail-chasing. All the other questions—who? what? when? where? and how?—are movement and solution-focused questions. But asking "why" doesn't bring about much change.

How I use this:
When clients are asking why life is the way it is, I suggest they may want to shift their question to something that offers them agency and authorship.

I sometimes playfully tell some clients that, "Hanging out at the Y (why) gives you a meal and a cot to sleep in but doesn't move you forward!"

The one place where "why" questions do seem valuable is when questioning one's own motivation. Why we chose what we did or acted as we did can be very instructive. It is when questions of "why" are focused on the behavior of others or on life's circumstances that they seem like a waste of mental energy and a way to **look** like you're doing something valuable without bringing about effective change.

Example from practice:
Marsha is a woman in a marriage she claims is "terrible." She had little respectful conversation, no joyful exchange, and this is all built on a history of her partner's infidelity, for which Marsha has no interest in forgiving. Marsha stays in her marriage feeling anxious and stuck. She came to therapy and frequently asked the questions, "Why am I suffering a miserable marriage?" and "Why is he such a jerk to me?" These are unanswerable questions. I find little value in her using her energy to discuss, debate, and attempt to understand **why** things are as they are. No adjustment and growth will come from these questions. On the contrary, Marsha might ask: "What do you want to do about it? When do you want to take a desired action? How would you like to respond to this situation?" These are all questions which interest me because they are movement questions. After years of therapy, Marsha can now hear herself asking the unsolvable "why" question and shift the focus of her attention to where she has power and agency. When she shifts her focus, her anxiety is greatly reduced.

Elsbeth Martindale
CLINICAL PSYCHOLOGIST

Why Questions

People often come to therapy and want to know the answers to "why" questions. Why are they depressed? Why can't they find lasting partnership? Why their friend stopped talking with them? And on and on. These are curious questions but often are very difficult to answer. More importantly, the answers don't often lead to solutions that bring about lasting change. Granted, "why" questions can make you feel like you're taking action, but, in fact, you are only pondering, not makeing a plan for change. The better option are the "movement" questions of who, what, when, where, and how. These give you agency and authorship, empowering you to grow.

Why?

- Past focused
- Passive not active
- Victim language
- Regurgitation of what's not working
- Distracts from moving forward
- Postpones change
- Fools you into thinking you're working
- Can be an invitation for a fight

Who?
What?
When?
Where?
How?

- Future focused
- Active not passive
- Change and solution focused

It's not always wise to insist on knowing the "why's"!

Five States of Being

elsbethmartindale.com/five-states-of-being

This handout can help clients see their tendencies and patterns as well as their options for conscious observation of these patterns. It is a simple example of how we often automatically react in ways that are emotionally harmful to ourselves. Clients can learn to observe their patterns, identify the conditions that can trigger these, and find tools to shift their inner state in the direction of their choosing. This ability offers clients true agency over their internal culture.

How I use this:

I have used this handout mostly in presentations and group therapy because of the great discussions that tend to evolve from this exercise. Seeing the common human experience of projection, mis-attribution, and habitual concluding is valuable. Everyone has the potential for misreading the environment in a harmful way. Giving clients the experience of, "It's not just me," can be very comforting.

Example from practice:

I keep my handouts at-the-ready in case I might need them. One evening in group, Rachel shared how she had misread her partner's actions and ended up in a huge argument over something which ended up being a misunderstanding. Others in group shared how they've done similar things. I pulled out this exercise in an attempt to deepen the conversation, sharing the common tendency to misread circumstances based on our history and expectations. The group had a great discussion of the ways they each get triggered and jump to automatic conclusions. They were particularly interested in talking about the things they each do to exacerbate their suffering and the power they have to diminish their pain when they become aware of their inner dialogue.

Elsbeth Martindale
CLINICAL PSYCHOLOGIST

Five States of Being

- Imagine walking down the street. You notice someone you know walking toward you. You wave "hello!" but there's no response. Notice your response to the lack of response.
- Imagine walking down the street. You notice someone you know walking toward you. You wave "hello!" and the person notices you and waves "hello!" back. Notice your response to the response of the person.
- Notice any differences in your responses.
- These responses can be called, "states of being."

Exercise adapted, with permission, from a workshop presentation by Linda Graham, MFT. www.lindagraham-mft.net

IDENTIFY FIVE STATES OF BEING, ONES FAMILIAR TO YOU	WHAT CONDITIONS TRIGGER THESE STATES?	WHAT TOOLS CAN YOU USE TO SHIFT (AMPLIFY OR DIMINISH) THESE STATES?
1		
2		
3		
4		
5		

Elsbeth Martindale
CLINICAL PSYCHOLOGIST

Four Versions of the Self
elsbethmartindale.com/four-versions-of-self

Our sense of self can be determined by a variety of factors, some internal and some external. This handout helps clients see the various ways they think about their self definition. Often clients sacrifice a great deal to preserve another person's perception of them. This kind of image control can lead to very interesting conversations. Some leading questions might include the following: "How important is it that others think good of you?" "What happens to your view of yourself when others are critical of you?" and "Is what others think of you more important to you than what you think of yourself?" The answers can be fascinating and telling insights about self-definition.

How I use this:
This is a handout I often use in presentations or with groups because of the feedback available about the perceptions of others and the impressions of individuals. This sort of objective observation of self-definition makes for fabulous conversation about values, locus of control, self-support, and self-authorship.

Example from practice:
The women in my Monday evening women's group are consistently driven to deeper understanding of themselves and others. The *Four Versions of the Self* gave each of them a chance to look at themselves in a new light. The participants were able to get honest feedback about the perception other group members had of them. Naomi was surprised to hear others saw her as tender and caring, while she views herself as impatient and short. Christina was curious to see that, over the course of her life, she has remained consistent in her dedication to family and finds a strong sense of herself in this context. Sasha realized, through this exercise, how much she wants others to see her persona of being a hard worker and someone who doesn't slack.

The group members had the most difficult time with identifying their ego view of themselves, finding it much easier to consider what others thought of them than what they, themselves, thought of themselves. Maybe not surprisingly, the woman found it even more difficult to identify the positive qualities they saw in themselves. I reminded the group of the lovely quote by Macrina Wiederkehr: "Oh, God, help me believe the truth about myself, no matter how beautiful it is."

Elsbeth Martindale
CLINICAL PSYCHOLOGIST

Four Versions of the Self

Look at the four different ways you can view your Self. Fill in the boxes as suggested:

1) Examine your Ego self. What words might you use to describe yourself?
2) What is the Perception others might have of you?
3) What is the Persona you wish to present to the world?
4) What are some of the qualities of your Self that have been consistent about you throughout your whole life? Describe these.

EGO - What do you think of you?

_____

_____

_____

_____

_____

PERCEPTION - What do others think of you?

_____

_____

_____

_____

_____

SELF - What is consistent about you through time?

_____

_____

_____

_____

_____

PERSONA - What do you wish others would think of you?

_____

_____

_____

_____

_____

Elsbeth Martindale
CLINICAL PSYCHOLOGIST

Therapy Summary Sheet

elsbethmartindale.com/therapy-summary-sheet

Because our job as therapists is to work ourselves out of a job, it is a thing to celebrate when clients finish their work in therapy. Note, though, that not all terminations come after clients have achieved all their desired goals. Therapy ends for lots of reasons. When clients end because they have gained the skills and tools for managing their lives effectively, this is an event to be marked and celebrated. This summary sheet gives a place to identify the achievements and the skills learned. It also offers a self-suggestion about what to do if a client slips into an old troublesome pattern.

How I use this:

Prior to a final session with clients, I will send them this Therapy Summary Sheet to fill out so we can discuss it together. I generally go through my notes and highlight the noteworthy achievements in skills and strategies. Reinforcing practiced and effective means for life management is a real gift to offer our clients as they end their treatment.

Example from practice:

It took many years for Silvana to heal from the injuries she sustained in childhood. Her parents neglected her emotional and physical needs. She made many desperate attempts to find acceptance and love, but her actions were ungrounded and led to further injury. Slowly, Silvana began to develop trust and confidence that her wounds could be healed. She built skills for both internal and external life-management. During her weekly appointments over the course of her therapy, she made steady and consistent progress. When Silvana announced she felt emotionally strong and ready to stop treatment, this was a thing to be celebrated. In our final termination sessions, we worked together to name the things she had learned and the skills she acquired. We needed more than three bullet points in each section of this Therapy Summary Sheet to contain all the wisdom and healing that Silvana gathered in therapy. We made a plan for what she could do if and when she felt "shaky." This review solidified Silvana's sense of accomplishment and triumph for all her hard work in reversing her expectations about life.

Elsbeth Martindale
CLINICAL PSYCHOLOGIST

Therapy Summary Sheet

Name _____ Date _____

The things I've learned in therapy include:

1 _____

_____

2 _____

_____

3 _____

_____

The skills I've acquired include:

1 _____

_____

2 _____

_____

3 _____

_____

If I begin to slip into old and ineffective patterns, I plan to...

_____

_____

Elsbeth Martindale
CLINICAL PSYCHOLOGIST

Elsbeth Martindale
CLINICAL PSYCHOLOGIST

PART II

Symptom Care

With clarity about the issues with which your clients are suffering, you can begin to focus your attention on the relief of specific symptoms. The handouts in this section address some of the typical symptoms that show up for clients in therapy. These handouts provide a springboard to look at symptoms with an intention to learn. With careful and tender presentation, clients can begin to transform suffering into opportunities for growth, the development of new skills, and a chance to heighten wisdom.

Stress Boulders...51
Crisis Management..53
Depression Pit..55
Critic Catcher...57
Hold Yourself in a Positive Light...59
Anger Balloon 61
Anger Continuum 63
Distress Tolerance Activities 65-67
Letters to Myself When I'm Depressed 69
Grief and Loss..71
Grief and Loss Ritual..73
Goodbye Letter 75

Stress Boulders

elsbethmartindale.com/stress-boulders

This visual handout offers an image of the potential avalanche that can occur when stress builds to a point when even a small event can seem unmanageable. Helping clients become conscious of all the stressors in their lives can both help them validate their inner experience and begin to see where adjustments and accommodations can be made.

I developed this handout as part of a presentation to professionals on self-care. It is important to practice effective stress management, especially if we work to assist others in this area. I have a sign I sometimes post on my bulletin board at work which states, "Take my advice; I'm not using it." This obviously is not the ideal. We are more able to teach, and be believable, if we actually practice what we preach.

How I use this:

I might pull out this handout in session or give it as homework as a way to talk about the precarious position of living with too much stress. I would give this to a client who is either denying the weight of the stressors or needs validation for its impact. I might say something like, ***"Let's have a look at all the current stressors in your life. It is sort of like this potential avalanche. If one thing starts to tumble, the results could be quite costly. Are you aware of this buildup? What can be done to shore things up and minimize potential damage?"*** Denial is not a good long-term strategy. This handout helps clients get real about the pressures in their lives.

Example from practice:

Tessa, a college freshman, called in a state of panic, asking for a letter to her school to extend her deadlines and postpone her finals. She came into my office and told me how she just couldn't get out of bed in the morning because she was so overwhelmed by her commitments and responsibilities. We began to look at all the stressors in front of her. The image of a field of boulders resonated with her. She was feeling "rumblings" and was fearful of being smothered and destroyed by the pressures. We took time to identify each individual stressor and what was possible to adjust to provide her a greater sense of stability. To ease the pressure of her school work, I did write a letter for Tessa. Then she identified several tasks and conflicts which could be set aside temporarily and focused her attention on the most pressing issues. The lesson of this overwhelm is clearly something Tessa took seriously. As a result, she developed a more structured plan of self-care and relaxation to prevent this sort of overwhelm from recurring.

Elsbeth Martindale
CLINICAL PSYCHOLOGIST

Stress Boulders

GET TO KNOW YOUR STRESSORS

- Identify the variety of stressors in your life. Be specific (e.g., working late on Tuesdays vs. job demands). Include professional, personal, relational, and physical stressors.

- Write the names of these stressors on individual rocks, assigning small rocks to small stressors and larger rocks to the heavier stressors in your life.

- If you'd prefer, make a list of small, medium, and large stressors on a separate piece of paper.

WARNING:
Stress can negatively "rock your world."

Crisis Management

elsbethmartindale.com/crisis-management

Not much is more stressful for a therapist than a client in crisis. When this occurs, it is essential to help clients make a personalized crisis management plan. This generic version can be a starting point for some of the basics.

How I use this:

If a client is in a state of crisis, I will pull out this handout and review its important features. The handout provides an outline of potential strategies for crisis management. An individualized plan can be designed on a separate page, specifying details of those to seek out for support, various options for body soothing, actual language of self-empathy (maybe making affirmation cards), and specific strategies for managing recurring distress.

Example from practice:

Celeste suffered from moderate-level depression for many years. As therapy unfolded, she told me how she uses cutting as a coping strategy when her pain becomes unbearable. We explored this pattern, its costs and benefits. As Celeste grew stronger in her relationship with herself, she decided she would like to find other methods for responding to her internal pain. When she felt in crisis, she wanted to consider new and more caring options for self-management. This handout gave her the basic steps to consider when the urge to cut became pronounced. Of course, this handout was not the only tool offered her to manage her self-harming behavior. It was, however, one which reminded her how she could respond to her pain in a new and more constructive manner.

Crisis Management

In the midst of a crisis, make it your goal to manage the situation from the perspective of your very best self. See the crisis as an opportunity to manage yourself at least one small step better than you did the last time you were in crisis. Here are some specific strategies to consider:

1) DON'T DO ANYTHING TO MAKE THE SITUATION WORSE!

Moly Ivins says, "The first rule of holes, when you're in one—stop digging."

Make it your intention to avoid creating drama. Don't make big decisions until you are in a calmer and a more receptive state.

2) SHOW YOURSELF SOME EMPATHY

Be gentle, kind, and loving with yourself. You're in the midst of pain. This is not the time for the critic to be let loose. Bring forward your kindest and wisest self to offer support, comfort, and clear strategies for making things better. Identify what you're feeling and acknowledge the validity of your human emotions.

3) ATTEND TO YOUR BODY

Eat some healthy food, especially protein. Avoid alcohol, sugar, and caffeine. Get needed sleep. Move your body to get your heart pumping. Create physical comfort for yourself (e.g., a hot bath, massage, cup of tea, etc.). Listen to what your body needs.

4) PAY ATTENTION TO YOUR THOUGHTS

Mindfully watch what you are thinking and concluding. Remember your skills, strengths, and intentions. You will do best if you steer your thoughts so they are:

- Realistic and reasonable
- Your own beliefs rather than those of others
- Life-enhancing and supportive of you
- Flexible and open to influence by those who are wise supporters
- Focused on solutions and removing obstacles
- Future focused, rather than retelling the story of how you got to where you are

5) REACH OUT

Surround yourself with supportive friends and family. Ask for support or help. Don't wait for others to notice your distress. Use your faith and spiritual traditions for support.

6) STEP BACK

Make time for reflecting, planning, and clarifying options. This may be a good time to take out your journal. Focus on yourself rather than others. Explore how you wish to handle things; this is where your power lies. Identify and commit to taking one small step in the direction of your mental health.

7) EXPRESS YOURSELF

Share your thoughts and feelings in a manner that supports you (e.g., conversation, prose, poetry, art, dance, and similar things). Practice stepping forward on behalf of yourself so others may know you and your needs.

Elsbeth Martindale
CLINICAL PSYCHOLOGIST

Depression Pit

elsbethmartindale.com/depression-pit

This handout offers a simple image of what happens during cycles of depression. It gives a chance to look at the external and internal factors which contribute to a dip in mood. It invites a discussion of the factors that can keep a person stuck in a depressed space as well as the known actions clients can take to help move out of the pit as soon as possible.

How I use this:

I use this handout as a representation of the common pattern of cyclic depression. The lines, on the handout, offer places to identify potential agency in three areas: avoidance, management, and recovery. It can be helpful for clients to see their power in stalling or preventing a slip into depression and to specify the actions which might be effective for them. Looking at what can be done to avoid swirling in the pit, and what steps can be taken to rise out of the pit, give clients some sense of agency to care well for themselves when depression shows up.

Example from practice:

I showed this illustration to Marcia after she had another bout of mild depression. "Yup," she said. "This explains everything." She then detailed how her extra hours at work and lack of adequate sleep led to her slipping again into the pit of depression. She was able to see how she kept herself swirling by being mad at herself, telling herself she is stupid, and wallowing in self-pity about how "this keeps happening." We looked together at her known handholds or steps for climbing out of the pit. She listed the things that have worked for her in the past and vowed to get busy utilizing these strategies to find her way back to a more contented place. Specifically, she agreed to connect with her girlfriend, go for a hike over the weekend, and call her naturopath about her supplements.

Elsbeth Martindale
CLINICAL PSYCHOLOGIST

Depression Pit

Depression is absolutely no fun. It can feel like you are in a pit out of which it is difficult to climb.

If you find yourself a frequent visitor to the depression pit, you might explore the pit and learn what you can from the experience. Three important questions you might want to consider include: What caused me to slip into the pit? What keeps or kept me stuck? And what steps helped me climb out of the pit in the past? The answers you find can help you navigate the pit in the future. Note: This exploration is easier to do when you are not at the bottom of the pit, but on your way out.

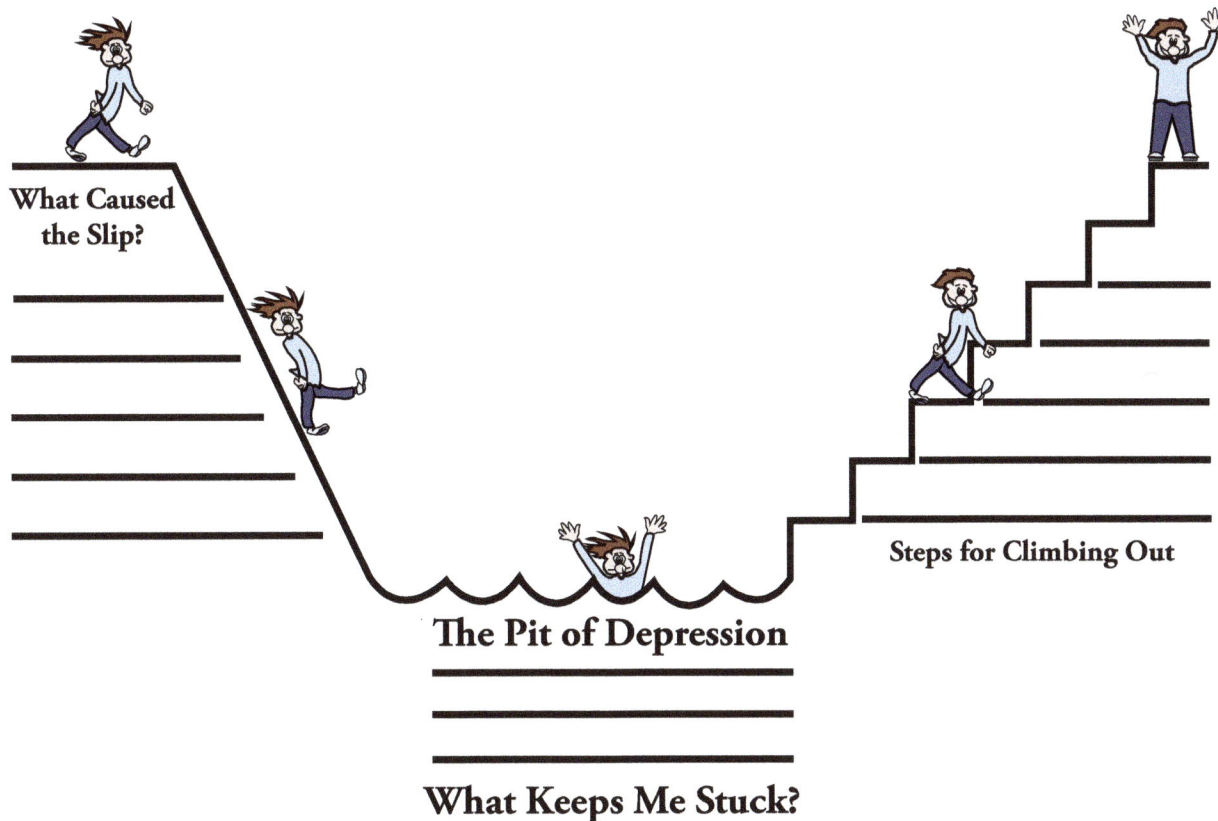

What Caused the Slip?

_____

_____

_____

_____

_____

Steps for Climbing Out

The Pit of Depression

_____

_____

_____

What Keeps Me Stuck?

Elsbeth Martindale
CLINICAL PSYCHOLOGIST

The Critic Catcher
elsbethmartindale.com/critic-catcher

This handout is a great summary of the three steps needed to reform an inner critic: (1) capturing the critic's message, (2) challenging the message in three important ways, and (3) rewriting the concern of the critic in a non-critical manner. Two additional handouts that can be helpful when teaching clients about the *Critic Catcher* are the *ROLF Filter* handout and the *Needs List* handout. When speaking of tone, in relation to "Examining the Message" (step 2), I often use the example of what my husband and I would say to our toddler when he demanded what he wanted. We'd say, "Can you say that in a way that would make me want to assist you?"

How I use this:

I use this handout at least once a month—probably because my clients' critics show up in session quite regularly. Clients need to see that "confronting the critic" is not an angry exchange or battle, but a careful exploration of how a message might land differently if the delivery were less hostile. When clients have a too-frequent inner critic, an active and persistent engagement in reforming the critic will need to be undertaken.

As a therapist, I demonstrate kind confrontation. If a client shares a self-criticism, I might start by saying, *"I don't like it when you talk that way to my client."* This shows clients the appropriateness of speaking up to disrespect and abuse. When clients see how I confront their negative internal tone, they learn they, too, can interrupt and challenge the way messages are delivered in their inner world. In short, I want my clients to be able to eventually say to their own critic, "You can't talk that way in my head!"

It is also useful for clients to help their inner critic feel respected by addressing the need that underlies its harsh message. The need is probably in service of the client's well-being but delivered in an unnecessarily harmful manner. In other words, the critic needs to learn how to talk more respectfully. The bottom line is that it is possible to create a collaborative inner system where bullying, criticism, and coercion are confronted.

Elsbeth Martindale
CLINICAL PSYCHOLOGIST

Critic Catcher

1

LISTEN

NOTICE SELF-CRITICISM

Feeling bad is often the first indication of the critic's presence. See if you can capture the critic.

I heard myself saying, "_____.

Is this voice similar to someone else's voice? Whose? _____

2

CHALLENGE

EXAMINE THE MESSAGE

THOUGHTS	NEEDS	TONE
What are the underlying beliefs or conclusions in this message? Are they true? Use the ROLF Belief Filter to examine and clean up the message. Make sure it is: • **REALISTIC** • **OWNED** • **LIFE-ENHANCING** • **FLEXIBLE**	What are the valid needs that underlie this criticism? Common human needs: safety, security, trust, growth, play, success, connection, respect, ease, nurturance, clarity, courage, empathy, freedom, accomplishment, adventure, solitude, independence, joy, expression, etc. Identify the needs: _____ _____ _____ _____	How was the message communicated? Possible tones: sarcastic, whiny, angry, rude, harsh, cold, playful, mean, unfriendly, challenging, and/or _____ _____ Does the tone used make you interested in having a conversation? Yes No Name some tones you would prefer? _____ _____

3

RE-TRAIN

DESIGN A NEW MESSAGE

Find a new way of speaking about the concerns and needs of the critic. This time say it with words that pass a ROLF filter and with a tone that keeps you engaged in the conversation. Write the new message here:

" _____."

Say this message aloud. Show the critic how to speak with respect, like a caring friend might speak.

Gently rubbing and cuddling your own arms while you speak will release oxytocin (the bonding hormone) to help you feel compassion and connection with your wiser self.

Elsbeth Martindale
CLINICAL PSYCHOLOGIST

Hold Yourself in a Positive Light
elsbethmartindale.com/hold-yourself-in-a-positive-light

It is sad to me how readily people (maybe especially in the beginning of therapy) like to tell stories of themselves which cast themselves in a terrible light (e.g., "I'm such a screw up; I can't do anything right," or "I totally blew it again. I broke down and called her. I have no discipline."). The common reasons for doing this are described in the handout. But, there are better ways to hold ourselves when we are trying to grow and evolve. I find great value in helping clients turn around their stories—from tales of defeat and stupidity to stories of their attempts, however feeble, to get their needs met. This adjustment can be quite challenging.

How I use this:
If I hear clients telling stories that feature self-criticism and judgment, I often will interrupt them to point out the added destruction to themselves caused by framing a tale in a manner that cements self-condemnation or informs me they see themselves as helpless. I might say, ***"You are really disappointed in your choices. Can you hear how hard you are being on yourself? Is it necessary/helpful to be so harsh about yourself?"*** This usually leads to an explanation of why they believe cruelness is required. From this point, I can then help them see other options for addressing their concerns in an attempt to set things right.

Using the examples in the handout, or their own stories, I help my clients reframe things in ways in which they "hold up themselves" as much as possible. If, as in Practice Suggestion #1, they forgot a doctor's appointment because of oversleeping, I might suggest they say something such as, "I was disappointed with myself for oversleeping and missing my doctor's appointment. I want to be more mindful about setting an alarm so I can make time to attend to my health."

In Practice Situation #2, telling the story as dramatically—a close call filled with panic and distress—only activates the neurological system. The body can't always discriminate story from active experience. Cortisol and adrenaline can be released in response to drama stories, even if the danger has long since passed. To "hold themselves in a good light," clients can experiment with retelling stories with a focus on their gratitude, persistence, and the soothing strategies employed to endure the former anxious moment. This method creates a more peaceful inner world.

Elsbeth Martindale
CLINICAL PSYCHOLOGIST

Hold Yourself in a Positive Light

You deserve to be respected, especially by yourself. Show others how you like to be treated by demonstrating kindness, honesty, and appreciation toward yourself.

CREATE AN INNER CULTURE OF GOODNESS

There is no need or value in living in a world full of belittlement and hate. This is true externally as well as in your inner world. Are you aware of your inner climate? Start with expanding your awareness by listening to your own self-talk.

Change it up if you find yourself being mean, excessively harsh, and impatient. Talk to yourself the way you would talk with a good friend. Confront inner bullying like a good mother by saying, "We don't talk that way in my house."

Learn to speak to yourself about your wants and needs by trying to win cooperation with all the parts of you. Even your resistance can be shown respect. Your entire inner world is within your power to create according to your own design.

WHAT GETS IN THE WAY

Three common reasons for treating yourself unkindly:

1. Others may have treated you with disrespect and you have followed their modeling. You may need to update your inner operating system.
2. Others currently treat you unkindly, so being harsh with yourself beats them to the punch. You may need a better set of friends.
3. You believe severe treatment is the only way to get yourself to behave. It's time for an internal parenting course to learn modern motivational strategies.

WHY CHANGE IT UP?

- You demonstrate confidence and self-respect.
- You show others how you desire to be treated by showing them how you treat yourself.
- Stories of triumph create good vibes and less drama.

GET SOME PRACTICE

Tell a story of a challenge you recently faced. Refrain from naming what you did wrong. Rather, tell the story from a place of what you did to cope, manage, or attempt to solve the problem. It's likely you brought your best to the problem, so tell it from this point of view.

You also can imagine yourself in one of these situations:

1. You forgot a doctor's appointment because you overslept.
2. You pulled into a gas station on empty. You'd been panicked for 20 minutes thinking you were running out of gas.
3. You poked fun at a friend's new haircut and accidentally caused hurt their feelings.
4. You chose to not go to a party because you were feeling too depressed.

> You can search throughout the entire universe for someone who is more deserving of your love and affection than you are yourself, and that person is not to be found anywhere. You, yourself, as much as anybody in the universe, deserve your love and affection. - Buddha

Elsbeth Martindale
CLINICAL PSYCHOLOGIST

Anger Balloon
http://elsbethmartindale.com/anger-balloon

I love the metaphor of a balloon expanding to represent the pressure unexpressed needs put on the psyche. When left unattended, needs begin to pressure the system and, if met with continued dismissal, can grow into anger. The end result of this build-up can be an explosion and a messy outcome. It is helpful to let clients know that at the core of anger is a legitimate need.

How I use this:

I tell my clients, as I show them this illustration, that there are conscious as well as unconscious strategies for managing needs. The unconscious strategies often require less effort, like going downhill, whereas conscious strategies can feel like an uphill grind. Although a conscious strategy may be more challenging in the moment, the effort of mindfully choosing a wise strategy will likely lead to a better outcome. This handout helps discuss the various strategies for dealing with tension at different levels, for finding release before getting to rage.

Example from practice:

Kate is not an angry person. She rarely lets herself raise her voice or show displeasure. She came to therapy, referred by her doctor, for unexplained intestinal pain. After building trust and acknowledging her peacekeeping values, I suggested we look at what happens when needs are not met and how unexpressed needs can turn into anger. This was a new concept for Kate. I showed her the handout, and the illustration helped her gain a sense of how the repression of needs can manifest indirectly, even as physiological symptoms. I suggested we scout around to see if she had needs that weren't being addressed. Gently, we looked at her long-standing need to please, her fear of rejection, and her exhaustion raising three children on her own. She realized she needed more contribution from her children, better boundaries at work so she could get home on time, and more support in her relationships. We looked at the tension in her system caused by not having these needs expressed. Then, we turned the focus of therapy to learning the skills of expression and advocacy. Kate read *Non-Violent Communication* and learned many peaceful ways to speak up about her needs, and she began to practice these skills with her kids and colleagues. Feeling more empowered to have her needs addressed helped alleviate Kate's stomach pain while keeping her identity as a peaceful woman.

Elsbeth Martindale
CLINICAL PSYCHOLOGIST

Anger Balloon

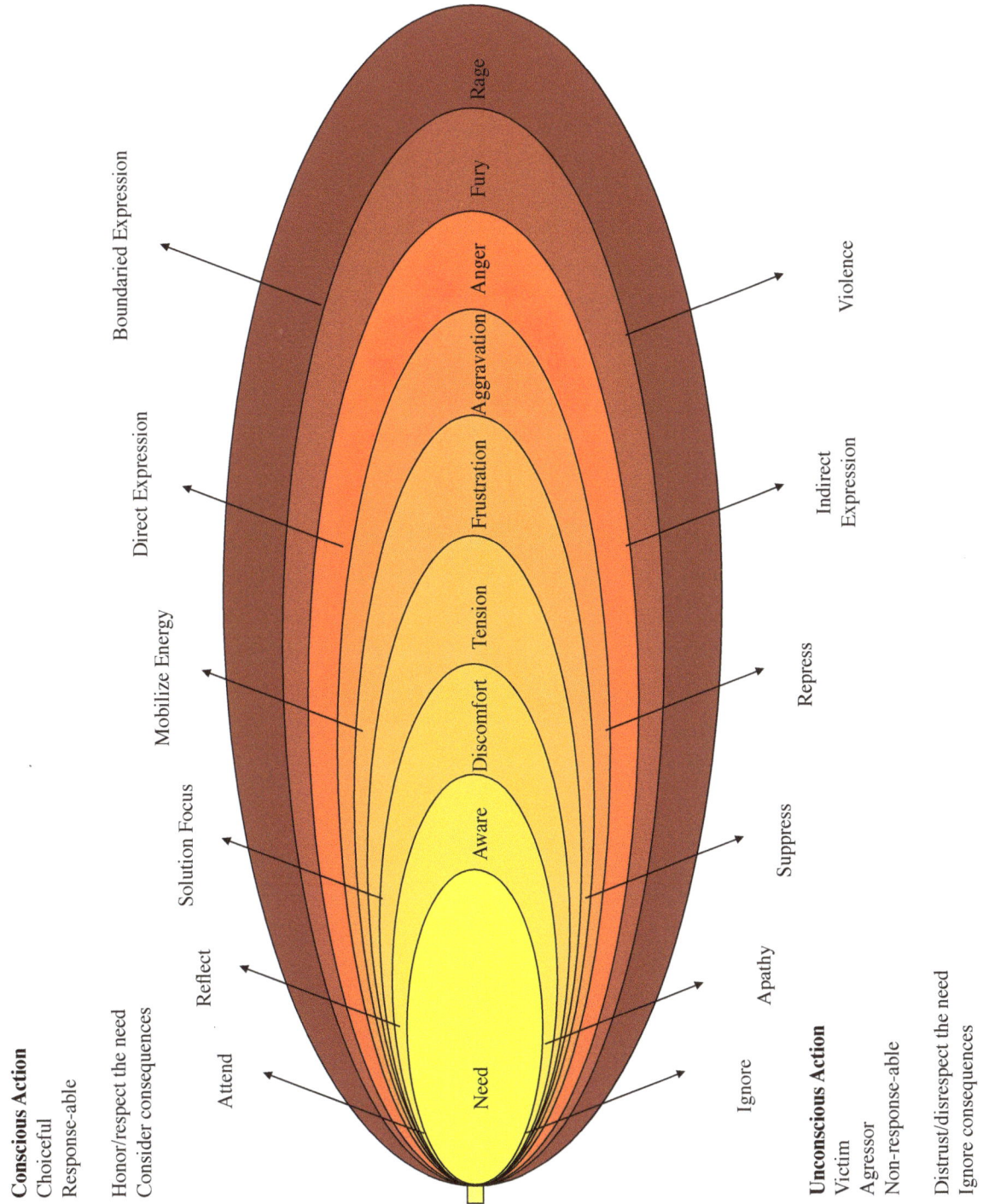

Rage

Fury

Anger

Aggravation

Frustration

Tension

Discomfort

Aware

Need

Boundaried Expression

Direct Expression

Mobilize Energy

Solution Focus

Reflect

Attend

Violence

Indirect Expression

Repress

Suppress

Apathy

Ignore

Conscious Action
Choiceful
Response-able

Honor/respect the need
Consider consequences

Unconscious Action
Victim
Agressor
Non-response-able

Distrust/disrespect the need
Ignore consequences

Elsbeth Martindale
CLINICAL PSYCHOLOGIST

Anger Continuum
http://elsbethmartindale.com/anger-balloon

The Anger Continuum handout shows an elaborated description of both the conscious and unconscious strategies for managing needs.

How I use this:
The point of explaining this to clients is to show them the various actions that can take them off the road to rage. Even when clients have a great deal of unexpressed emotion, resulting from a poorly managed need, healthy solutions can be found for dispelling negative feelings without doing damage to self or others.

Example from practice:
Growing up in an angry household didn't help Lilly learn skills for dealing effectively with her own unmet needs. She learned to suppress her desires to avoid meeting with reactivity on the part of her parents. This stuffing of her feelings and needs set up Lilly for having angry outbursts in her marriage. She hadn't learned to take her needs seriously and make clear requests as an advocate for herself. This *Anger Continuum* helped show Lilly the path she had been trained to walk in an unconscious reaction to her family. This handout outlined a clear path toward being more successful in having her needs recognized within herself and then represented effectively to others. This relearning of the conscious path for managing her feelings was something Lilly had to understand and then practice over and over until it became the well-worn and chosen path for caring for herself.

Elsbeth Martindale
CLINICAL PSYCHOLOGIST

Anger Continuum

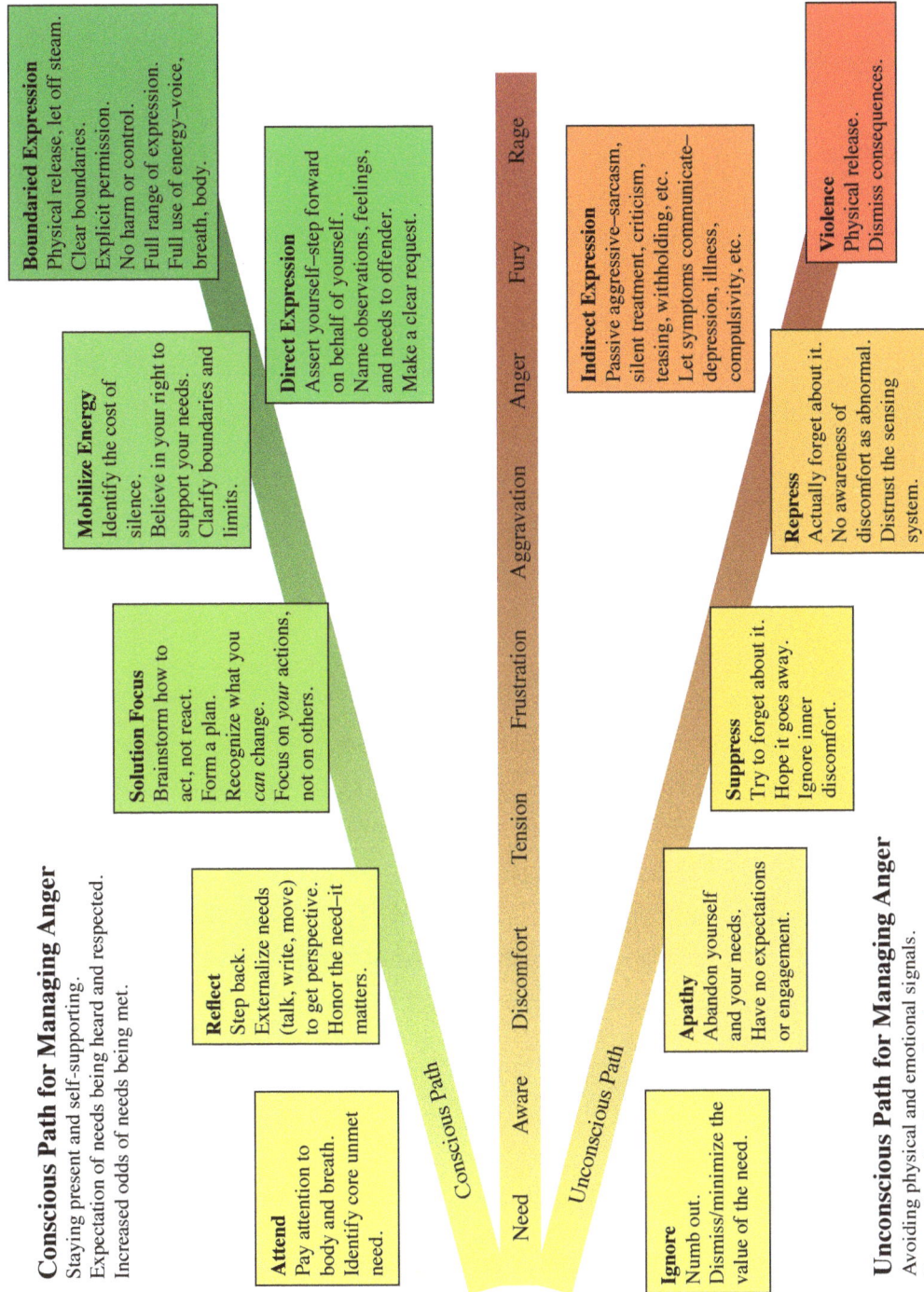

Conscious Path for Managing Anger
Staying present and self-supporting.
Expectation of needs being heard and respected.
Increased odds of needs being met.

Boundaried Expression
Physical release, let off steam.
Clear boundaries.
Explicit permission.
No harm or control.
Full range of expression.
Full use of energy—voice, breath, body.

Mobilize Energy
Identify the cost of silence.
Believe in your right to support your needs.
Clarify boundaries and limits.

Direct Expression
Assert yourself–step forward on behalf of yourself.
Name observations, feelings, and needs to offender.
Make a clear request.

Solution Focus
Brainstorm how to act, not react.
Form a plan.
Recognize what you *can* change.
Focus on *your* actions, not on others.

Reflect
Step back.
Externalize needs (talk, write, move) to get perspective.
Honor the need–it matters.

Attend
Pay attention to body and breath.
Identify core unmet need.

Violence
Physical release.
Dismiss consequences.

Indirect Expression
Passive aggressive–sarcasm, silent treatment, criticism, teasing, withholding, etc.
Let symptoms communicate—depression, illness, compulsivity, etc.

Repress
Actually forget about it.
No awareness of discomfort as abnormal.
Distrust the sensing system.

Suppress
Try to forget about it.
Hope it goes away.
Ignore inner discomfort.

Apathy
Abandon yourself and your needs.
Have no expectations or engagement.

Ignore
Numb out.
Dismiss/minimize the value of the need.

Unconscious Path for Managing Anger
Avoiding physical and emotional signals.
Expectation of neglect or abandonment.
Needs left ungratified.

Need · Aware · Discomfort · Tension · Frustration · Aggravation · Anger · Fury · Rage

Conscious Path · Unconscious Path

"Violence is the language of the unheard." - Dr. Martin Luther King Jr.

Distress Tolerance Activities

elsbethmartindale.com/distress-tolerance-activities

This list of distress tolerance activities includes many of the items discussed in Dialectical Behavioral Therapy. I organized and expanded the distress management ideas into seven categories. The handout is helpful in showing clients they have many supportive options from which to choose when they are distressed. Once empowered, clients begin to see their agency and capacity to choose their responses for self-management while they build new skills to reduce the frequency of distress in their lives.

How I use this:

I generally use this handout in conjunction with my *Distress Tolerance Cards* (http://elsbethmartindale.com/product/distress-tolerance-cards/). I give my clients the stack of cards and ask them to sort the cards into three categories: useful, possible, and not helpful strategies. I then mark this handout with all the methods for distress management the client identified as useful or possible. I send them home with a copy of the marked sheet, so they can see their options for caring well for themselves in moments of distress.

Example from practice:

Terry was overwhelmed by emotion on a fairly frequent basis. She had little skill in speaking up for herself and used primitive strategies for dealing with her frustration. Like many clients who haven't yet learned good coping and problem management skills, Terry would often resort to burning herself as a way to release and distract herself from her emotional pain. She needed alternative actions which would offer her the needed release or distraction without causing injury and harm to herself. She needed ideas for how to care for herself with more tenderness and respect. We sorted the Distress Tolerance Cards and discussed the options as we went through the deck. I marked this *Distress Tolerance Activities* handout for her with all the things she determined might be useful when she felt overwhelmed. This list gave Terry many ideas for comforting herself and helped her feel her power to consciously choose how to respond to distress when it arose.

Elsbeth Martindale
CLINICAL PSYCHOLOGIST

Distress Tolerance Activities

Review this list of activities which often help people manage distressing situations. There are seven different categories of activities from which to choose. Keep this list close at hand so you can more easily respond with intention rather than reacting with old habits or unconscious patterns.

BODY-MOVING ACTIVITIES

These activities encourage you to move your body to increase circulation, distract you from your worries, & burn off energy. They are most effective when you feel either agitated or lethargic.

- Bike ride
- Chop wood
- Clean
- Climb stairs
- Dance
- Garden
- Go for a run
- Hit or throw a ball
- Kick something
- Play a sport
- Stretch your body
- Walk or hike
- Work out/Exercise
- Wrestle
- Yoga, Tai Chi, or Qigong
- _____
- _____

SOCIALIZING ACTIVITIES

These activities engage you with others. They help you see that you are not alone.

- Ask for support
- Be with people you admire
- Call a friend or family member
- Give something to someone
- Go to a religious service
- Go to a support group
- Go to an event
- Help someone in need
- Listen to another's perspective
- Make eye contact and smile at others
- Random act of kindness
- Reconnect with an old friend
- Spend time with positive and uplifting people
- Visit family or a friend
- Volunteer
- Write, text, or email
- _____
- _____

IN-THE-MOMENT ACTIVITIES

These activities bring your focus to making things better, as best you can, in the moment. Some activities are easy to do without any preparation, some set you up for pleasurable experiences in the future, and others require that you prepare a space to make your situation different.

- Affirm yourself
- Be gentle with yourself
- Compare
- Distract yourself with entertainment
- Emulate someone you admire
- Imagine a wall
- Make a massage appointment
- Make therapy appointment
- Make a reservation
- Observe without judgment
- Packaging - box up a thought & set it aside
- Practice acceptance
- Practice gratitude
- Practice relinquishment
- Pray
- Read uplifting material
- Recall a past pleasant moment
- Repeat a mantra
- Reward yourself
- Root your feet
- Schedule a retreat or vacation
- Shout "stop"
- Sing or hum a joyous tune
- Speak up
- Visualize a screen or shield
- Wear your favorite color
- _____
- _____

SENSATION-FOCUSED ACTIVITIES

These activities shift your attention to your senses. They stimulate sensory awareness and can be used as a distraction. Most are pleasurable but some are not. Never do anything harmful to your body.

- Burn incense
- Buy or pick flowers
- Cup of tea or coffee
- Cold washcloth
- Crumble herbs
- Eat something tasty
- File your nails
- Five senses stimulation
- Go out to eat
- Go somewhere new
- Hold an ice cube
- Hot bath or shower
- Lay on a heating pad
- Light a candle
- Listen to a story
- Listen to music
- Listen to nature
- Paint your nails
- Pamper yourself
- Physical sensations in the moment
- Put on lotion
- Put on scented oils or perfume
- Seek beauty
- Sex
- Snap a rubber band
- Splash cold water on your face
- Suck on hard candy
- Warm your hands, cup over eyes, breathe
- _____
- _____

Elsbeth Martindale
CLINICAL PSYCHOLOGIST

Handouts for Psychotherapy

RELAXING ACTIVITIES

These are activities that relax and calm your body.

- Breathe deeply
- Create art
- Create silence
- Exercise hard
- Fire in fireplace
- Go for a drive
- Go to bed early
- Hobby or craft
- Listen to a guided relaxation
- Massage
- Nap
- Play a game
- Play with an animal
- Play with clothes
- Progressive relaxation from toes to head
- Rock in a rocking chair
- Sauna
- Sit in the dark
- Sit in the sun
- Take a break from problem-solving
- Visualize a mini-vacation
- Visualize a peaceful place
- Visualize a secret room
- _____
- _____

EMOTIONAL-EXPRESSION ACTIVITIES

These activities get you in touch with your feelings and help you express them. Some activities require words but many are designed just to allow you to feel or see the extent of your distress.

- Assert feelings and needs
- Bite something
- Break plates
- Cry
- Empty-chair technique
- Grunt, stomp, shout
- Identify feelings and needs
- Journal or doodle
- Look for meaning & purpose in the struggle
- Pound a pillow
- Rip something
- Scream while driving
- Squeeze a rubber ball
- Stir opposite emotions
- Talk in a loving way
- Vesuvius release
- Visualize a drain
- Write a letter expressing yourself
- _____
- _____

THOUGHT-CHALLENGE ACTIVITIES

These activities take your mind to a task that requires thought or sharp focus. These actions help you steer your mind away from things that are troubling by giving you a problem to solve or question to ponder.

- Color name
- Count backwards by 3's from 100
- Count things
- Count to 10 slowly
- Creative writing
- Examine pros and cons
- Focus on what you like, not on what's wrong
- Identify your thoughts
- Mindfulness
- Name favorites
- Opportunity to learn
- Plan a joyous event
- Play a musical instrument
- Read
- Recite Serenity Prayer
- Sing something complex
- View long-term goals
- Visualize your success
- Work
- Work a puzzle
- _____
- _____

DISTRESS TOLERANCE CARD SET

You can find a set of the Distress Tolerance Cards at:
http://elsbethmartindale.com/product/distress-tolerance-cards/

The cards provide a detailed description of each strategy. You might find it helpful to have your clients sort the cards into piles of what works, what might work, and what does not work for them in managing distressful situations. Then, by marking this handout with your clients' preferred distress-managing strategies, you'll be able to offer them a roadmap for being proactive in calming themselves and responding mindfully to their next distressful situation.

Elsbeth Martindale
CLINICAL PSYCHOLOGIST

Letters to Myself When I'm Depressed

elsbethmartindale.com/letters-to-myself-when-im-depressed

Clients who struggle with repeated episodes of depression often feel defeated and angry when the signs of "another round" begin to manifest. This handout can be given to such clients when they are not depressed as a way to help them respond to their depression from a place of self-support. These pre-written letters help clients manage a depressive dip, not with self-hatred and dread, but with a bit of kindness and care for themselves. This tool increases self-agency and self-soothing. It helps clients see their role in attending to and easing the challenges in their lives.

How I use this:

I suggest clients write three letters to themselves when they are not depressed, thinking about and addressing the specific actions they might take when they are at each of the **three stages of depression**. The goal is to set clients in the role of self-manager, even in the midst of their suffering, to help them see their power to step into a position of self-comforter and caregiver. The idea is to make the letters sweet and tender, like little gifts to the part of themselves that is suffering.

Although the handout doesn't specify this, I prefer to have clients write their letters in longhand. I then ask them to store the letters in an envelope they are likely to see often enough that they know where to reach for it when depression shows up. This feels more personal than letters on their phone or computer.

Example from practice:

Lynn has had many bouts of depression in her life. Part of her healing involved coming to a place of acceptance for the management and care of herself from the beginning and all the way through a depressive episode. This role as self-caregiver shifted her from a victim perspective to a place of self-advocacy.

In the first letter to herself, Lynn included a list of the strategies she found helpful for staving off depression. She invited herself to implement as many of these as possible. With her second letter, she included a set of affirmation cards to remind herself of her ability to weather her depressive dips. She decided to amend her last letter with a self-care box of goodies. Shifting her focus from self-hatred to self-care, Lynn was actually able to avoid the deep pit of depression and never needed the third letter during the remaining time we worked together.

Elsbeth Martindale
CLINICAL PSYCHOLOGIST

Letters to Myself When I'm Depressed

Depression comes in waves, sometimes gently and sometimes like a crashing thunder storm. Getting to know your rhythm, pattern, and the various levels of depression can help in depression management. Here is a simple method for identifying and addressing the stages of your depression. Writing letters to yourself at each of the stages can help you respond to your depression with the best care possible.

Start by identifying three distinct phases in your depression cycle. I often refer to them as, "falling," "fallen," and "can't get up." Place the names in the blanks for each of these three different stages.

1 _____

LETTER #1: Now, face the person you are when you are at the first stage of depression. Look at what generally happens at this stage. What do you think about, act like, tend to do, or not do? Step back and just observe yourself in this early stage of depression. See if you can develop a compassionate attitude toward this part of yourself. Without judgmentt, see the ways this part is hurting, struggling, and full of needs. Notice s/he/they is not evil or bad, just hurt and trying to survive the best way s/he/they can. From this place of compassion and clarity, write a letter to yourself expressing your care and concern. Offer ideas of what might help lighten the depression. Do not scold or be critical of yourself. Just gently invite yourself to take good care during this gray time. Maybe you'll want to remind yourself that, "this too shall pass."

2 _____

LETTER #2: Next, look at the person you are in the second phase of your depression cycle. Notice that this stage is more challenging. Do as you did in the first letter. Start with observing, then sit in a place of compassion and write a different letter to yourself at this stage of moderate depression. Think of what would be helpful to hear when you're in this place. What would soothe and comfort you? Think of words and actions that might be helpful at this stage.

3 _____

LETTER #3: Finally, look at yourself at the last and most severe stage of your depressive cycle. This may be a place you go to rarely or a place you go more frequently than you'd like. Imagine yourself in the midst of the struggle and pain of this stage. See the chaos, loneliness, and desperation that can be felt here. Access as much empathy toward yourself as possible. Stay out of judgment and write a brief letter sharing your concern, compassion, and care. At this last stage, you may want to make a care package for yourself. This would be a way of showing support and comfort. You could include bubble bath, a coupon for a massage, the phone numbers of friends or babysitters, your favorite candy bar, or some other "goodie." The goal is to comfort and soothe yourself, letting yourself know you will be okay and reminding yourself of the steps that lead to feeling better.

Elsbeth Martindale
CLINICAL PSYCHOLOGIST

Grief and Loss
elsbethmartindale.com/grief-and-loss

This handout summarizes both the symptoms and the process of grief and loss. It helps normalize the experiences of clients and shows them their path is well trodden and familiar to many.

How I use this:
When clients experience a loss, I offer this handout to them so they know what they can expect. It often serves to validate what they are already experiencing. Grief is often extremely personal, but hearing the commonality of human reactions can bring a bit of comfort and acceptance of the journey.

Example from practice:
Roz lost her best friend in a tragic accident. Roz was overwrought with grief. She began therapy, at the recommendation of her primary care physician, because there was concern about the possibility of depression. Roz was having trouble with sleep and had lost weight since the accident. Indeed Roz was depressed but, upon full evaluation her symptoms didn't meet the criteria of a full depressive episode. We looked at this *Grief and Loss* handout together. When Roz saw many of her symptoms listed as symptoms of grief rather than clinical depression, she was relieved. Roz turned her focus to allowing the sorrow to be expressed and ushering the grief through its process. Although this undertaking was painful, Roz was relieved to understand the symptoms she experienced were normal reactions to loss and not pathological. Roz tracked these symptoms, using the list on the handout. With time, she was able to watch as the signs of grief and loss subsided and she came to a place of acceptance and peace.

Elsbeth Martindale
CLINICAL PSYCHOLOGIST

Grief and Loss

Because grief can be so painful, and sometimes seems overwhelming, it often frightens us. Many people who are in a grief situation seem to wonder if they are grieving in the "right" way and wonder if the feelings they have are "normal."

There are **five common stages** associated with loss and grief.

Denial - "No, not me, it cannot be true."
Anger - "Why me? This isn't right!"
Bargaining - "One more chance. If only ..."
Depression - "I'm lost. I'm broken."
Acceptance - "So what's next?"

These five stages don't necessarily happen in this order, but all of these stages are typically associated with the experience of loss.

It may be reassuring to know that most people who suffer a loss experience one or more of the following:

- Tightness in the throat, or heaviness in the chest
- An empty feeling in the stomach; loss of appetite
- Guilt at some times, anger at others
- Restlessness (looking for activity, but finding it difficult to concentrate)
- A sense of unreality, as if the loss didn't actually happen
- Sensing the loved one's presence (expecting the loved one to walk through the door, hearing his/her/their voice, seeing the loved one's face, etc.)
- Aimless wandering; forgetfulness; inability to finish things once begun
- Difficulty sleeping; frequent dreams of the loved one
- Intense preoccupation with the life of the deceased
- Assumption of loved one's mannerisms or traits
- Guilt or anger over things that did or did not happen in the relationship with the deceased

- Intense anger at the loved one for leaving
- A need to tell, retell, and remember things about the loved one and the experience of the death
- Mood changes over the slightest things
- Tears at unexpected times
- Feeling "out of place" when with others
- Repeated sighing or difficulty breathing
- Lower resistance to infection

The experiences listed are all natural and normal reactions to loss. These symptoms come and go and affect individuals in different ways. Probably of greatest concern are any physical symptoms. If symptoms are causing you worry, it is a good idea to check with your doctor. Keeping yourself physically healthy will help you manage all the emotional aspects associated with grieving.

Grief and Loss Ritual

elsbethmartindale.com/grief-and-loss-ritual

My colleague, an acupuncturist who works in hospice, shared this beautiful ritual with me. I love its simplicity and grace.

How I use this:

I've used this ritual only in group work, although I've sent it to clients to consider outside of therapy. In group it has been very powerful. Having a witness to grief seems to ease its pain, if ever so slightly.

Example from practice:

My Monday evening women's group has eight members. Recently four of the eight members experienced a significant loss. I took this opportunity to offer the group this simple grief ritual. The women were all moved by this opportunity to both support and be supported around the challenging experience of loss.

Elsbeth Martindale
CLINICAL PSYCHOLOGIST

Grief and Loss Ritual

Grief and loss can shake your world like no other experience. It's helpful to have some methods for encountering and enduring this challenging emotional experience. The ritual presented here is simple yet quite profound. It was developed and taught by Rachel Naomi Remen, MD. She recommends doing this ritual a week after the passing of a loved one. You can do this ritual after any loss—such as the death a loved one, the loss of a pet, or the ending of a relationship. You may wish to journal about your experience or practice this ritual with a group of trusted friends. Repeating the ritual over time can reveal new layers of insight.

SET THE STAGE

Begin by **lighting a candle.** This designates the time as separate from "ordinary life." It allows for a clear beginning and ending. In this prepared place, **imagine the person or pet you lost**. Picture that loved one in whatever way comes to mind–perhaps as you last saw him/her/them or as he/she/they were long ago.

RECEIVE THE GIFT

Open your hands in a gesture of reception and ask yourself, **"What am I learning from this ending?"** (with regard to life, death, work, love, and so on). Picturing your loved one again, bring your hands together and thank him/her/them, saying something such as, **"I thank you for this gift. I honor you for it."**

HOW HAVE I GROWN?

Open your hands again, and, with a receptive stance, ask yourself, **"How have I grown or been changed by this experience and this learning?"** Again, picturing your loved one, bring your hands together and say, **"I thank you for this growth."**

ACKNOWLEDGE REGRET

With another gesture of receptiveness, open your hands and ask, **"What do I regret or wish I had done differently?"** Then, picturing your loved one, and bring your hands together, offer an apology, and say something such as, **"I did not want it to be this way. I'm sorry and I ask for your forgiveness."** Take several moments to listen, then ask if there is anything he/she/they want you to know in response to this acknowledgment of sorrow.

OFFER BLESSINGS

With a final gesture of receptiveness, open your hands and consider, **"What do I wish for you on your journey?"** After considering your response, bring your hands together and say something such as, **"This is what I wish for you on your journey. I bless you with this gift."**

Elsbeth Martindale
CLINICAL PSYCHOLOGIST

Goodbye Letter
elsbethmartindale.com/goodbye-letter

Here's a simple structure for the challenging task of accepting a loss. This offers clients some language for speaking about the specifics of their loss and an invitation to practice letting go when they are ready.

How I use this:
I've not used this handout often but it has come in handy a few times in my many years of practice. Although this handout doesn't cover the enormity of what needs to be expressed in loss, it offers a starting point and a vision for a desired outcome.

Example from practice:
Ky felt strongly connected to his aunt. She had been like a second mother to Ky, caring for him when his own mother was absent. It was quite a shock when he got the call from his sister announcing his aunt's passing. Although he hadn't seen her in several years, he was deeply distressed by her unexpected death. He felt regret and guilt, in addition to sorrow, for not having stayed in more regular contact. Ky had been in therapy for many months working on issues related to his partnership, but his aunt's death became the focal topic for several sessions. After exploring the mix of emotions surrounding this loss, Ky came to a place of acceptance. He was ready, within himself, to say goodbye. I gave him a copy of this handout as a template for constructing a letter to assist him in letting go. Ky came back to his next session with a sweet goodbye letter to his aunt. He was able to thank her for all her tenderness and care. He was able to ask for forgiveness for being distant the past several years. This writing process freed Ky of his guilt and allowed him to appreciate the beauty of this meaningful relationship.

Elsbeth Martindale
CLINICAL PSYCHOLOGIST

Goodbye Letter

Saying goodbye is often very difficult, especially when an ending happens without your choice. You may need to go through much sorrow, anger, and denial before you can settle into acceptance of losing something or someone you treasured. When you're ready, saying good-bye will free you to move on to new possibilities. Writing a goodbye letter can be helpful with this process. It is a way to put down thoughts and ideas and to see what gets revealed. When you write your goodbye letter, don't censor! In writing freely, you will learn what you may still need to work on in order to truly be free.

SOME HELPFUL PROMPTS MIGHT INCLUDE:

Dear _____ ,

There are several things I want you to know but never said to you. I wish I would have told you ...

The things I enjoyed about you include ...

The things you did which hurt, angered, or scared me are ...

IN THE END, YOU MAY BE ABLE TO WRITE SOMETHING SUCH AS:

I choose to let you go. I no longer need to hold on to my feelings of _____ toward you.
I let these feelings go. I wish you peace and invite your spirit to live happily and free.

Elsbeth Martindale
CLINICAL PSYCHOLOGIST

Part III

Self-Care

Handouts for improving self-care give clients tools for assessing their current and ideal levels of care for their own needs. Whether the needs are relational or internal—supporting attitudes and actions—these handouts help clients see the importance of their commitment and participation in creating the life they want.

Assess Your Support 79

Restoration and Rejuvenation 81

Resilience Building 83

Resiliency Factors 85

Self-Encouragement 87

Self-Care 101 89

Selfishness Defined 91-94

Give Yourself a Hand 95

Gratitude Homework 97

Making Life Sweeter 99

Savoring the Moment 101

Stages of Change 103

Motivation to Change 105

Self-Reinforcement 107

Landing Pads 109

Journal Protector 111-113

Caregiving Assessment 115-123

Commitments to Better Self-Care 125

Gems of Wisdom 127

Assess Your Support

elsbethmartindale.com/assess-your-support

It can be valuable to help clients step back and assess the relationships in their life. Sometimes people hold on to relationships which are not nourishing without even being aware of the costs. This handout helps clients think about the qualities that matter to them in friendship and then rate their close companions to see how well they match their ideas of supportive connection.

Many clients are resistant to evaluate honestly their friendships, feeling that doing so may be an act of disloyalty. This barrier is a delicate one and needs to be respected. When clients embrace the challenge, however, and mindfully examine the relationships with which they surround themselves, they can gain great insights.

How I use this:

When clients are dissatisfied with their support system—needing to expand their contacts or complaining frequently about those in their inner circle—this handout can be instructive. I start by asking them to identify the qualities they find valuable in friendship. This is a powerful task on its own. Then, taking one companion at a time, we go through the prompts on the handout. This process opens my clients' eyes to what is lacking in their current support network. The process also illuminates where they may need to invest less or more energy in order to build more meaningful connections.

Example from practice:

Liz had a number of "good friends" in her life but often felt longing for deeper emotional involvement. In reviewing this handout together, she discovered how a peripheral friend was more in alignment with her intimacy needs than the women she claimed were her closest friends. This led Liz to reconsider her energy expenditure in her relationships. She decided to engage more with the peripheral friend, inviting her to activities and sharing her appreciation of the friendship more openly. Liz kept her other friends but looked less to them for the emotional contact she so craved.

Elsbeth Martindale
CLINICAL PSYCHOLOGIST

Assess Your Support

Social support is an important factor in emotional health. Many people will come into your life just as, over time, other people leave and move on. It is important to continue to form new friendships, so you have access to support and connection when you need it. Make a new friend every year. Doing so allows you to let go of friendships when you out-grow them or when they no longer provide the nourishment you need.

QUALITIES OF GOOD FRIENDS	Friend #1	Friend #2	Friend #3	Friend #4
They speak of uplifting, hopeful, positive ideas.				
They are open to talk about struggles, losses, or challenges, theirs and mine.				
I feel listened to and heard by them.				
I feel safe to share personal and vulnerable parts of myself with them.				
I am able to receive empathy and support from them.				
I receive affirmation or supportive words from them.				
I have received encouragement toward my goals from them.				
They make time for our relationship.				
I can laugh or cry with them.				
They give and/or receive affection from me.				

1. Read the qualities of good friends. Add additional qualities which are important to you in friendship.

2. Write the names of four of your most significant friends in the top of each column.

3. In the columns below each friend's name, rate each from one to five (this will be difficult) to show the degree to which each exhibits a particular quality in his/her/their friendship with you.

4. Reflect on what this shows you about your closest friendships. Are there adjustments or changes you'd like to make to increase the value of your connections?

Elsbeth Martindale
CLINICAL PSYCHOLOGIST

Restoration and Rejuvenation

elsbethmartindale.com/restoration-rejuvenation

This is a fabulous handout for discussing with clients the need for balancing input and output of life energy. Unless enough energizing activities are invited into one's life, his/her/their personal "cup" can easily run dry. Various questions can help to assess a client's depletion: *"Are your expending your energy with consciousness and choice? Are you making time for restoration? Are you clear about what restores you? Are you giving too much away without replenishing?"* This handout captures each of these questions with a clear, memorable illustration.

How I use this:

I will pull out this handout in session so I can discuss all the aspects of restoration with my clients. Sometimes they need help in identifying what feels restorative. Sometimes they need to loosen the valve that allows the energy to flow into their personal cup. Sometimes they could use some washers on the dripping faucets to stop the drain of their energy. I might spend a whole session just talking through the details of this handout.

The best way to use this handout is to have clients fill it out. Invite them to name the things that restore them and write them down. Before talking about how to "open the tap and fill the cup," I find it helpful to have them list all the drains on their personal cup and decide if these are choiceful or automatic. I end with a discussion of how to shut down the flow of some of the spigots, if appropriate, and then examine how and when to open the valve from the reservoir. Getting out of the theoretical and into actions for change is a hallmark of a useful handout.

Example from practice:

Kat had a busy professional life on top of raising two children and visiting her ailing mother on a weekly basis. She lived a good but exhausting life. When physical symptoms of stress became unbearable, she began therapy. You can imagine the problem: all the spigots on her personal cup were fully open and not enough flow was coming into her cup to replace the output—a recipe for depletion and stress. Kat knew what was in her preferred "reservoir of energy" but wasn't turning the tap to bring the restorative actions into regular practice. This image helped her see her dilemma clearly. After taking time to prioritize her own rejuvenation needs, Kat was able to request more support from her kids, set time boundaries on her visits to her mother, and make space to meet a friend at the gym twice a week for a good workout. All this allowed Kat to keep giving, but from a place of peace and abundance.

Elsbeth Martindale
CLINICAL PSYCHOLOGIST

Restoration and Rejuvenation

Reservoir of Energy

Making Art   Watching Sports   Time With Friends

A Good Book   Music   Parties

Being in Nature   Good Food

Exercise

Playing Sports   Massage   A Nap

Reading the Newspaper   Viewing Art   Time Alone

Reservoir of Energy

Personal Cup

WHAT ENERGIZES ME?

_____

_____

_____

_____

_____

_____

WHEN DO I PLAN TO TAP INTO WHAT RESTORES, REJUVENATES, AND FULFILLS ME?

_____

_____

_____

_____

_____

WHAT DRAINS MY PERSONAL CUP? IS IT CHOICEFUL?   Y/N

_____   ___

_____   ___

_____   ___

_____   ___

_____   ___

_____   ___

Elsbeth Martindale
CLINICAL PSYCHOLOGIST

Resilience Building

elsbethmartindale.com/resilience-building

My colleague, Dr. Catherine Becket, gave a presentation on resilience and drew a similar illustration on the board. I loved her representation of the need for balance between stressors and uplifting actions and have adapted it for my handout.

How I use this:

I combine this handout with the *Resiliency Factors* handout. The illustration on this handout helps clients see the mechanics of how stressors need to be balanced with buoyancy factors to avoid feeling weighed down by the demands of life.

Example from practice:

Keisha was a recent college graduate. She moved home, after college, to live with her parents while she looked for work. She came to therapy feeling lost, stressed, and fearful. Her degree in theatre arts was not leading her to the job opportunities for which she had hoped. She claimed she had always been a bubbly person but found herself feeling gloomy and down. After verifying she was not clinically depressed, I suggested we look at the balance of stressors versus uplifting features of her current life. This diagram helped her see how out of balance she was. Her weights were many and heavy: unemployment, loss of a familiar social network after graduation, the demands of living with parents after years of independence, and no money. We then examined the *Resiliency Factors* handout and identified five things Keisha was interested in doing to build her capacity to manage her current life stressors. By implementing these resilience strategies, Keisha was able to manage the stress without getting depressed. Her bubbly self could once again shine through. She was able to find a job, build new relationships, and work toward moving out on her own.

Resilience Building

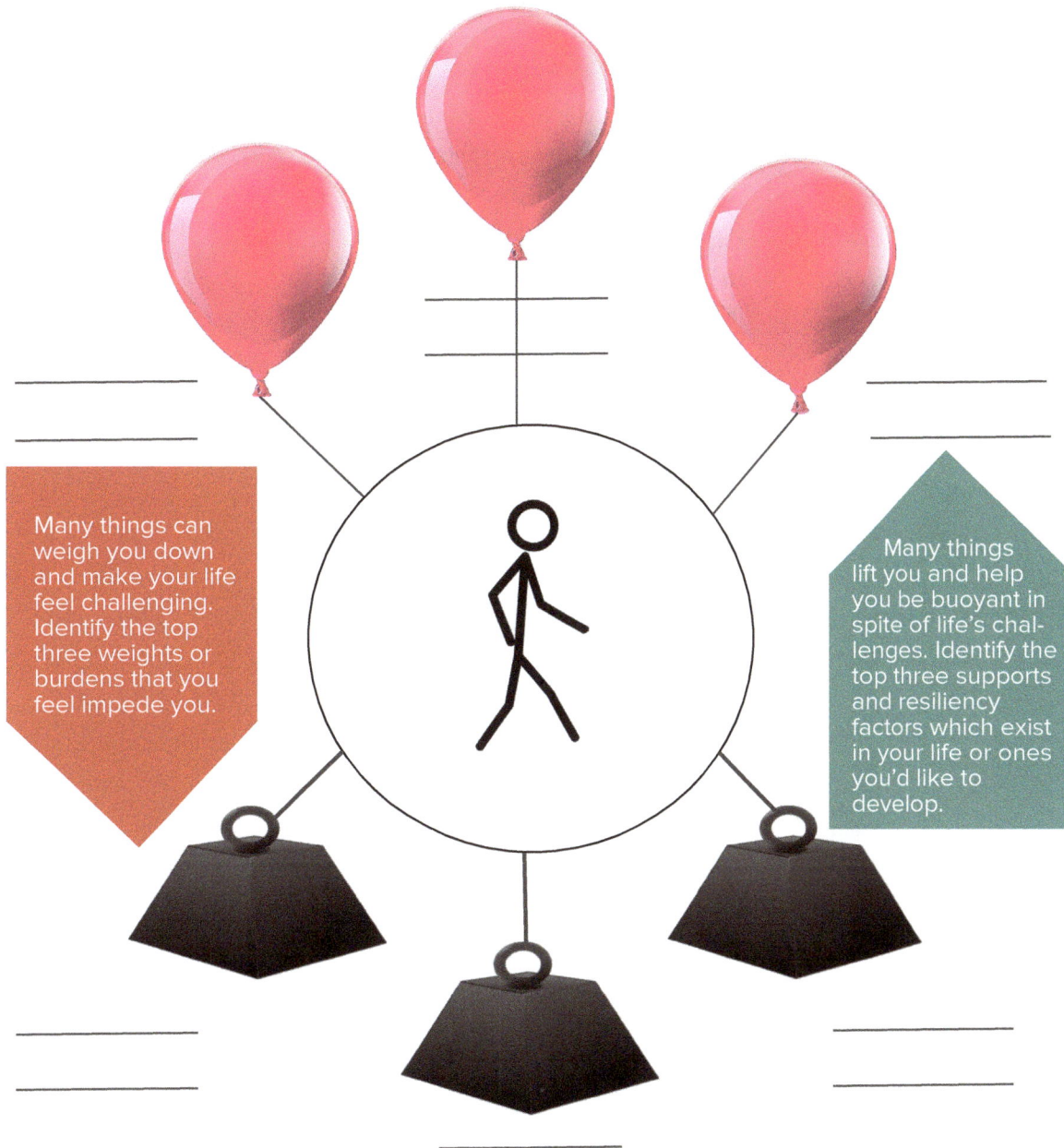

Many things can weigh you down and make your life feel challenging. Identify the top three weights or burdens that you feel impede you.

Many things lift you and help you be buoyant in spite of life's challenges. Identify the top three supports and resiliency factors which exist in your life or ones you'd like to develop.

Elsbeth Martindale
CLINICAL PSYCHOLOGIST

Resiliency Factors

elsbethmartindale.com/resilience-building

Much research has gone into the factors which increase resiliency. This handout offers a list of seventeen of the most common resiliency factors.

How I use this:
After looking with clients at the balance between the weights (stressors) and balloons (buoyancy factors) illustrated in the *Resilience Building* handout, I will talk through the seventeen resiliency factors on this handout. I explore with my clients how they could improve in each of the areas and identify a specific action plan. Some of the factors are abstract (e.g., practice flexibility) and need to be fleshed out with discussion about how the particular action applies specifically to their lives and challenges. We also take time to identify actions clients are already taking which support their resilience. A little celebration of these can be reinforcing.

Example from practice:
Zachary lost his job after eight years. His company downsized and Zachary was let go. He was a father of two young children and felt devastated by this change. We looked at the various stressors in his life and I validated the weight of each. In addition, we explored the buoyancy factors that were keeping him afloat in the midst of the stress. Looking together at the *Resiliency Factors* handout, Zachary was able to identify ten of the seventeen factors he currently had in place in his life. Zachary was glad to see he was doing many of the "right" things to buoy himself in the midst of challenging times. He was grateful he had these practices as a regular part of his life. He was able to identify two additional resiliency factors he could add. He decided he would rejoin his church study group as a way to both increase his social connections and allow more spiritual exploration. The focus on resiliency helped Zachary navigate this stressful period while he kept his hopes high and looked for new employment.

Elsbeth Martindale
CLINICAL PSYCHOLOGIST

Resiliency Factors

Here are seventeen proven ways to build resiliency. Mark the strategies you are already using to keep yourself buoyant. Identify new ideas, for your current situation, to add more resiliency to your life.

1. **Invest in Relationships**
   Engage in new social activities. Befriend someone new. Be more positive and practice in the relationships you currently have.
   My specific plan: _____

2. **Perform an Act of Service**
   Give yourself in service to others and/or a cause.
   My specific plan: _____

3. **Improve Your Life Skills**
   Build skills in decision-making, assertion, impulse control, and/or self-compassion.
   My specific plan: _____

4. **Find Humor**
   Let your heart be light. Put a smile on your face. Bring joy and playfulness to your day.
   My specific plan: _____

5. **Build Inner Directedness**
   Make choices and decisions based on your own inner evaluation of what's right for you.
   My specific plan: _____

6. **Put Things in Perspective**
   Step back and see your life from a distance. Understand others in the context of their own struggle. Offer compassion and grace to yourself and others.
   My specific plan: _____

7. **Be Independent**
   Actively distance yourself from unhealthy people and situations. Act with autonomy.
   My specific plan: _____

8. **Take a Positive View of Your Personal Future**
   Actively imagine things "going right" for you. Tell your positive story to others.
   My specific plan: _____

9. **Practice Flexibility**
   Think in shades of gray. Let go of rigidity. Demonstrate a willingness to bend as a way to cope.
   My specific plan: _____

10. **Learn Something New**
    Find something new to explore and learn about. Let yourself be curious and invested in a new understanding.
    My specific plan: _____

11. **Practice Self-Motivation**
    Take initiative and positively motivate yourself to achieve your personal goals.
    My specific plan: _____

12. **Recognize Your Strengths and Competencies**
    Know what you are good at and involve yourself in activities that allow you to live from these strengths.
    My specific plan: _____

13. **Find Ways to Support Your Self-Worth and Confidence**
    Talk supportively about yourself internally and externally. Affirm your goodness, skills, and positive intentions.
    My specific plan: _____

14. **Touch Spirituality**
    Explore and support your personal faith in something greater than yourself. Practice spiritual attitudes.
    My specific plan: _____

15. **Persevere**
    Keep on going in spite of difficulties and challenges. Believe in your dream, hopes, and possibilities.
    My specific plan: _____

16. **Be Creative**
    Find ways to express yourself. Play with art in all its forms. Focus on the process rather than the result.
    My specific plan: _____

17. **Practice Gratitude**
    Actively identify things for which you are thankful. Name these things out loud to yourself and others.
    My specific plan: _____

Resiliency Resources:
American Psychological Association - http://www.apa.org/practice/programs/campaign/resilience.aspx
Resiliency in Action, Nan Henderson - http://www.resiliency.com/what-is-resiliency/
How People Learn to Become Resilient, M. Konnikova - https://www.newyorker.com/science/maria-konnikova/the-secret-formula-for-resilience

Elsbeth Martindale
CLINICAL PSYCHOLOGIST

Self-Encouragement

elsbethmartindale.com/self-encouragement

The contrast between praise and encouragement was something I discovered when teaching Systematic Training for Effective Parenting. The idea that too much praise can lower a child's self-esteem because it teaches them to look externally for validation had a huge impact on me. External validation, or other-esteem, can be fleeting and shifting. True self-esteem comes from making an internal evaluation of behavior and changing the behavior or celebrating it depending on one's evaluation.

In helping clients build self-esteem, I find it useful to support them with a means for self-evaluation in the form of a simple question: ***"Do you or do you not like your behaviors and choices?"*** This handout suggests making a bracelet out of a rubber band that has the question, "Do I Like It?" written on it. The bracelet reminds them to ask themselves many times throughout the day if they like whatever it is they are doing. This shift to self-evaluation and self-encouragement is the key to building self-esteem.

How I use this:

I made dozens of bracelets with the question, "Do I Like It?" I offer these to my clients, along with this handout, so they can learn the value of checking in with themselves to evaluate if they like how they are acting and being in the world. I've had many clients tell me how useful this bracelet is in helping them turn their focus inward. These Self-Esteem Builder bracelets are available on my website (http://elsbethmartindale.com/product/self-esteem-builder/).

Example from practice:

Rebecca was a fit and attractive woman. She has loved the attention she got from others and has worked hard to keep herself in shape. When her husband stopped showing his affection by extolling her beauty, she began to wonder what she was "doing wrong." She became obsessed with worry that her husband was no longer in love with her. There was a lot to unpack in therapy, but one of the key changes came when Rebecca began turning inward to make her own evaluation of her beauty. Indeed, she liked her own body. She liked keeping fit and strong. She stopped trying to get her sense of value from others, including her partner. This, of course, shifted the focus of her conversations with her husband from worry about his approval to deeper exploration of how to enhance intimacy between them. Rebecca loved the "Do I Like It?" bracelet. It helped her stop her habit of looking externally for her worth and reminded her to decide for herself if she was being the woman she wanted to be.

Elsbeth Martindale
CLINICAL PSYCHOLOGIST

Self-Encouragement

THE PROBLEM WITH PRAISE

Did you know that praise can actually cause your self-esteem to plummet? Praise is a form of *other*-esteem. It tells you whether someone else thinks your actions are acceptable or valued. Both praise and criticism are external perspectives on your worth or contribution. In contrast, self-esteem is built from the inside; that's why it's called *self*-esteem. Self-esteem is built through encouragement and self-evaluation.

WHAT IS ENCOURAGEMENT?

Encouragement invites you to assess for yourself if you are pleased or not with your production, behaviors, and contributions. When asked by a child to evaluate a drawing, an encouraging mother, instead of pointing out what she likes in her child's artwork, would ask her child, "What do *you* like about your drawing? You seem happy with it. Tell me about it." This response encourages the child to assess personally what he/she/they like or don't like about the artwork. If the child wishes the drawing were different, an encouraging mother would help the child explore how to make the drawing more satisfying. When children learn to evaluate their own behavior, they are less dependent on what others think and more focused on designing their actions to be satisfying and pleasing to themselves. This results in high self-esteem.

The same principles for creating self-esteem in children can be applied to adults in the form of self-encouragement. You can begin to assess for yourself whether you believe your actions are pleasing or worthwhile. You can ask yourself, "Am I being the kind of person I desire to be?" You can listen to your own critique, whether positive or negative, to determine if you are pleased with the way you are living your life. With self-encouragement, you own the responsibility for assessing and adjusting things to meet your own values and expectations.

HOW TO BUILD SELF-ENCOURAGEMENT

Make a Self-Esteem Builder bracelet, a wristband (rubber bands work great) on which you have written the question, "Do I like it?" The bracelet simply asks you to evaluate, many times a day, if you like how you're living the detailed aspects of your life (e.g., Do I like how I'm talking to my friend? Do I like how I'm driving the car? Do I like what I'm eating?). Whenever you notice the bracelet, check in with yourself by asking yourself if you like what you are doing, thinking, or feeling in that very moment.

If your answer is "yes" - smile at your success at living your life as you desire.

If your answer is "no" - you have some work to do. Start by visioning how you would rather be living your life. This is a powerful exercise. It's an opportunity to focus on what you want and how you want to be. Design a response that meets with your own standards, desires, and vision of the self you want to create. Make sure to keep your focus on *you* and your power to choose, rather than concocting a story about how others should be different.

Wear the bracelet until it loses its potency to remind you to check-in. Then, pass the bracelet along to someone else and teach that person how to build his/her/their own self-esteem.

It's not your job to like me; that's my job.

Elsbeth Martindale
CLINICAL PSYCHOLOGIST

Self-Care 101
elsbethmartindale.com/self-care-101

I created this handout twenty years ago and have used it frequently ever since. I had a client who was not in the habit of "watching" himself—his actions, thoughts, feelings, and needs. He tended to just be reactive to the events in his life without seeing his agency to steer his life. I made this handout for this man but actually never gave it to him; I assessed he was not in a place to actually be successful with it. Instead, I have used this gem with many others clients with positive outcomes.

The notion of stepping into the role of the wisest part of self to address the concerns of the neediest parts of self is a concept familiar to me from Psychosynthesis training. I find that helping clients take the position of the Wise Inner Guide in response to their needs is one of the most powerful strategies I employ in therapy.

How I use this:

I will send this handout home with a client after we've had a discussion of agency and self-authorship. This topic comes up often in my work because I believe it is one of the most foundational concepts in consciousness. So, when I'm talking with a client about the importance of recognizing and attending to their own needs, I might suggest a formal process for doing daily check-ins as a way to build the habit.

I might ask, ***"How can you make sure your needs are addressed?"*** We'd then look at the necessity of turning inward with a willingness to observe and assist the parts of self with unmet needs. We'd explore how this simple process is often neglected and leaves no one but self to blame if a bad day ensues. It can be challenging to take full ownership and responsibility for one's life, but, as I tell my clients, if you don't take care of you, who will?

Example from practice:

Luke seemed to step on the toes of his colleagues with regularity. He often told an off-color story or joke and was perplexed when others were offended. Luke needed more conscious guidance of his behavior and this handout gave him a framework. Luke began his days by acknowledging his desire to connect well with his coworkers. He appealed to his own watchful Wise-Man to assist him in being mindful of the potential impact before blurting out a joke. His inner guide was able to assist him in engaging in meaningful dialogue so his need for connection could be met.

Elsbeth Martindale
CLINICAL PSYCHOLOGIST

Self-Care 101

The core of our being is filled with needs and desires. When we listen to our inner yearnings and make efforts to meet these needs, we find contentment. A history and habit of self-neglect leads to dissatisfaction, depression, and tension. To change this pattern, check in with your self every morning. At the end of the day, you might check in again about your successes attending to and caring for your inner needs.

AT THE BEGINNING OF THE DAY

Take the position of your core self (inner child, needy one, deepest longing, essential self) and ask:
What do I hope to get out of my day today?
1)

2)

3)

From the position of your care giver (adult self, nurturing parent, wise inner guide), ask your core self:
How can I help today?

Here's what I, your care giver, am willing to do to support your needs today.
1)

2)

3)

AT THE END OF THE DAY

Take the position of your core self (inner child, needy one, deepest longing, essential self) and ask:
Did my needs get met today?

From the position of your care giver (adult self, nurturing parent, wise inner guide), ask your core self:
What did you like about the ways I took care of you today?

How could I have done a better job of caring for you?

SUGGESTION

Try lighting a candle when you check in. Doing so will separate this self-care time from your "regular life," and help you take this endeavor seriously and with clear intention.

Elsbeth Martindale
CLINICAL PSYCHOLOGIST

Selfishness Defined - Part A

elsbethmartindale.com/selfishness-defined

I struggled for years to clarify the distinction between healthy self-care and selfishness. Some clients have been taught that any action which does not put others above themselves is "selfish." Many are so afraid of this label they become easily manipulated by anyone who would accuse them of being selfish if they didn't do what was requested of them.

Then, one day the light bulb went on: I could contrast selfishness with self-neglect and self-disrespect. This seemed to drive home the message. You need to care for and respect yourself just as you care and respect others. This handout captures the distinction and provides examples clients can use to explore the lesson.

How I use this:

If someone is caught in the "fear of being called selfish," by others or by oneself, I pull out this handout and have a conversation about what selfishness looks like. I might say, *"Selfishness is the blatant disregard for the needs and rights of others. Self and other respect, however, is something everyone deserves. Sometimes, out of fear of being called "selfish," people go all the way to self-neglect, putting others' needs above one's own to the detriment and disrespect of self. This constitutes hidden abuse. No one sees how disregarding you are of yourself."*

I go through one or more area on the handout and talk about what selfishness, self-neglect, and self and other respect looks like. In the first box, regarding needs and wants, I would discuss with clients what constitutes selfish behavior. *"Being selfish might involve demanding that one's needs are met without regard for how others might feel. Self-neglect, in contrast, would involve ignoring one's own needs or being silent about them. Self and other respect would involve considering the needs and wants of others, while also examining one's own needs and speaking up for these as necessary."* Engaging in a similar process with several of the topics helps clients see the contrast between the three options. This can be very helpful in retraining an automatic deferential response to others' requests.

Elsbeth Martindale
CLINICAL PSYCHOLOGIST

Selfishness Defined - Part A

Fill in the chart to see the differences between each position	Selfish	Self-Neglecting	Self and Other Respecting
My needs and wants			
My limits and boundaries			
My possessions			
My time			
Comforting and soothing			
My health			
Speaking up			
Responding to others' needs			
Listening to others			

Selfishness Defined - Part B

elsbethmartindale.com/selfishness-defined

And the answer is...

In this handout, I offer some suggestions of what selfishness, self-neglect, and self and other respect might look like. I usually print Part A and Part B of the *Selfishness Defined* handout back-to-back so clients can easily see how I think about the distinctions between these terms.

How I use this:
I often give this handout as homework to encourage clients to grapple with the concept that standing for self does not always meet the criteria of "selfishness."

Example from practice:
Esther was raised in an authoritarian home. Her parents were religious and believed that obedience to authority was virtuous and right. They expected Esther to follow their rules. When she "disobeyed," she was often condemned as being "selfish." It was important to Esther to please her parents and to be a good daughter. She was mostly compliant, which served her well in her family home. Unfortunately, this agreeable style became quite problematic for Esther when she moved into the world, especially with regard to her relationships with men. She found she had great difficulty saying "no" when others asked her to go along with their wishes. She was afraid to displease and had no practice standing up for herself. After several painful relationships, Esther came to therapy. She needed to develop self-defining skills as she was dangerously ill-equipped to manage herself effectively in relationships. One of the topics that came up early in her work was the fear of being called selfish. She feared this judgment more than most. The ideas in this handout were unfamiliar to Esther. Eventually, she began to see that being aware of having needs did not make her selfish, nor did speaking up about her needs. Sadly, this fear was so deeply ingrained that it took her years to turn around her thinking.

Elsbeth Martindale
CLINICAL PSYCHOLOGIST

Selfishness Defined - Part B

Here is some suggested language for exploring the distinctions between these concepts Compare your responses to see how closely they match the suggested language.

This filled-in chart shows some options for responding to the presented issues.	Selfish	Self-Neglecting	Self and Other Respecting
My needs and wants	Demanding others fulfill my needs, maybe even without my having to ask.	Ignoring or dismissing my needs, believing others are more important.	Being aware and response-able to meeting my needs as well as hearing and respecting the needs of others.
My limits and boundaries	Expecting others to know my limits and getting angry when they don't.	Being silent or indirect about my limits for fear of imposing on others.	Speaking up and letting others know my expectations.
My possessions	Acquiring more and more things.	Ignoring the care of my things.	Taking care of things and asking others to treat them kindly as well.
My time	Requiring others to comply to my timing and being angry when I'm inconvenienced.	Not being watchful of time, so often feeling like I don't have enough.	Being attentive to time and setting limits to make sure I use it well.
Comforting and soothing	Believing it's someone else's responsibility to comfort and soothe me.	Believing I don't need comfort and/or not trusting I will get it from others.	Recognizing it's my job to ask for and/or comfort myself.
My health	Focusing on health, body, and self exclusively. Not caring how this may effect others' needs.	Ignoring my health.	Attending to my health with regular practices.
Speaking up	Speaking without respect for how my words might affect others.	Prioritizing others' needs and comfort over my own, so I won't speak if I will inconvenience them.	Speaking up with respect for others.
Responding to others' needs	Ignoring others' needs and focusing mostly on my own.	Making others' needs more important than my own.	Being willing to listen and take others' needs into consideration.
Listening to others	Only listening to others when it serves me.	Listening (or looking as though I am) so others are happy.	Listen to enhance my understanding of others.

Elsbeth Martindale
CLINICAL PSYCHOLOGIST

Give Yourself a Hand

elsbethmartindale.com/give-yourself-a-hand

This handout is a gem, one of my favorites. It offers clients an understanding of the power of gratitude and gives them a "handy" means for focusing on several areas where gratitude can be easily identified—within one's self, in nature, in helping others, in the experience of love, and in the little pleasures of life.

How I use this:

When clients are interested in the idea of gratitude as a life-enhancer, I will bring out this handout. I briefly name the benefits known about practicing gratitude and then launch into the simple ways to find gratitude in daily living. I sometimes suggest they "pick a finger" at every red light they encounter while driving and practice gratitude. This gives them the encouragement to find simple, everyday ways to practice gratitude.

This is one of those concepts about which I might "quiz" a client during a session after discussing this tool. I might ask the client to tell me what each finger represents to help seal the practice in their memory.

Example from practice:

I have used this gratitude tool around my own dinner table many times. After explaining the gratitude fingers, I ask someone to pick a finger of the person next to him/her/them and invite the person to share his/her/their related gratitude with the table. After that person does this, he/she/they pick a finger of another person to repeat the pattern. This adds a bit of playfulness to the notion of saying grace before a meal.

Elsbeth Martindale
CLINICAL PSYCHOLOGIST

Give Yourself a Hand

Positive emotions can have long-term benefits in your life. Aside from making you feel good in the moment, attending to positive emotions brings a variety of other positive side effects. Fredrickson's Broaden-and-Build Theory of Gratitude suggests positive emotions both broaden your momentary mindset and build your enduring resources for managing stress. Also, the more you savor your experience, the deeper the gratitude will sink in. So take the time to really feel your gratefulness in your whole body.

Experiment for Yourself

Use your five fingers to stir positive emotions. Pick a different finger throughout the day (e.g., after your morning shower, at each red light you encounter, before each meal) and give yourself a hand at feeling good now and for your future.

REVERSE FLIP-OFF
Name something you have done to bless someone else's life.

POINTER
Point to something beautiful in nature.

RING FINGER
Recall a time when you have loved another or felt loved by another.

THUMBS UP
Name something you have done for which you feel proud.

PINKIE
Name a-little-something for which you are grateful.

Research demonstrates that people who experience frequent positive emotions tend to:

- live up to ten years longer
- store resources for solving problems
- have a broader perspective with more options
- think more creatively
- integrate information more quickly and easily
- be less likely to jump to conclusions
- be less depressed
- undo the negative effects of stress and emotions
- increase physiological recovery after anxiety
- feel good in the future
- create positive feelings in others

Fredrickson, Barbara L. 2003. "The Value of Positive Emotions: The emerging science of positive psychology is coming to understand why it's good to feel good." *American Scientist* 91, 330-335.

Gratitude Homework

elsbethmartindale.com/gratitude-homework

For those who want more opportunities to practice gratitude, this handout expands the look into the things for which one might be thankful. At times, you can get so used to the goodness around you that you can neglect to appreciate the blessings of life.

Gratitude journals are "a thing." Many examples are available online of how to keep such a journal. Some of my clients really love this type of journaling focus.

Some clients have been stymied by believing gratitude must be outwardly directed toward someone specific or to a deity. Whereas this is a fine direction, when desired, it is the experience of feeling grateful and expressing this feeling that seems to create the emotional and psychological benefit.

How I use this:

I will send this home or email it to clients if they are interested in experimenting with adding more gratitude into their lives.

Example from practice:

Lian had been feeling down for several months. She had been hit with several losses and disappointments and life seemed heavier than she had experienced it in the past. While Lian wasn't clinically depressed, she was feeling less joy and excitement in her day-to-day life. She asked, "Isn't there something I could do to start feeling better right away?" While gratitude isn't a magic answer, it has been shown to have an immediate effect on increasing positive affect and well-being. I gave Lian the *Gratitude Homework* handout and suggested she identify the areas of her life where she felt even small levels of gratitude. I encouraged her to try the ideas listed in the Challenge section of the handout. Several weeks later, we explored the benefits of intentionally increasing her gratitude. She reflected that turning her focus to the things for which she was grateful had indeed made her mood lighter and her enthusiasm for life brighter.

Elsbeth Martindale
CLINICAL PSYCHOLOGIST

Gratitude Homework

Research shows that experiencing and expressing gratitude increases your emotional as well as physical health. Here are some ideas for increasing your sense of gratitude.

NAME ONE OR MORE THINGS FOR WHICH YOU ARE GRATEFUL IN EACH OF THESE AREAS:

Your Health:

Your Partnership:

Your Friendships:

Your Work:

Your Physical Surroundings:

Your Financial Situation:

_____:

HERE'S A CHALLENGE

Try doing one or two of these activities in the coming week. Write or talk about your experiences afterward.

- Intentionally express gratitude to your partner or friend.

- Go out of your way to be "nice." (e.g., let someone in front of you in traffic, hold open a door for someone, Intentionally smile at and wish someone a great day, and the like)

- Tell a child in your life, "I feel really grateful/ delighted/happy when I see you doing..."

- Go to a place in nature and use all your senses to experience the beauty.

- Look at your body in a mirror. Identify the part of your body you most like or appreciate. Specify the reasons you like and appreciate this body part.

- Tell someone at work one of the things that make you appreciate your job.

- Give thanks for your food before you eat it.

- Bring home fresh-cut flowers and place them in a central place in your home. Stop for several seconds to appreciate them each time you pass by.

Elsbeth Martindale
CLINICAL PSYCHOLOGIST

Making Life Sweeter

elsbethmartindale.com/making-life-sweeter

I once overheard someone saying to a friend, "What doesn't kill you makes you bitter." I thought this was a funny twist on the old adage, but unfortunately, life seems to have made many clients bitter. Their cup is half full all the time, their problems are rehearsed and repeated, and their spirits seem weighed down. Dysthymia? Depression? Or just a bad habit of keeping one's focus on what's wrong?

When clients are caught in this negative space, I want them to know some things they can do to turn their attention toward something "sweeter." I like the idea that the sweetness is an additive—no need to battle with the negative, trying to make it go away. Just add a little sweetness to make life more palatable!

Please don't use this as a tool to tell your clients not to feel what they feel. Bitterness and defeat are sometimes honest reactions to the harshness of life. But when clients want to nudge their attitude toward something more uplifting, these eight additives offer a means for doing so.

How I use this:

After hearing and empathizing with clients' suffering, they may be ready and interested in lightening their burdens. When the clients make it clear they seek some strategies to lift themselves, this is a great handout to offer. I might say, *"You sure have a bunch of legitimate pain in your life. It is hard when the pain is all around you all day long. Would you like to consider some actions that might lighten your load just a bit? There are eight things you might consider adding, one at a time, to see if they provide a bit of relief or counterbalance to your struggle. Would you like to see what these include?"* We might then discuss the handout and see if the client can find one additive to consider exploring before the next session. I remind clients this exercise is only an experiment, with no attachment to "making everything better." It is just a nudge in the direction of goodness.

Example from practice:

Debbie Downer is a client I'm sure many of you have had. She is habitually focused on what isn't working in her life, how others have done her wrong, and what terrible thing is likely to happen next. Debbie clearly needs some validation for her struggle, but after a time it would be helpful to present to her some alternative places to put her mental energy. If she is willing to experiment, she might find a beautiful blue sky behind all those dark clouds. Just sayin'.

Elsbeth Martindale
CLINICAL PSYCHOLOGIST

Making Life Sweeter:
What to do when life's got you bitter

Life can be harsh and the negative experiences can add up, making you feel bitter and resentful. You might conclude your whole life is miserable and sour.

When life feels bitter, we often tell ourselves we need to stop being negative, angry, sad, or upset. Stopping these feelings can be like trying not to think about a pink elephant. The more we remind ourselves what we shouldn't be thinking, the more time we spend engaged with that topic.

Instead of trying to stop the negativity, try adding something new to the mix. Consider that you can't take out a seasoning from a pot of soup once it's been added! But you can fix the taste of the soup by adding ingredients that make the pot more tasty.

WHEN LIFE'S GOT YOU BITTER...
ADD A LITTLE...

COMPASSION
Show kindness and deep concern for your struggles and suffering and make an effort, no matter how small, to make things better.

ACCEPTANCE
Acceptance takes the fight out of the situation and allows things to be as they are.

CREATIVITY
This is a form of play that allows you to discover something new and/or express yourself, both the good and the bad.

GENTLENESS
When life is hard, the last thing you need is a beating. Try being gentle with your struggling self.

SUPPORT
Reach out and let someone help you. Just talking about your struggle can lighten the load.

CURIOSITY
This is an antidote to judgment. It allows you to explore yourself and your circumstance with an openness to learning.

GRATITUDE
Appreciate what you do have. Find something good in your life and notice, appreciate, and celebrate it.

EXPERIMENTATION
Allow yourself to risk, to be imperfect, and to explore something new.

Elsbeth Martindale
CLINICAL PSYCHOLOGIST

Savoring the Moment

elsbethmartindale.com/savoring-the-moment

Another great life-enhancer is the power of savoring. Fred Bryant and Joseph Veroff's book, *Savoring*, explains the research behind this important appreciation enhancer. Interestingly, an Oregon candy company advertises a caramel with the slogan was, "Suck, don't chew." What a great description of savoring, staying with pleasure and letting it be amplified and fully experienced! I like to think of savoring as "permitted indulgence," with a big dose of mindful awareness and gratitude thrown in.

How I use this:

I offer this handout to clients who are working on living fully and appreciating the goodness in their lives. The section about what can interfere with savoring is particularly helpful, as it features typical ways you can block yourself from feeling goodness.

Example from practice:

Megan is a successful professional. She has completed several years of empowering psychotherapy and now comes to therapy on a monthly basis to keep her skills sharp and to process the challenges of her work and family life. In one recent session, Megan told of her success at work managing a crisis and successfully leading her team to receiving public recognition for its achievement. Megan was amazed that she had been able to "pull this off." She marveled at the accomplishment and expressed appreciation for all that went in to the success. I then introduced Megan to the concept of savoring, suggesting it might be a good thing to do with her jubilation. So we took time to reflect on her achievement, recognized we were allowing that achievement to be honored and felt, and localized the feeling of goodness in her body. This further deepened Megan's experience of delight. Sometimes life is really, really good. We don't want our clients to miss feeling the joy of those moments.

Elsbeth Martindale
CLINICAL PSYCHOLOGIST

Savoring the Moment

Savoring is a way to take an active role in deriving pleasure and fulfillment in the midst of a positive experience. Savoring allows you to step outside yourself to see, feel, review, and appreciate your experience–resulting in increased joy and meaning. In savoring, you not only enjoy an experience but you also enjoy that you are enjoying that experience!

BENEFITS OF SAVORING

- Increases noticing and awareness
- Overrides heuristic adaptation
- Intensifies any pleasant experience
- Keeps your attention on a good thing a bit longer to lengthen your positive feelings
- Reinforces your capacity to bring and hold goodness in your life
- Increases positive mental health and buffers against stress
- Increases joy and happiness

STEPS TO FOLLOW TO SAVOR

1. Find a positive experience to truly savor every day Maybe it's a warm cup of tea, beautiful object in nature, scrumptious thing to eat, refreshing shower, connection with a good friend, or a beautiful poem. Do this **now**.

2. Feel into the experience. What's good here? What do you like about this? Why does this make you happy? What's happening in your body? What sensations are you aware of? **How** does it feel?

3. Reflect and notice yourself doing this activity. Be amazed and delighted that it's happening. **Wow!**

Actively and Choicefully
SEEK (NOW)
Pleasurable Experience

Mindfully Observe
REFLECT (WOW)
Be aware you're in it

Clearly and Completely
FEEL (HOW)
Embody and Name

Explore More: *Savoring: A New Model of Positive Experience* by Bryant & Veroff, 2007.

ENHANCE SAVORING

1. Consider **sharing your savoring experience** with someone else. Research shows that telling others about your savored experiences increases the joy and positive effect of the experience (Gable, et al, 2004; Langston, 1994).

2. Feel into the complexity of the experience. Notice different perceptual elements and multiple sensory inputs.

3. Find words for both your internal and external experience.

4. Find a situation **free from social or esteem needs** as motivators.

5. Imagine this might be the **last time** you will ever experience this.

6. Slow down so you can notice the smaller units of what is being experienced. Notice more detail of both surroundings and of self.

7. Recall and review your savored experience in the future. Remembering a positive experience in an embodied way increases positive emotion for as many as four weeks after recall (Lyubmirsky, et al, 2006).

WHAT TO AVOID

Some actions can hurt or diminish a savoring experience.

1. Focusing on the future, thinking about what it will be like when the savoring experience is over.

2. Reminding yourself, in the midst of a savoring experience, that the **experience will soon end**. Telling yourself, "Nothing good lasts forever."

3. Comparing the current experience with past experiences and finding your current experience lacking in some way.

4. Telling yourself **things will never be this good again**. Missing it before it's even gone.

5. Looking for how the **current situation could be better** or improved. "This would be even better if..."

6. **Telling yourself you don't really deserve**, or you don't have time for, a savoring moment.

Elsbeth Martindale
CLINICAL PSYCHOLOGIST

Stages of Change

elsbethmartindale.com/stages-of-change

Prochaska's Model of Change is an important framework for all therapists to understand. He suggests, as I'm sure most therapists can verify, people don't change until they're good and ready. Pressure from others may bring them into the office, but that doesn't mean they are ready to jump into the challenging work of making a shift in their behavior. Understanding and appreciating this is essential for effective and non-defeated therapy.

How I use this:

I use this model mostly for myself, as a therapist, when I want to assess my clients' current desire for change, so I can know the focus and pace of therapy. If client is not even contemplating change, therapy will likely progress slowly, if at all. In this scenario, my best chance at helping the client is to have him/her/them assess his/her/their circumstances and consider what he/she/they think would make things better. If clients are at a contemplating stage of change, then my focus will likely involve looking at the costs and benefits of shifting behavior. Some people start therapy when they are in the preparation stage, wanting to make changes but in need of support, strategies, or a clear plan. Clients can also start therapy when they are in the action or maintenance stage, but this is less common. So, understanding where a client is starting can be valuable to me as a therapist. It helps me gage the process and hold realistic expectations for the work.

My clients like this handout. It helps them see change as a progression. The stages can help clients be less judgmental of themselves. It offers permission to hang out in the contemplation stage as long as they need. It is also helpful for clients to understand the need for maintenance and celebration once changes are implemented.

Example from practice:

Tye was referred to me by her healthcare provider after coming out of rehab for alcohol abuse. The provider told me, "Tye is sober and ready to do some deep psychological work." I needed to assess Tye's readiness myself, in order to have realistic expectations for treatment. It was made clear, in my intake session, that Tye was in the Maintenance Stage as related to alcohol use, but was she only in the Contemplation Stage for doing "deep psychological work." This awareness helped me have realistic expectations for therapy. I helped Tye understand what "deep" work would look like and what results might be expected were she to dive in. She stayed in Contemplation for several months before she began to take realistic preparation action. I could meet Tye where she was, work at her pace, without imposing a "deep work" agenda.

Elsbeth Martindale
CLINICAL PSYCHOLOGIST

Stages of Change

The Transtheoretical Model of Change (TTM), researched by Prochaska and others, examines and explains intentional behavior change. Based on more than two decades of research, the TTM has found that individuals move through a series of six stages in the adoption of healthy behaviors or cessation of unhealthy ones.

THE SIX STAGES OF CHANGE

PRE-CONTEMPLATION STAGE

This is the stage in which an individual has no intent to change behavior in the near future. Pre-contemplators are often characterized as resistant or unmotivated and tend to avoid information, discussion, or thought with regard to the targeted behavior. They lack awareness that life can be improved by a change in behavior. They would prefer to have others change rather than change themselves.

CONTEMPLATION STAGE

Individuals in this stage openly state their intent to change in the near future (six months). They are aware of the problem and are more aware of the benefits of changing, but they remain keenly aware of the costs. This is a stage of information gathering about solutions and actions. Contemplators are often seen as ambivalent to change or as procrastinators, because change is only planned, not yet acted upon. Substituting thinking for action can make one a "chronic contemplator." Movement will begin when the focus shifts from problems in the present or past to solutions and the future.

PREPARATION STAGE

This is the stage in which individuals intend to take steps to change, usually within the next month. Preparation is viewed as a transitional rather than stable stage, with individuals intending progress into action.

ACTION STAGE

The action stage is one in which an individual has made overt, perceptible lifestyle modifications for fewer than six months.

MAINTENANCE STAGE

Individuals in the maintenance stage are working to prevent relapse and consolidate gains secured during action. Maintainers are distinguishable from those in the action stage in that they report the highest levels of self-efficacy and are less frequently tempted to relapse.

TERMINATION STAGE

Individuals in the termination stage see the problem behavior as in the past and no longer desirable.

WHAT STAGE OF CHANGE ARE YOU IN?

To assess your stage, answer the following questions:
1. I solved my problem more than six months ago. Yes/No
2. I have taken action on my problem within the past six months. Yes/No
3. I am intending to take action in the next month. Yes/No
4. I am intending to take action in the next six months. Yes/No

All 'No' responses = Pre-contemplation
'No' on questions 1, 2, & 3 = Contemplation
'No' on 1 & 2 only = Preparation
'No' on 1 only = Action
All 'Yes' responses = Maintenance

Motivation to Change

elsbethmartindale.com/motivation-to-change

This is a twenty-year-old handout, made at a time when I was first exploring how to help people change. The strategies start small and get more challenging. This is a dose of behaviorism—what reinforces and rewards change. I don't use this very often now in my practice, perhaps because each of these strategies is woven into other discussions. But, at times, clients are unable to follow through on a commitment they want to make to themselves, and this handout can show them some strategies for holding themselves accountable. These days, I'd probably show more interest in the resistance, and the message of resistance, instead of encouraging clients to override it. But, on occasions, it is absolutely right to explore strategies for holding oneself to commitments to change.

Looking at the *Stages of Change* handout might also be valuable before implementing change strategies. If clients are not ready to shift, it is helpful for them to recognize this and not feel pressured by others to change.

How I use this:

When clients says they want to shift a behavior yet continue to fall short of doing so, this list of options for self-motivation can be explored. My approach is to lean toward strategies of invitation and request, grounded in adherence to values. Occasionally, however, it seems some folks need a bit of a kick in the hind end, so a strategy on the harsher end (e.g., punishment) can do the trick.

Example from practice:

Lisa claimed she wanted to try to reduce her alcohol consumption. She'd been saying this for months with no significant change in behavior. I knew she had been at the contemplation stage for quite some time. I showed her this sheet of strategies for motivation to change. I suggested that, when she was ready, she might try one or more of these strategies to help anchor her desire to be successful in changing her drinking patterns. She eventually made an agreement with her sister to hold her accountable to drinking no more than one glass of wine in the evening. Having committed this to someone else was enough to hold her in check, and Lisa successfully began to limit her consumption of alcohol.

Elsbeth Martindale
CLINICAL PSYCHOLOGIST

Motivation to Change

Yup, change is difficult. You can make it easier on yourself by adding some of these motivators. They start out easy and become more difficult and costly. Sometimes the threat of a negative consequence is the only thing that seems to work. Begin more gently and see if you can motivate yourself with a carrot rather than a stick. Choose a motivator, work with it, then assess the results. Switch strategies as necessary.

MAKE A SIGN
Print out a note or sign that will remind you of the change you want to make. Target a specific behavior. Putthe sign(s) up in a prominent place in your home, car, or work. (e.g., Do fifty sit-ups before eating dinner tonight. Get off the computer after forty-five minutes.)

KEEP A RECORD
Records help you remember as well as monitor your intentions and accomplishments. Sometimes just marking a success on paper can be rewarding. (e.g., Move a marble from a basket to an empty jar every time you catch yourself talking kindly to your children. Put a check mark on paper each time you floss your teeth.)

WRITE AN AFFIRMATION
Affirming yourself is a kind and gentle reminder of the person you wish to become. Make sure the affirmation is truthful, named in the positive, and not too far out of reach. Display your affirmation and read it out loud when you notice it. (e.g., I am willing to take better care of my body. I can set limits when I begin to feel badgered.)

MAKE A CONTRACT
Write up a contract for yourself specifying the behavior you want to change, your plan for making the change, and the reward for making the change. Sign it and have someone witness and sign it with you. (e.g., Write a contract that specifies how many times per week you will go to the gym and what you will give yourself after thirty days of success.)

COMMIT TO ANOTHER
Make a verbal or written commitment to a friend and ask that friend to call you to check up on your behavior. (e.g., Ask your friend to call you on Friday to check if you went to your 12-Step meeting.)

REWARD YOURSELF
Set aside some money ($20, $40, or $100) and take yourself shopping when you accomplish the goal you set for yourself. Similarly, you could identify something you want and hold off buying it until a desired change has happened. Another option is to buy an item and give it to a friend to hold for you when your goal is reached. (e.g., Buy yourself a new wardrobe when you lose the weight you desire.)

WRITE THE VISION OF THE NEW YOU
Write a letter to yourself from your future self, the self that was able to accomplish the set goal. Tell your current self you can do it! Have the future self write about how good it feels to have made the desired changes. (e.g., Have the nonsmoking future self write about how good your body feels and the benefits you feel having quit smoking.)

PUNISH YOURSELF
If you must, you can create a negative consequence for yourself if your goal is not met within a specified time frame. (e.g., Write a check to a political organization that you despise, then give the check to a friend, instructing the friend to send it off if you do not do as you intend.)

Elsbeth Martindale
CLINICAL PSYCHOLOGIST

Self-Reinforcement

elsbethmartindale.com/self-reinforcement

Yup, stuff that is reinforced persists. This simple concept from behaviorism is often neglected and under-utilized. But, because it works, it needs to be something we help our clients understand. The human animal responds to reinforcement just like other creatures. If clients like their new behavior, or the behavior of others, show them how to reinforce this behavior to maintain it.

How I use this:

I have a string of beads I show clients, with beads that spell out, "I'm proud of myself." The beads are on a ribbon with a clasp, so they can be worn as a bracelet. This bracelet is a great example of a simple and accessible tool that can be used to mark successes. Clients can slide beads down the ribbon one at a time, until they can celebrate pride in an accomplishment.

I show people this reinforcer tool and talk about my other favorite reinforcer tool, marbles in a jar, to show how easy it is to create a way to mark success. Really, a simple smiley face on a calendar is adequate. Just recognizing improvement and success will keep progress coming.

This handout lays out the simple steps of reinforcement and encourages clients to use these principles on themselves. I find clients often enjoy designing their own reinforcement methods. More buy-in on the process of reinforcement can be found when clients choose or develop a strategy unique to their circumstance and preferences.

Example from practice:

Judy wanted to improve the bedtime routine with her seven-year-old daughter. She wanted to do less nagging and reminding. She wanted the process of preparing for sleep to be peaceful for both herself and her daughter. Judy introduced the idea of a marble jar to her daughter, telling her they could each get a marble in the morning if they had a good bedtime the prior night. They spelled out the specifics of what constituted a "good bedtime" and then began watching and reviewing their individual behaviors. Her daughter was eager to reward herself with a marble in the morning, as was Judy. Just setting up this plan helped them both be more mindful of their actions and to make choices which supported their intentions. It was a great success!

Elsbeth Martindale
CLINICAL PSYCHOLOGIST

Self-Reinforcement

Success in making changes can be secured by the principle of positive reinforcement. Self-reinforcement is simply a process of rewarding yourself for the small steps you take toward your goals. You can reinforce yourself by simply acknowledging the actions you are taking in the service of these goals. Recognition of movement reinforces change, and this will keep you moving toward your long-term desires.

STEPS TO TAKE

1) IDENTIFY YOUR GOAL

Start by naming the thing you wish to accomplish. Make SMART goals, goals that are Specific, Measurable, Attainable, Realistic, and Time-bound (a clear time-frame for achievement).

2) BREAK DOWN THE GOAL

Break down any long-term goal into small and manageable steps. Make the steps small enough that they are achievable, yet big enough that your action demonstrates movement in the direction of your long-term goals. If the long-term goal is to be healthier, then a small step might be to start moving your body. A SMART goal might look like, "I will walk a minimum of one mile on Monday, Wednesday, and Friday mornings before work for the next two weeks."

3) REINFORCE YOUR STEPS

Each time you are successful at taking the desired step toward your goal, notice it and reinforce it. Give yourself credit for becoming the person you want to be. Watching your success pile up makes you want to continue to move forward.

4) CELEBRATE YOUR SUCCESS

When you achieve your goals, make sure you take time to celebrate and do a little happy dance. You just took action and achieved a goal to become more of the person you desire to be. This is totally worth celebrating!

IDEAS FOR REINFORCERS

- Put a **check mark** on a calendar, in a journal, or on a piece of paper. This is a simple way to give yourself credit for your action. Seeing the check marks add up will show evidence of your effort and success. Simple, but effective.

- Put a marble in a **marble jar.** Fill the jar, one by one, with colorful marbles to mark your success. Keep this jar on a window sill so you can see the light shine through the success markers. Very reinforcing.

- Start the day with five polished **rocks in your pocket**. Every time you act in a manner which supports your goals, move a rock from one pocket to another. See if you can get all rocks moved by the end of the day.

- Write a **word of affirmation** in your journal or on a scrap piece of paper. Say the kinds of things to yourself you wish another might say to you. "Good job," "At-a-boy," "You totally rock," might be good reinforcers. Recognition is important and feels fabulous, so load yourself up.

- Move a **bead on a string**. String a set of beads tightly on a string or bracelet. Keep the string nearby and every time you act in accordance with your values or goals, move a bead down the string. Make it your goal to move all the beads by the end of the day.

A journey of a thousand miles begins with a single step - Chinese proverb

Landing Pads

elsbethmartindale.com/landing-pads

This handout addresses the idea that thoughts can be observed and directed. Some clients have not considered their power to determine where they "land their thoughts." Identifying favorite places they would like their thoughts to land makes the steering of thoughts just a little bit easier, and it is so much more effective than telling the brain to just stop an unwanted thought. The handout suggests clients identify several places they would like to put their mental attention when their thoughts are going in a less desirable direction.

How I use this:

After some awareness and practice of mindfulness, clients can recognize their capacity to steer their thinking. This handout encourages them to take their minds to places of their own choosing and to identify them in advance so they are clear about their enticing options. The more enticing the landing pad, the more easily they can shift their focus. I use this often with clients who ruminate on topics which are not emotionally nourishing.

Example from practice:

Rose has a habit of worrying about her adult daughter's decisions and behaviors. Rose recognizes she can do very little to make her daughter choose more wisely, and worrying, she understands, has absolutely no power to make things better. But the habit is hard to break. We talked about the places she'd rather have her mind land if it were not on worry. She identified three places she could bring her thoughts which could give her more enjoyment and have a greater outcome: her artwork, her desired travel, the friends with whom she wanted to socialize, and the specifics of the get-togethers. Having clarity that thinking about art, travel, and friends would be a worthy distraction from worry made it easier for Rose to steer her thoughts in a more productive direction.

Elsbeth Martindale
CLINICAL PSYCHOLOGIST

Landing Pads

Sometimes your thoughts can get away from you and take you to places which can be painful, annoying, or overall not nourishing. With some awareness this is happening, you can gently steer your thoughts to places you'd rather visit such as a future plan, a joyous memory, or a creative project. Don't try to outrun or chase away the unwanted thoughts. Instead, take your mind to a place where you choose to go and get lost in the details of this idea. Your unwanted thoughts will fade in the background as you fully attend to your preferred thoughts.

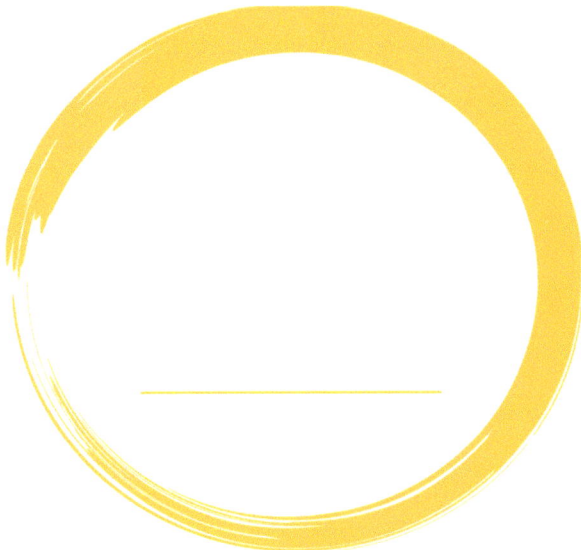

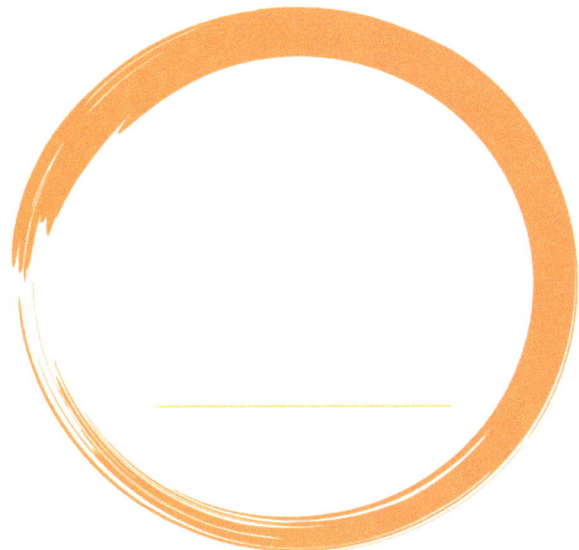

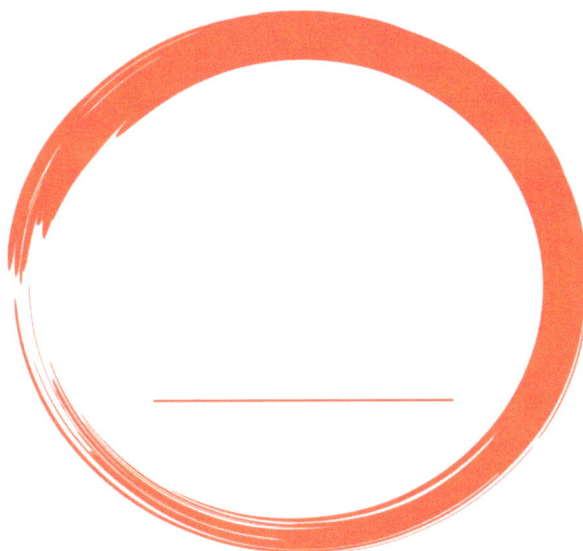

TRY THIS

Identify three thoughts you enjoy pondering. You might consider what brings you joy to think about. I suggest something delightful, playful, creative, challenging, or future focused. Write three of these thoughts in the circles. When you are stuck in the swamp of negative thinking, bring your attention to one of these circles and play, in as much detail as you can, within these spaces. Your spirit will thank you.

Elsbeth Martindale
CLINICAL PSYCHOLOGIST

Journal Protector

elsbethmartindale.com/journal-protector

My journal was violated by my grandfather when I was twelve years old. I felt so invaded and powerless, I stopped keeping a journal for many years. Then I created what I thought was a way to protect myself from such an invasion again: I made a simple sticker to insert in all my journals, letting anyone who opens my journal know my intention—which is NOT to have anyone read it. Of course, this simple tactic doesn't prevent an intruder, but it does give a clear message to the reader that he/she/they are violating my wishes. I showed my sticker to my good friend Karin, and she loved it. We sat for hours afterward coming up with a variety of playful and direct journal protector scripts.

How I use this:

If clients want to keep a journal but fear others may intrude into their private space, I suggest they consider this sort of sticker. Of course, I remind my clients that having agreements in place with others around privacy is preferable, but sometimes that doesn't seem like enough. Putting the boundary in writing in an obvious place helps clients know they have done what they can to set a clear boundary. The handout provides language for boundary setting, starting off kind and becoming more fierce if the message isn't respected.

Example from practice:

Nineteen-year-old Hanna enjoys writing but has been hesitant to use a journal as a way to explore and process her personal concerns. After suggesting several homework exercises that involved writing, I realized Hanna was unwilling to put her thoughts to paper out of fear her mother would read what she'd written. I showed her these journal protector ideas, which she loved. We then role-played ways of telling her mother about her desire to have her writing remain private and of asking for her mother's cooperation. The combination of setting both a verbal and a written boundary made it safe for Hanna to begin using a journal in a therapeutic manner.

Elsbeth Martindale
CLINICAL PSYCHOLOGIST

Journal Protector

Life is messy. The things you need to explore and understand about life are not always easy, pleasant, or well organized. A journal can be your best friend, helping you uncover, discover, and resolve both the big and small concerns of your life.

Everyone deserves to have a safe place to write, draw, and doodle—a place to reflect, process, express, and dream. Consider protecting your journal by installing a Journal Protector.

Journal Protectors make it apparent to others that they are not welcome to look at your musings. It sets a very clear boundary and tells others, in no uncertain terms, that they are violating you if they look through your journal without your explicit consent. Of course, there is no guarantee that others will respect your expressed boundaries, but the Journal Protector makes any violation of these boundaries crystal clear.

EXAMPLES: Copy and paste into your journal or write your own version.

OMG! Stop! I can't believe you picked this up. What are you thinking? You SO cannot read my journal. I'm totally serious.

I'm so mortified and mad. I can't believe you're doing this to me. That is so rude! This is my private journal. It is a place where I get to think what I want, name what I feel, and dream about my future. None of the contents were written for you.

Did I mention, this is private? Stop being a jerk. Show some respect. Close this now, put this down, and walk away. NOW!

Apparently, you aren't the person I thought you were. I can never trust you again.

When you cross someone's explicit boundaries, you become the enemy, I guess that's what you are to me now. I'm really sad.

Hello, I see you've found my journal. Please set it down. The contents on these pages were not meant for you. Simply put this back where you found it. Do not read on. Trust me.

Well, I see you don't trust me. I asked you to put this down. I'll say it again. This is NOT for you to read. Set it down NOW! Speaking of trust, it is very clear I cannot trust you. The fact that you are reading this suggests that you are willing to cross my boundaries, intrude into my space, and disregard my wishes. This is really sad.

The hardest thing now is that I will have to confront you. We will need to talk, and I will need to rethink being close to you. This is SO messed up.

Elsbeth Martindale
CLINICAL PSYCHOLOGIST

Journal Protector - continued

Here are more examples of journal protectors.

Excuse me. Apparently you don't know that journals are private and should be respected. Did I tell you you could read the contents of these pages? I think not!

Now, be a good citizen and put this journal down. Do not flip through even one page. Trust me, if I have something I want you to know, I will tell you to your face.

Don't even read the next sentence in this paragraph ...
... okay, you are a low-life violating piece of scum. May karma have its revenge on you, jerk!

WARNING

This journal is private. If you are reading it without my consent, please STOP NOW! It is a violation of my privacy and my wishes for you NOT to read anything within these pages without my explicit invitation. Think about what you are doing. You have the choice in this moment to be the kind of person you want to be. I want you to be the kind of person that respects my boundaries. Please put this back where you found it and read no further.

Should you need to know, the irreparable costs of continuing to read on include:
- loss of my respect
- loss of your self-respect
- loss of my trust
- an overall feeling of discomfort, especially in my presence

Please put down my journal!

Thank you for demonstrating respect.

DO NOT ENTER

THIS BOOKMARK WAS PLACED IN MY PRIVATE PROPERTY.
YOU ARE NOT WELCOME TO EXAMINE THESE PAGES.
IF YOU PERSIST, YOU WILL BE CROSSING A DANGEROUS LINE FROM WHICH YOU WILL NOT BE ABLE TO RETURN.

PUT THIS DOWN NOW.
DO NOT READ ON.

YOU DON'T SEEM TO GET IT.
YOU ARE INVADING AND VIOLATING MY WISHES.
I CURSE YOU FOR STEALING MY PRIVACY.
YOU ARE DESPICABLE, SCUM OF THE EARTH, THE UNTRUSTABLE LOWEST OF LOW.

MAY YOU SUFFER A MISERABLE LIFE AND A TORTUOUS DEATH FOR YOUR INVASIVE AND UNFORGIVABLE ACTIONS. I MAY NEVER FORGIVE YOU.

Caregiving Assessment

elsbethmartindale.com/caregiving-assessment

I developed this assessment recently for a retreat I was leading on Accessing the Wise Inner Guide. I understand the Wise Inner Guide (WIG) as including the four elements or archetypes Angeles Arrien discussed in her book, *The Four-Fold Way*: The Warrior, Healer, Visionary, and Teacher. Dr. Arrien says; "Optimum health is considered to be the equal expression of these archetypes." She believes that calling on the power of these four archetypes allows us to live in harmony with our environment and our inner nature. I have been greatly influenced by Dr. Arrien's perspective as a cultural anthropologist and have woven her work into my therapeutic model.

The other influence in creating this *Caregiving Assessment* is Jean Clarke's work as expressed in her book (with Connie Dawson), *Growing Up Again*. This is one of the most valuable books I have found for talking with clients about inner parenting and relationship with self. One of the gems from her work is the identification of the message parents should give their child in each of the stages of development. Clarke has devised a set of *Affirmation Ovals* which capture each of the seven messages for each stage. She has given me permission to reprint the *Affirmation Ovals* and sell them on my website at http://elsbethmartindale.com/product/affirmation-ovals/.

How I use this:

Combining Jean Clarke's identified messages of a good parent with the four archetypal qualities from Angeles Arrien's work, I created this assessment. I have used it with many clients to help them assess the caregiving their parents provided and to contrast this with their own current level of caregiving for themselves. This has led to many excellent conversations about the challenge of good self-care and the role models who showed us how, skillfully or not, to care for ourselves.

Example from practice:

I love running weekend retreats for my clients. A recent retreat focused on Accessing the Wise Inner Guide (2019). I asked my clients to fill out this assessment prior to attending the retreat. I wanted them to come into the weekend with clarity about the kind of parenting they received in each of the four areas of wisdom (Teacher, Healer, Warrior, and Visionary). I also wanted them to assess their current level of self-care in each of these four areas. We spent time at the retreat reviewing their scores and learning how to be a more skilled Wise Inner Guide in each of these domains. It was the best retreat ever!

Elsbeth Martindale
CLINICAL PSYCHOLOGIST

Caregiving Assessment

How you were cared for growing up has had a powerful effect on how you currently care for yourself. Your parents and care providers showed you their version of caring for your needs. Their style is easily replicated, and often done without conscious consideration. It is helpful to look with open eyes at how you received parenting so you can determine if you wish to carry forward or adjust this style for your own self-parenting. The following Caregiving Assessment gives you a means for doing just that.

WHAT IS GOOD CAREGIVING?

Ideally, you want to be parented from a place of care and wisdom. I like the notion of guiding or steering the inner world with a sense of doing this from a Wise Inner Guide. A Wise Inner Guide, if not modeled by your own parents, can be learned and practiced. It may take time to reprogram your style of self-care, but with persistent intention and action you can develop a sense of guiding inner wisdom. From this place, you can become your own source of comfort, guidance, strength, and encouragement.

FOUR WISDOM ARCHETYPES

Angeles Arrien, a cultural anthropologist and author of *The Four-Fold Way*, talked about four main archtypes, across all cultures, to which people ascribe wisdom. These include The Warrior, The Healer, The Visionary, and The Teacher. Angeles Arien says, "Optimum health is considered to be the equal expression of these archetypes." You can use these archtypes as a way to assess the wisdom of your previous care givers. You can also use this measure to evaluate your own developing Wise Inner Guide.

THE HEALER

The healer pays attention to what has heart and meaning. The healer offers soothing and comfort when hurt.

THE TEACHER

The teacher guides, warns, advises, and looks for the best path forward. The teacher is able to speak the truth without blame or judgment.

THE WARRIOR

The warrior knows how to show up and be present. The warrior stands up, defends, and asserts itself for your needs.

THE VISIONARY

The visionary is open to outcome but does not get attached to it. It sees your potentials and possibilities.

TAKE THE ASSESSMENT

Use this assessment first to examine your caregiver's skillfulness in parenting you in each of the four areas described. Then evaluate your own ability to provide these essential qualities of self-care to your current life.

Elsbeth Martindale
CLINICAL PSYCHOLOGIST

Caregiving Assessment

Name _____   Date _____

Growing up, my **CAREGIVER** offered…

		minimally ……………….. completely
1	proper nutrition and tasty food.	1…2…3…4…5…6…7…8…9…10
2	encouragement to exercise regularly.	1…2…3…4…5…6…7…8…9…11
3	an appreciation of rest and relaxation.	1…2…3…4…5…6…7…8…9…12
4	medical care when needed.	1…2…3…4…5…6…7…8…9…10
5	to work through her own losses and pain.	1…2…3…4…5…6…7…8…9…10
6	to take good care of her own needs through action and declaration.	1…2…3…4…5…6…7…8…9…10
7	loving touch.	1…2…3…4…5…6…7…8…9…10
8	to look at their self/himself/herself/ with love, objectivity and forgiveness.	1…2…3…4…5…6…7…8…9…10
9	comfort and tenderness.	1…2…3…4…5…6…7…8…9…10
10	loving and consistent care.	1…2…3…4…5…6…7…8…9…10
11	to seek to understand and support my needs.	1…2…3…4…5…6…7…8…9…10
12	to make time for me.	1…2…3…4…5…6…7…8…9…10
13	acceptance of my feelings, both positive and negative.	1…2…3…4…5…6…7…8…9…10
14	patience toward me and others.	1…2…3…4…5…6…7…8…9…10
15	kindness toward me and others.	1…2…3…4…5…6…7…8…9…10
16	empathy and compassion around my pain and struggles.	1…2…3…4…5…6…7…8…9…10
17	genuine expressed love.	1…2…3…4…5…6…7…8…9…10
18	acceptance of my uniqueness and differentness from him/her/them.	1…2…3…4…5…6…7…8…9…10
	Add total points from questions 1 - 18 = _____ ÷ 18	**HEALER** Qualities = _____
19	to talk and make time for connection.	1…2…3…4…5…6…7…8…9…10
20	time for playing together.	1…2…3…4…5…6…7…8…9…10
21	to find joy and delight in me.	1…2…3…4…5…6…7…8…9…10

22	affirm, encourage, and support for my growth.	1...2...3...4...5...6...7...8...9...10
23	to be reliable and trustworthy.	1...2...3...4...5...6...7...8...9...10
24	to teach me ways to express feelings positively.	1...2...3...4...5...6...7...8...9...10
25	to teach me cause-and-effect thinking.	1...2...3...4...5...6...7...8...9...10
26	to think about others' feelings.	1...2...3...4...5...6...7...8...9...10
27	to help me see the consequences of my actions and be responsible for them.	1...2...3...4...5...6...7...8...9...10
28	to be a reliable source of information about the world.	1...2...3...4...5...6...7...8...9...10
29	to support me as a sexual being.	1...2...3...4...5...6...7...8...9...10
30	to celebrate my successes, large and small.	1...2...3...4...5...6...7...8...9...10
31	flexibility and willingness to adjust.	1...2...3...4...5...6...7...8...9...10
32	enjoyment of simple things.	1...2...3...4...5...6...7...8...9...10
33	an acceptance of loss and grief.	1...2...3...4...5...6...7...8...9...10
34	to teach me without being judgmental of me.	1...2...3...4...5...6...7...8...9...10
35	encouragement to reach out to others for support and information.	1...2...3...4...5...6...7...8...9...10
36	to allow me to be separate and independent.	1...2...3...4...5...6...7...8...9...10
37	to help me be engaged in my community.	1...2...3...4...5...6...7...8...9...10
38	listening without interrupting.	1...2...3...4...5...6...7...8...9...10
	Add total points from questions 19 - 38 = _____ ÷ 20	**TEACHER** Qualities = _____
39	willingness to stand up to injustice around me.	1...2...3...4...5...6...7...8...9...10
40	to remain constant in the face of challenges.	1...2...3...4...5...6...7...8...9...10
41	to challenge negative behavior and decisions.	1...2...3...4...5...6...7...8...9...10
42	encouragement to stand on my own, take a stand, and/or make clear when I am unwilling to stand.	1...2...3...4...5...6...7...8...9...10
43	perseverance, persistence, and willingness to work hard.	1...2...3...4...5...6...7...8...9...10
44	an ability and willingness to set limits and boundaries.	1...2...3...4...5...6...7...8...9...10
45	encouragement to not "need" him/her/them.	1...2...3...4...5...6...7...8...9...10
46	encouragement to be courageous.	1...2...3...4...5...6...7...8...9...10

47	to teach me to honor and respect myself and others (including him/her/them).	1...2...3...4...5...6...7...8...9...10
48	time for quiet, stillness, rest, and solitude.	1...2...3...4...5...6...7...8...9...10
49	to help others make space for me.	1...2...3...4...5...6...7...8...9...10
50	a safe and secure environment.	1...2...3...4...5...6...7...8...9...10
51	to set reasonable limits and enforce them.	1...2...3...4...5...6...7...8...9...10
52	protection from harm.	1...2...3...4...5...6...7...8...9...10
53	to grow and change their self/himself/herself and encouragement for me to do the same.	1...2...3...4...5...6...7...8...9...10
54	encouragement to inspire and contribute to others.	1...2...3...4...5...6...7...8...9...10
55	to teach me the importance of being kind to myself and to others (including him/her/them).	1...2...3...4...5...6...7...8...9...10
56	encouragement to seek mentors, guides, and support as needed.	1...2...3...4...5...6...7...8...9...10
57	permission to disagree with him/her/them.	1...2...3...4...5...6...7...8...9...10
	Add total points from questions 39 - 57 = _____ ÷ 19	**WARRIOR** Qualities = _____
58	freedom and curiosity to see me for who I am.	1...2...3...4...5...6...7...8...9...10
59	freedom and encouragement to explore.	1...2...3...4...5...6...7...8...9...10
60	to celebrate my independent thinking and problem-solving.	1...2...3...4...5...6...7...8...9...10
61	to model and teach conflict-resolution skills.	1...2...3...4...5...6...7...8...9...10
62	willingness to make sacrifices for the greater good.	1...2...3...4...5...6...7...8...9...10
63	to help me see my possibilities and potentials.	1...2...3...4...5...6...7...8...9...10
64	to name my strengths and gifts.	1...2...3...4...5...6...7...8...9...10
65	encouragement to follow my own dreams and set my own course.	1...2...3...4...5...6...7...8...9...10
66	encouragement to speak my truth.	1...2...3...4...5...6...7...8...9...10
67	encouragement to know and invest in my own inner life.	1...2...3...4...5...6...7...8...9...10
68	understanding of the value of creative expression.	1...2...3...4...5...6...7...8...9...10
69	an appreciation of the value of silence, stillness, and reflection.	1...2...3...4...5...6...7...8...9...10
	Add total points from questions 58 - 69 = _____ ÷ 12	**VISIONARY** Qualities = _____

Elsbeth Martindale
CLINICAL PSYCHOLOGIST

Name _____   Date _____

In my **CURRENT LIFE**, I offer myself…

minimally ……………….. completely

#		
1	proper nutrition and tasty food.	1…2…3…4…5…6…7…8…9…10
2	regular exercise.	1…2…3…4…5…6…7…8…9…11
3	time for rest and relaxation.	1…2…3…4…5…6…7…8…9…12
4	medical care when needed.	1…2…3…4…5…6…7…8…9…10
5	trust in others' capacity to work through their own losses and pain.	1…2…3…4…5…6…7…8…9…10
6	awareness of and respect for the needs of others.	1…2…3…4…5…6…7…8…9…10
7	loving touch.	1…2…3…4…5…6…7…8…9…10
8	willingness to look at myself with love, objectivity, and forgiveness.	1…2…3…4…5…6…7…8…9…10
9	comfort and tenderness.	1…2…3…4…5…6…7…8…9…10
10	loving and consistent care.	1…2…3…4…5…6…7…8…9…10
11	understanding of my needs and action in support of them.	1…2…3…4…5…6…7…8…9…10
12	time for me.	1…2…3…4…5…6…7…8…9…10
13	acceptance of my feelings, both positive and negative.	1…2…3…4…5…6…7…8…9…10
14	patience toward myself and others.	1…2…3…4…5…6…7…8…9…10
15	kindness toward myself and others.	1…2…3…4…5…6…7…8…9…10
16	empathy and compassion around my pain and struggles.	1…2…3…4…5…6…7…8…9…10
17	demonstrations of self-love.	1…2…3…4…5…6…7…8…9…10
18	acceptance of my uniqueness and differentness from others.	1…2…3…4…5…6…7…8…9…10
	Add total points from questions 1 - 18 = _____ ÷ 18	**HEALER** Qualities = _____
19	time and opportunities for connection with others.	1…2…3…4…5…6…7…8…9…10
20	time for play.	1…2…3…4…5…6…7…8…9…10
21	to find joy and delight in myself.	1…2…3…4…5…6…7…8…9…10
22	to affirm, encourage, and support my growth.	1…2…3…4…5…6…7…8…9…10

Elsbeth Martindale
CLINICAL PSYCHOLOGIST

23	to be reliable and trustworthy.	1...2...3...4...5...6...7...8...9...10
24	to express my feelings effectively.	1...2...3...4...5...6...7...8...9...10
25	to learn about cause-and-effect.	1...2...3...4...5...6...7...8...9...10
26	to think about others' feelings.	1...2...3...4...5...6...7...8...9...10
27	to see and be responsible for the consequences of my actions.	1...2...3...4...5...6...7...8...9...10
28	to give myself reliable sources of information about the world.	1...2...3...4...5...6...7...8...9...10
29	to support and expand my sexuality.	1...2...3...4...5...6...7...8...9...10
30	celebration of my successes, large and small.	1...2...3...4...5...6...7...8...9...10
31	flexibility and willingness to adjust.	1...2...3...4...5...6...7...8...9...10
32	enjoyment of simple things.	1...2...3...4...5...6...7...8...9...10
33	acceptance of loss and grief.	1...2...3...4...5...6...7...8...9...10
34	support to grow without being judgmental.	1...2...3...4...5...6...7...8...9...10
35	encouragement to reach out to others for support and information.	1...2...3...4...5...6...7...8...9...10
36	allowance to be separate and independent.	1...2...3...4...5...6...7...8...9...10
37	engagement in an experience of community.	1...2...3...4...5...6...7...8...9...10
38	listening without interrupting.	1...2...3...4...5...6...7...8...9...10
	Add total points from questions 19 - 38 = _____ ÷ 20	**TEACHER** Qualities = _____
39	willingness to stand up to injustice around me.	1...2...3...4...5...6...7...8...9...10
40	to stay centered in the face of challenges.	1...2...3...4...5...6...7...8...9...10
41	to challenge my negative behavior and decisions.	1...2...3...4...5...6...7...8...9...10
42	the ability to stand on my own, take a stand, and/ or make clear when I am unwilling to stand.	1...2...3...4...5...6...7...8...9...10
43	perseverance, persistence, and willingness to work hard.	1...2...3...4...5...6...7...8...9...10
44	the ability and willingness to set limits and boundaries.	1...2...3...4...5...6...7...8...9...10
45	the ability to accept if my preferences aren't met.	1...2...3...4...5...6...7...8...9...10
46	support to be courageous.	1...2...3...4...5...6...7...8...9...10
47	honor and respect, for myself and others.	1...2...3...4...5...6...7...8...9...10

Elsbeth Martindale
CLINICAL PSYCHOLOGIST

48	time for quiet, stillness, rest, and solitude.	1...2...3...4...5...6...7...8...9...10
49	the ability to request others make space for me.	1...2...3...4...5...6...7...8...9...10
50	a safe and secure environment.	1...2...3...4...5...6...7...8...9...10
51	reasonable limits and followthrough.	1...2...3...4...5...6...7...8...9...10
52	protection from harm.	1...2...3...4...5...6...7...8...9...10
53	to grow and change and allow others to do the same.	1...2...3...4...5...6...7...8...9...10
54	to be my own authority of my needs and feelings.	1...2...3...4...5...6...7...8...9...10
55	to inspire and contribute to others.	1...2...3...4...5...6...7...8...9...10
56	to seek mentors, guides, and support as needed.	1...2...3...4...5...6...7...8...9...10
57	permission to disagree with others.	1...2...3...4...5...6...7...8...9...10
	Add total points from questions 39 - 57 = _____ ÷ 19	**WARRIOR** Qualities = _____
58	curiosity about who I am and who I am becoming.	1...2...3...4...5...6...7...8...9...10
59	freedom and encouragement to explore.	1...2...3...4...5...6...7...8...9...10
60	independent thinking and problem-solving.	1...2...3...4...5...6...7...8...9...10
61	skills for conflict-resolution.	1...2...3...4...5...6...7...8...9...10
62	a willingness to make sacrifices for the greater good.	1...2...3...4...5...6...7...8...9...10
63	curiosity about my possibilities and potentials.	1...2...3...4...5...6...7...8...9...10
64	to know my strengths and gifts.	1...2...3...4...5...6...7...8...9...10
65	the ability to follow my own dreams and set my own course.	1...2...3...4...5...6...7...8...9...10
66	the ability to speak my truth.	1...2...3...4...5...6...7...8...9...10
67	knowledge and investment in my own inner life.	1...2...3...4...5...6...7...8...9...10
68	opportunities for creative expression.	1...2...3...4...5...6...7...8...9...10
69	time for silence, stillness, and reflection.	1...2...3...4...5...6...7...8...9...10
	Add total points from questions 58 - 69 = _____ ÷ 12	**VISIONARY** Qualities = _____

Elsbeth Martindale
CLINICAL PSYCHOLOGIST

Caregiving Assessment - Summary

Now you have a chance to look at the wisdom with which your care-giver was able to provide care for you. You can assess where they were strongest as well as where they were less skilled.

You can also look at the wisdom you bring to your own self-care, noting where you are strongest and where you might want to improve.

Compare your caregiver's skills in caring for you with your own.

	Caregiver's Score	Self-Care Score
Healer	_____	_____
Teacher	_____	_____
Warrior	_____	_____
Visionary	_____	_____

Are you as skillful as your caregiver in caring for yourself? What do you make of this?

Are you more skillful in self-care than your caregiver was in caring for you? What do you make of this?

In what aspect of self-care are you seeing the need for improvement? How would improvement in this area enhance your life? What steps could you take to build wisdom in this area?

Elsbeth Martindale
CLINICAL PSYCHOLOGIST

Commitments to Better Self-Care
elsbethmartindale.com/commitments-to-better-self-care

This handout was developed for a self-care workshop for professional therapists. At the training, participants were asked to look at the cost of caring for others day in and day out. They were then directed to assess their own self-care and identify areas where improvement could be made. The handout helped them commit to improving their own level of self-care.

I often post a card on my bulletin board that says, "Take my advice; I'm not using it." Sadly, this is often the case in our profession. We can be generous to the needs of others while neglecting to attend to our own. This tendency, of giving to others without attending to self, is not just an issue among therapists. Parents, professionals of all types, and caring people in general can be so focused on the needs of others that they forget to attend to themselves. This handout is a great tool for making self-care a priority.

How I use this:
When clients are struggling to prioritize their own needs, I pull out this handout and discuss with them their challenge and help them identify small steps of change that might shift their pattern. Habits don't change quickly. They require commitment and persistence. The handout addresses the specifics of changing the negative pattern of self-neglect and provides examples of small changes for improving one's investment in self-care.

Example from practice:
Karla is a veterinarian with a thriving practice. She absolutely loves her work but often prioritizes it above her own self-care. She is able to manage a fairly stressful life without much debilitating distress but is aware her pace is not likely sustainable. Karla was able to identify the costs of this chosen lifestyle. She didn't have enough time to play with her own dog, she didn't have much intimacy with her partner, and she had little time for introspection and reflection. Knowing these were consequences of a harried life, Karla made a small-step commitment to walk her dog each evening. She asked her partner to join her and to hold her accountable to going even if she claimed she was "too busy." This, of course, didn't solve the problem of being overextended, but it allowed her to prioritize one important aspect of her life and commit to following through. Her success in this one small area gave her hope of taking another small step in the future to help her balance her personal and professional life effectively.

Elsbeth Martindale
CLINICAL PSYCHOLOGIST

Commitments to Better Self-Care

Commitments will allow you to ground your intentions. They are hard to hold unless they are crafted in several important ways:

- They must truly be in sync with your personal goals and grounded in your own longings and hopes, not just something others think you should do.
- They must be realistic and achievable.
- They must embody all three types of self-care strategies: preventative, protective, and curative.
- Small-step commitments often work best, like rungs on a ladder. Find a small step that can be taken toward your ultimate goal.
- Frame commitments as specifically as possible. Avoid general, undefinable terms.
- Following through on commitments is more likely if they are reinforced. A simple smiley face on a calendar or a self-administered pat on the back will do. Just recognize and honor your success.
- You may find it helpful to share your commitment with another person and ask him/her/them to help hold you accountable to achieving your intended goal.

EXAMPLES OF SELF-CARE COMMITMENTS

- I will sit in my comfortable chair and look out at the garden every morning next week while I have my first cup of coffee.
- I will take a stretch break between my morning and afternoon clients. I will close my office door, get on the floor, and stretch my body for five minutes. I will do this every day I see clients next week.
- I will be silent for at least five minutes each day for thirty days.
- I will take at least five minutes every day in the mid-afternoon to step outside and be silent. I'll check in with my body, notice what's inspiring, and give myself a moment of appreciation.
- I will practice speaking truthfully without blame or judgment. I will do this more consistently with my spouse and smile inwardly when I am successful.
- I will sign up for singing lessons before the end of next week.

- I will be more compassionate and gentle with myself. When I notice inner harshness, I will gently tug my right ear lobe to remind myself of my capacity for kindness, even toward myself.
- I will start each day with permission to disappoint someone. I will practice living free of the fear that the unhappiness of others is my fault.

Use a separate sheet of paper to write three very specific self-care goals. To what could you commit that would be both supportive and sustainable in the care of yourself?

HERE'S AN IDEA

Check out the app *Intend - The Change Reminder.* This app allows you to name your goal, set reminders, and track your progress. Cool, huh?

Elsbeth Martindale
CLINICAL PSYCHOLOGIST

Gems of Wisdom

elsbethmartindale.com/gems-of-wisdom

This is a great reinforcement tool to help solidify client learning. It is a playful tool and needs to be offered in this spirit.

How I use this:

When clients have that ah-ha experience of really having been able to grasp and use a concept discussed in therapy, this is a great reinforcer. I might say to clients, *"You've really got this! This is a gem of wisdom you can hold on to the rest of your life. Here (handing them a paper gem), write down this notion so you won't ever forget it. You've got this!"*

Example from practice:

Arma had been working hard in therapy. He had become more willing to assert his needs and desires in his relationship with his wife, leading to greater satisfaction in his marriage. He came to a session, full of joy, stating, "I get it now! It's not selfish to tell my wife what I want. It actually helps her know me better." Arma, who was raised to be attentive to the needs of his depressed mother in order to keep her from being emotionally absent from the family, had learned the bad habit of shutting himself down so no one would be bothered by his needs. This strategy had been causing apathy and indifference in his marriage. When Arma "got it," I suggested he take a *Gem of Wisdom* and write the newly discovered truth on the back side of a gem. He wrote, "It is okay for me to have and express my needs. Doing so helps me be seen and not feel alone."

Elsbeth Martindale
CLINICAL PSYCHOLOGIST

Gems of Wisdom

Successful therapy generates wisdom for clients. They may have understood something in a new way, found actions that support their goals with more ease, or learned something that has enhanced their sense of well-being. When an ah-ha moment reveals itself, it may be helpful to reinforce it with a "gem of wisdom." When clients have ah-ha moments, hand them a "gem," suggesting they write their new wisdom on the back of the gem and collect the gems as reminders of their growth.

Gem of Wisdom   Gem of Wisdom   Gem of Wisdom   Gem of Wisdom

Gem of Wisdom   Gem of Wisdom   Gem of Wisdom   Gem of Wisdom

Gem of Wisdom   Gem of Wisdom   Gem of Wisdom   Gem of Wisdom

Gem of Wisdom   Gem of Wisdom   Gem of Wisdom   Gem of Wisdom

Part IV

Healthy Connection

These handouts give clarity to and encourage the practice of the skills needed to attract and keep healthy relationships—whether the connection is romantic, familial, or a friendship.

RELATIONSHIPS
Differentiation vs. Fusion 131
Ladder of Differentiation..133
Managing Self in Conflict..135
Conflict in Relationships...137
I'm Sorry vs. What I Wish I Would Have Done Differently 139

COMMUNICATION
Hidden Feelings and Needs...141
Five-Finger Communication...143
Reflective Listening 145
Reflective Listening Practice 147
Who Owns the Problem?...149
Five Ways to Say It.. 51
Reflective Shield...153-155
Content-to-Process Shift...157

BOUNDARIES
Boundary Fences..159
Characteristics of Healthy Boundaries 161

MAKING CONNECTION
Encouragement...163
Twenty-Second Hug 165
Kudos Catcher 167
Phone Nap Pad..169

Elsbeth Martindale
CLINICAL PSYCHOLOGIST

Differentiation vs. Fusion

elsbethmartindale.com/differentiation-vs-fusion

Differentiation is a valuable concept to teach clients in therapy. I use the lists in this handout to talk about the distinction between healthy connection and enmeshed connection. The book, *If the Buddha Dated*, by Charlotte Kasl, from which this list was developed, is my favorite summary of David Schnarch's research on Passionate Marriages.

How I use this:

At least once a month I am pulling out this handout to help clients understand the notion of differentiation. I love Schnarch's definition that *differentiation* is, "The ability to hold a non-anxious position in the presence of a loved one's anxiety." I tell my clients this definition and then look through this handout, reading the qualities of both fusion and differentiation and stopping along the way to discuss the effect of these qualities and actions in relationships.

Example from practice:

Adam was dating his first serious partner. He talked frequently in therapy about the struggles and challenges he faced in his relationship. One of the most difficult aspects of his partnership involved his frequent fear that he was displeasing his boyfriend. Adam attempted to do the "right things" to not make his partner upset but felt as though he was constantly failing in his attempts. Adam worried his partner would be disappointed in him and that the relationship would end. It was hard to watch Adam's distress and constant worry. We looked at the qualities of differentiation and fusion outlined in this handout. It became clear just how fused Adam was in his partnership. In reviewing the defining features of differentiation, Adam was intrigued and interested in moving his relationship in a more differentiated direction. The work of building skills for self-validation and self-soothing was not an easy task, but little by little Adam experimented and practiced a healthier way to hold himself in his relationship. He and his boyfriend were able to work through their challenges and develop a stronger and more rewarding partnership.

Elsbeth Martindale
CLINICAL PSYCHOLOGIST

Differentiation vs. Fusion

QUALITIES OF DIFFERENTIATION

- Maintaining one's center in relationships. Able to define one's self, knowing one's own feelings and able to articulate these. Truthful even when it's difficult. Able to care for one's self.

- Having one's self-esteem and mood remain constant in the presence of others' anxieties and worries. Able to remain a loving witness; compassionate and supportive without entanglement.

- Knowing that one's value is a given. One's self-worth remains constant, not challenged by circumstances or others' beliefs.

- Developing a set of values through reflection, awareness, learning, and experimentation.

- Feeling comfortable or fascinated by different theories, belief systems, and perspectives. Secure enough in your own values and beliefs that you are not threatened by differences and allow yourself to be curious.

- Recognizing seduction, control, and manipulation—yours and others. Not trusting blindly but trusting based on evidence and history.

- Being able to self-reflect and self-confront. Owning responsibility for your choices, mistakes, and decisions.

- Asking for and receiving support without feeling weak or compromised. Accepting your humanness and fallibility.

- Giving without an agenda or the feeling you are giving away a part of yourself. Giving from a place of abundance.

- Seeing others clearly, not categorizing others. Not having preconceived beliefs or expectations of others.

- Learning to comfort and soothe yourself when faced with stress or difficulties. Not responding in haste to defend or react.

QUALITIES OF FUSION

- Losing oneself in close relationships. Second-guessing, monitoring one's behavior to please others, and worrying what others think of you.

- Having one's self-esteem/mood infected/affected by the anxieties and worries of (an)other(s).

- Measuring one's self-worth by external validation: praise, grades, money, status, looks, weight, etc.

- Reacting unconsciously out of childhood conditioning, teachings, or trauma. Having a stronger emotional reaction than the current situation warrants.

- Blaming others. Not seeing your part in the dramas and problems you experience.

- Defensiveness in the face of criticism, different ideologies, approaches, or beliefs.

- Needing to be right or always believing you are wrong.

- Being dependent on others to comfort and soothe you.

- Having difficulty giving to others, or giving with an agenda.

- Bonding in righteousness, pain, or as "victims."

- Engaging in compulsive and addictive behavior.

- Changing your persona or behavior to please or control others.

- Rescuing people, worrying for them, being overly dramatic about problems.

- Staying in harmful, painful relationships out of fear and dependency, or out of fear of being on one's own.

Source: Taken in part from, *If the Buddha Dated,* by Charlotte Kasl, 1999

Ladder of Differentiation

elsbethmartindale.com/ladder-of-differentiation

I appreciate the idea that every relationship conflict offers the opportunity to move up the ladder of differentiation one rung at a time. The steps/rungs of the ladder explain movement toward more and more differentiation. More importantly, with each step, the relationship strengthens and grows.

How I use this:

When discussing differentiation, this visual of one-rung-at-a-time can be helpful. When moving from the theoretical understanding to the practical implementation of differentiation, this handout demonstrates the specific steps or progression from a fused position to a more differentiated stance. Taking small steps makes it easier to feel hopeful and will empower clients to take on the challenge of movement toward differentiation. As with many aspirations of health and wholeness, it is not the arrival that counts but the steady investment in working toward the goal.

Example from practice:

Helen has struggled in her marriage for many years. She sees little hope in her partner ever changing to be the person she desires him to be. When we return the discussion to what she can do for herself rather than what she is frustrated about in him, she is able to consider the next small step she can take in caring for herself. Helen has been able to see the difficult work of supporting herself and staying focused on soothing her own distress instead of blaming her husband for his "many faults." This ladder of differentiation helped her see each conflict as an opportunity to practice her self-care skills and to focusing on where she has the power to make a difference—managing herself.

Elsbeth Martindale
CLINICAL PSYCHOLOGIST

Ladder of Differentiation

The qualities of differentiation include the ability to: 1) maintain a clear sense of self when you are in close proximity to important partners, 2) regulate your own anxiety (self-soothing), 3) hold a non-anxious presence in the face of another's anxiety, and 4) be willing to tolerate pain for growth. David Schnarch, author of *Passionate Marriage*, says, "Every conflict is a chance to move up one rung on the ladder of differentiation." Here are the main rungs on that ladder.

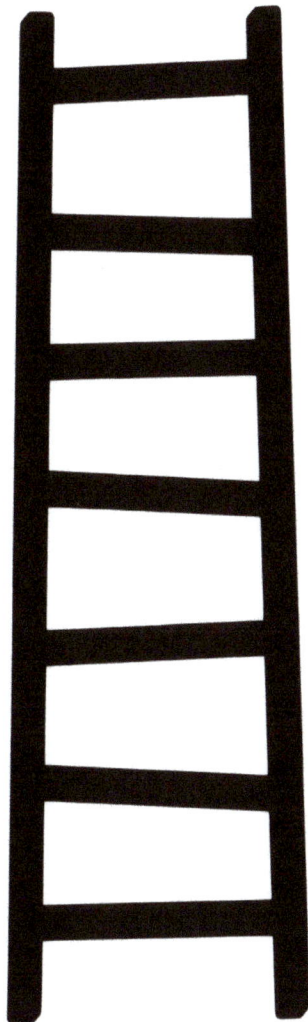

QUALITIES OF THE LEVELS OF DIFFERENTIATION

The **most differentiated** position is one in which you have a **clear sense of yourself** and have the **ability to self-soothe**. Even in midst of conflict you **actively try to get back in synch and repair** the mismatches in your partnership.

↑

When there is conflict, you may need to **break contact briefly**, focusing on a different interest, with **intention to replenish** yourself and **renew your efforts to regain connection**.

↑

You **take yourself toward activities which replenish you**. You **begin to make attempts to reestablish connection** with your partner after conflicts.

↑

Rather than fully avoiding your partner, you focus on **minimizing any negative interactions**. You keep a safe distance and **focus on your own replenishment**. You may still have trouble making active attempts to repair disconnection.

↑

When conflict is experienced you may actively avoid contact with your partner and be **aware of the disconnect**. You are **unable to initiate repairs in the relationship and within yourself**. You may also resist your partner's repair attempts.

↑

In this **most undifferentiated** position, the functioning of the relationship is severely affected because of continual disruption in your connection with your partner. You may feel **unable to reestablish connection**. You may be **unable to replenish yourself** when there is conflict.

Managing Self in Conflict

elsbethmartindale.com/managing-self-in-conflict

This scale was devised using the concepts of David Schnarch's qualities of differentiation. It is a way for clients to assess their levels of differentiation in their partnerships.

How I use this:

If clients are working on differentiation skills in their partnerships, I might offer them this scale so they can get a sense of where they currently stand and what specific skills might need improvement. Because they are trying to move up one rung of the ladder of differentiation in each conflict, this scale can be a measure of that movement.

Example from practice:

Estella is in a tough partnership. Her husband is a daily cannabis user and, as a result, is not emotionally present in their family much of the time. Estella wants to stay in this marriage. She and her husband are raising a child together, and Estella loves her partner in spite of his behavior. Over the years, Estella has become more skillful at taking a differentiated position in this relationship. She is practicing acceptance, because she has no power to change her husband's decisions. This scale has helped her see her progress.

Elsbeth Martindale
CLINICAL PSYCHOLOGIST

Managing Self In Conflict

Because you can't always get others to act the way you think they should, and because you aren't in charge of designing their life for them, maybe you can focus on what you do have power to do—managing yourself and your own reactions.

David Schnarch defined *differentiation* as, "The ability to hold a non-anxious position in the presence of a loved one's anxiety." Here is a way to score yourself in your attempts to be differentiated in your next relationship conflict—with one meaning you never do this and ten meaning you do this regularly.

SCORE CARD

1. I don't take my partner's behavior (or lack of change) personally. It's actually not all about me!

    1...2...3...4...5...6...7...8...9...10

2. I look for purpose and meaning in my dilemma. I see it as something I will need to confront again, so I'm invested in learning how to best manage it.

    1...2...3...4...5...6...7...8...9...10

3. I know that if I can't regulate my emotions, I can, at least, control my behavior. I don't do anything to make things worse.

    1...2...3...4...5...6...7...8...9...10

4. I can stop the negative mental tapes/stories. I can accept things as they are and figure out a plan for who I want to be in the middle of this reality.

    1...2...3...4...5...6...7...8...9...10

5. I don't ask or expect my partner to change his/her/their personality. I might make a request for behavior change or accommodation, if desired (e.g., "Would you be willing to..."), and offer this as a choice and not a demand.

    1...2...3...4...5...6...7...8...9...10

6. Self-soothing may require breaking contact with my partner. This is especially necessary if I am physiologically activated (i.e., heart rate above 15% of resting rate). I'm willing to break contact for the sake of self-repair and self-soothing. I can make it clear that my "time out" is for regaining balance and not dismissing him/her/them. When I take a break, I am willing to set a time to reconnect.

    1...2...3...4...5...6...7...8...9...10

7. I use my time out-of-sync effectively. I replenish myself. I don't plan my next attack or review my defense. I come back to being good with me so I can speak effectively about my needs.

    1...2...3...4...5...6...7...8...9...10

8. I don't use self-soothing to self-indulge, regress emotionally, or binge on food or substances. I know the purpose of my self-soothing is to promote resilience so I can keep striving toward my goal.

    1...2...3...4...5...6...7...8...9...10

9. I promote myself. I move up one rung of the ladder of differentiation in each conflict. I make myself as available for contact as possible.

    1...2...3...4...5...6...7...8...9...10

Conflict in Relationships

elsbethmartindale.com/conflict-in-relationships

Conflicts are inevitable in relationships, but they can create disconnection and animosity if they are managed from an inner primitive place. This handout explains the need to keep your physiology calm in order to resolve conflicts effectively. Many people don't know the importance of self-regulation.

Clients often believe walking away from a conflict is a sign of weakness and defeat or silent hostility. Actually, walking away may be the wisest move one can make. If the desire is to resolve the conflict and bring one's best self to the task, disengaging for the sake of restoring one's balance (physiologically and emotionally) can be the biggest gift to the partnership. Knowing when to pull away is important, as is identifying a time for return after disengagement, which helps the other not feel abandoned. As with most skills for self and relationship care, the practice of good self-management gets honed one conflict at a time.

How I use this:

When clients fight or argue in a way such that either partner becomes physiologically overheated (heart rate up), they need to know the value of stepping back until their Wise Mind can get back "online." If they are often accused of walking away as a sign of weakness, this handout can help clients see the wisdom in choiceful disengagement. Clients need to learn how to use the time away to restore themselves, rather than working on one's defense or next offense, so they can come back to a more conscious strategy for resolving the conflict.

Example from practice:

Tina felt the need to stay in the heat of an argument with her partner so as not to be accused of dismissing her partner. She would stay and fight because she didn't want to be seen as a wimp by allowing her partner to walk all over her. But, as the arguments and fights progressed, she and her partner became more and more unrefined in their strategies. Tina had not understood how her primitive mind took over when her body perceived a threat, how her frontal lobe disengaged and her "lizard" brain left her with only fight, flight, or freeze strategies. When she learned this, she was able to see the importance of removing herself from the downward spiral as soon as she became aware of her elevated heart rate. She was able to talk about this with her partner and make plans for disengagement for the sake of supporting their relationship and bringing their best selves to their conflicts.

Elsbeth Martindale
CLINICAL PSYCHOLOGIST

Conflict in Relationships

Conflict in relationships is inevitable, not wrong and not to be avoided. Skillful conflict management is key to the success in resolving challenges as they arise. To manage conflict effectively, it is helpful to know about your heart rate and arousal. For most people, resting heart rate is generally between 60 and 100 beats/minute.

THE TROUBLE IS...

If your heart rate increases 15 - 20% above your resting rate, then your system is FLOODED. Adrenalin overwhelms your nervous system, your frontal lobe disengages, and your primal brain takes over. Fight, flight, or freeze are the best you'll be able to do.

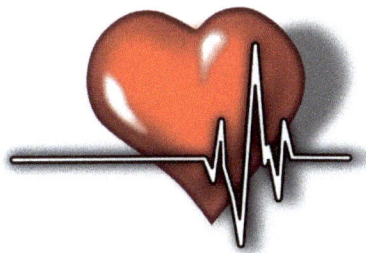

YOU CAN HELP...

Calm your physiology before you attempt to solve a conflict. With a relaxed nervous system, you have access to your prefrontal cortex, the part of your brain that helps with complex cognitive functions including planning, decision making, and moderating social behavior. Do you really want to go into a conflict without access to these capacities?

CONSCIOUS ACTIONS TO CALM YOUR PHYSIOLOGY

- Take personal action to restore yourself (discover what works for you, write down and post your best strategies).
- Discuss the new strategies you plan to use in advance, so others know your intention.
- Take time away, but don't review the problem or plan your defense. Focus on your restoration and your planned intention.
- Experiment with calming strategies such as deep breathing, progressive relaxation, splashing cold water on your face, or engaging in hard exercise.
- Adrenalin takes twenty minutes to wash out of the body, so you'll need at least that long to calm your physiology.
- Come back to the issue when your body is relaxed (heart beat at resting rate).
- Repair damage and re-focus on solutions.

HELPFUL WAYS TO UNDERSTAND RELATIONSHIP CONFLICTS

- Conflicts can be seen as opportunities to learn.
- Practice the magic ratio: 5 positives for every 1 negative equals relationship success.
- Define the problems as belonging to the relationship not to an individual.
- Keep a present-moment and solution focus.
- Reflect what you hear your partner saying.
- Remember that understanding does not mean agreement.
- Keep eye contact. Stay connected.
- Research has shown that 69% of problems in a relationship are unsolvable.
- Invest in loving acts: show appreciations, give regular attention to the relationship, add to your emotional bank account, continue courting, and clean up your own emotional messes.

Elsbeth Martindale
CLINICAL PSYCHOLOGIST

I'm Sorry vs. What I Wish I'd Done Differently

elsbethmartindale.com/im-sorry-vs-what-i-wish

Here is another gem I developed years ago. It speaks to the importance of unpacking a regret, learning from it, and using it to clarify a more desirable path, for self and for another. Too often an "I'm sorry" is thrown over a rupture or relational injury, as if this cover were all that were necessary to repair the wound and prevent its recurrence. To take an injury more seriously, one has to look at how it came about and make plans to choose a different path in the future. Demonstrating this conscious response to relational wounds can be beneficial to the individual who caused the injury as well as to the receiver of the wound.

How I use this:

I discuss the concepts in this handout when clients are not getting what they want out of an apology. If they aren't feeling like their relational ruptures are healing, they may need to go a bit deeper than just saying they are regretful. If they get at what they could have done to prevent an injury or mitigate its pain, they can then bring that to their partner with a description of what they would have liked to have done differently. This shows their partner they are serious about not repeating the wounding, and the action rebuilds trust.

Example from practice:

Lee came home late, once again, from a long day at work. They knew their partner would not like this. Indeed, they were hit with a barrage of anger when they walked in the door. In therapy, Lee talked about their dismay that their partner didn't accept the apology and move on; instead, the anger persisted several days. I suggested that a more caring response might require them to identify what they could do differently in the future to not repeat this scenario. This would require Lee to examine options for attending to their partner's needs and preferences and speaking about this—a much more challenging task than just apologizing. Together we looked at what could be done to address their partner's concerns, what commitments would be realistic, and how to communicate these. Lee went home and told their partner, "I was late from work last Thursday. I saw this greatly upset you because it is a repeated pattern. What I wish I'd done differently is to have called you as soon as I knew I'd be behind schedule. I wish I had been clearer with you about my need to respond to obligations at work while the boss is gone. I wish I'd been able to tell you all this Thursday night, so we could have had a good weekend." This made things better in that Lee's partner saw how much concern was being shown to them and how there was a plan for avoiding similar discomfort in the future. And everyone lived happily ever after!

I'm Sorry vs. What I Wish I'd Done Differently

Because hindsight is 20/20, you can often see things with much more clarity after an event than in the middle of a situation. You can use this clearer vision to learn about yourself and improve your skills. When you realize you have done something for which you feel regret and you want to repair the damage, you have a few options.

I'M SORRY

Saying a simple, "I'm sorry" is a quick and easy solution allowing you to:

- acknowledge your misstep
- show some regret and remorse
- try to put the situation behind you and move on
- make the other person possibly feel better, at least superficially
- stop any further discussion of the problem or mistake
- believe the problem has been solved

This approach can have unexpected **negative consequences**. These "magic words":

- can lack heart or true remorse
- offer no acknowledgment of the specifics of a misdeed
- used frequently or repeatedly, quickly lose their soothing or reparative power
- offer no plan for better choices in the future

HERE'S AN IDEA

If you have trouble coming up with alternatives for how you could have acted, try these suggestions:

- Imagine what someone whom you greatly respect would have done in a similar situation.
- Ask what the wisest part of you might have done.
- Think of the advice you would give someone else facing this situation.
- Don't think in terms of right and wrong. Focus instead on your desired outcomes.

WHAT I WISH I'D DONE DIFFERENTLY IS...

Provides a more satisfying way to deal with regret by allowing you to:

- rethink your part in the misdeed
- demonstrate regret and remorse
- attend to the conflict as a way to learn
- identify a clearer sense of how you want to act and describe the person you want to be
- offer a plan to prevent the problem from reoccurring in the future

There are some **excellent benefits** to spelling out what you could do differently, even though it requires more effort than a simple "sorry." Defining a new path of action:

- allows you to learn from your mistakes
- allows you to retrace your steps and find the junctures where you could have taken a different action
- allows you to design a different path, in your imagination, and rehearse this possibility
- increases the odds of choosing a more desired option in the future
- keeps the focus on you, which is where your power lies
- allows you to design the kind of life you want
- demonstrates your investment in decreasing conflict and injury in your relationships
- increases your influence and effectiveness in relationships
- increases trust in your relationships
- demonstrates openness and vulnerability
- increases the odds of a successful and evolving relationship

Elsbeth Martindale
CLINICAL PSYCHOLOGIST

Hidden Feelings and Needs

elsbethmartindale.com/hidden-feelings-needs

A simple practice sheet is sometimes the best tool in a therapy session. When clients aren't experienced at identifying feelings and needs, this handout can assist them in practicing these skills.

How I use this:

I often use this in group sessions when I am teaching clients to identify and express their feelings and needs. I will pull out a *Feelings List*, *Needs List*, and the *Five-Finger Communication* handouts as additional tools for exploring inner emotional experience. Together, these tools can help clients develop language and methods for practicing the skills of listening for the often hidden aspects of another person's experience.

Example from practice:

Judd is a successful businessman. He prides himself in being skillful in working with others. In group therapy, however, he was often given the feedback that he seems aloof and not fully present. With feedback from the group, he began to see he was good at explaining and telling stories but not so practiced in revealing his inner experience or listening to try to understand the needs and feelings of others. We used this sheet, in group, to practice identifying underlying feelings and needs. Judd had the chance to hear others model the use of these skills as well as practice them himself. This gave Judd a new way of being skillful in his relationships, a way that brought him into deeper connection both in expression as well as in reflecting others' emotional experience.

Hidden Feelings and Needs

Sometimes feelings and needs are hard to read. People often send "smoke-signal" communication rather than a clear declaration of what they want. Read the following sentences and assess the need of the person making each statement. What feeling is this person experiencing? For a further challenge, name three different strategies the sender of this message could use to increase the odds of getting his/her/their needs met.

1. After all I've done for you, and you can't even call me when you know I'm sick!

2. If you wanted me to pick you up, why didn't you just tell me?

3. I don't know why my husband has to be so mean when he gets drunk.

4. Why are you always picking on me?

5. I can't stand that he thinks I wasn't paying him attention.

6. I've never been treated so good in my life.

7. I hope I don't run out of insurance coverage before I learn all this stuff.

8. I can't wait to get home tonight and put my feet up.

9. I'm so fed up with this job, I want to tell the boss to shove it

10. How am I supposed to get all this done in one night?

11. If you would just tell me you love me once in a while, then I wouldn't have to worry so much.

12. No one seems to care about my feelings around here.

13. It's so much fun to be with you. We should hang out more often.

14. You're working again tonight?

15. Can't you see I'm trying my hardest?!

Five-Finger Communication

elsbethmartindale.com/five-finger-communication

If I had to pick a favorite handout, this would be it. It highlights the basics of Non-Violent Communication (NVC) on your hand. I find NVC to be the most powerful and thorough communication skill-building model. Its focus on underlying needs makes it super effective both in sending as well as listening. This Five-Finger Communication handout covers the sending aspect of healthy communication.

How I use this:

Here's what I would say to clients, "The basics of sending a message are all represented on the hand. Start with the **thumb**. You want to know if the other person is available to listen to you, so you want to name the topic. You want to state this in a manner which increases that person's willingness to talk. You want to get a 'yes' response. For example, you don't want to say, 'I want to talk about what a jerk you are.' Instead, you want to try something like, 'I'd like to talk about the way we've been getting along lately.' You want to get a thumbs-up or a "yes" in response to the question, 'Is this a good time?' **So the thumb represents the naming of the overall issue and asking if this is a good time.** Secondly, **use the pointer finger to point to the facts**—not interpretations or judgments, just facts. For example, you might say, 'We have been arguing and raising our voices toward each other often lately.' Next, the **middle finger is for naming feelings.** You might say, 'I'm feeling sad and frustrated.' There should be no explaining, just feeling words. Avoid saying, 'I feel that...,' as it will take you to a thought and not a feeling. **The ring finger is used to remember to name needs.** Use the statement, 'I have a need for...,' in order to avoid naming a strategy rather than a need. 'I have a need for connection and harmony,' not 'I need you to be nicer to me,' as this is a strategy for getting the need met, not the need itself. Finally, **the pinky is for naming your request**. The language of a request is, 'Would you be willing to...' For example, 'Would you be willing to take time each evening to talk about what we appreciate about each other and what we'd like to request from each other so we might live more harmoniously together?'"

This handout is made even better by the practice suggestions at the bottom. When clients can practice Five-Finger Communication with non-heated and non-personal issues, they can gain skillfulness. I ask a client to practice as many situations as possible before moving to examples from his/her/their own life. This is also a great handout to ask clients to take home and teach to someone else. Teaching is a great way to cement learning.

Elsbeth Martindale
CLINICAL PSYCHOLOGIST

Five-Finger Communication

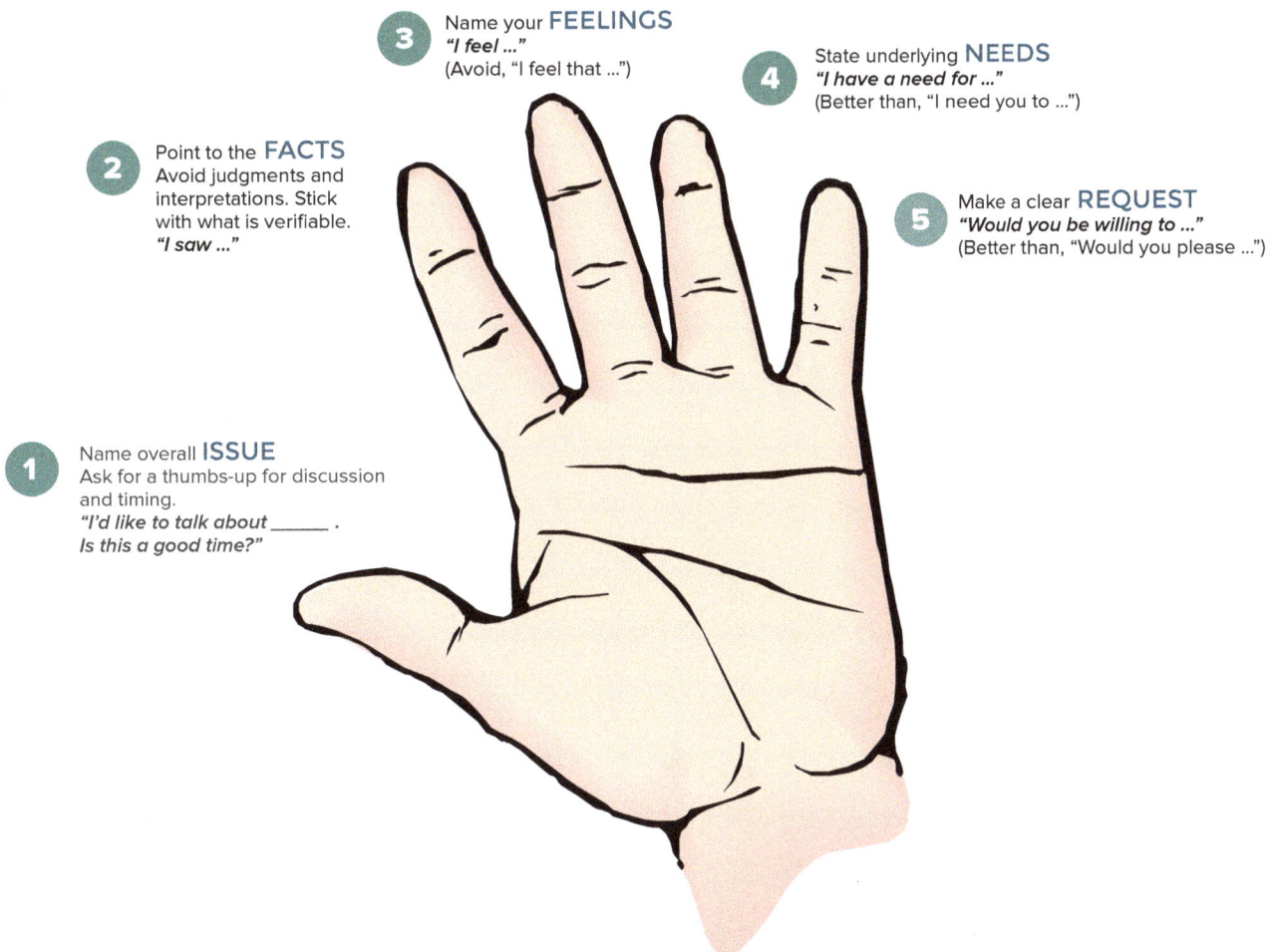

3 Name your **FEELINGS**
"I feel …"
(Avoid, "I feel that …")

4 State underlying **NEEDS**
"I have a need for …"
(Better than, "I need you to …")

2 Point to the **FACTS**
Avoid judgments and interpretations. Stick with what is verifiable.
"I saw …"

5 Make a clear **REQUEST**
"Would you be willing to …"
(Better than, "Would you please …")

1 Name overall **ISSUE**
Ask for a thumbs-up for discussion and timing.
*"I'd like to talk about _____ .
Is this a good time?"*

PRACTICE

1. You are angry because your partner came home late from work and you were planning on going out to dinner together.
2. Your child leaves a mess in the kitchen after making a snack.
3. Your boss gave the project you were hoping to work on to a less skilled coworker.
4. You mother calls to criticize you for not taking her to lunch on her birthday.
5. Your partner left your new camera at the park.

Elsbeth Martindale
CLINICAL PSYCHOLOGIST

Reflective Listening

elsbethmartindale.com/reflective-listening

The other half of good communication is being able to really listen. Reflective listening is not just a skill therapists need to know. You are withholding if you don't teach this essential skill for healthy relationships with your clients! This handout might have been the first handout I made, over twenty years ago. I pull it out at least once a month in order to teach this powerful tool.

How I use this:

I usually take out this handout and just read it. It says everything clients need to know in order to practice. And, practicing is exactly what is needed to learn this skill. I usually read through the examples, letting my client be the sender in the first example and the receiver in the second. Once they have practiced this, I will move to the *Reflective Listening Practice* sheet and give clients lots of opportunity to practice this essential skill.

Example from practice:

Kate and Jon came into their couples' therapy session after a six-month absence from therapy. Kate had a significant loss in her family, and the loss had taken much of her focus and energy. Jon stated he felt Kate was "far away" and wanted to find a way to have her come close again. The session was emotional, as both claimed they were missing one another but didn't know how to reconnect. We spent the remaining part of the session recognizing the longing they both shared for connection and intimacy and the pain they each feel when this is absent. Because the session was nearing the end, I told them I would email this *Reflective Listening* handout so they could continue to move toward each other on their own. I emailed the handout to them with instructions to read it aloud together, role-play the examples, and, if they wanted to move deeper, to practice the examples from the *Reflective Listening Practice* handout. It was helpful to have this tool at the ready. It allowed me to continue my "teaching" after their session and gave them more opportunity to practice listening to one another from the heart.

Elsbeth Martindale
CLINICAL PSYCHOLOGIST

Reflective Listening

Reflective listening is also called empathic listening. It is a way to respectfully attend to what is going on emotionally in another person. Like a mirror reflects the image it sees, you, as a reflective listener, mirror back what you hear someone else saying. Defenses, excuses, and differing opinions are withheld until your partner feels completely understood, and you, the reflector, feels as though you fully understand.

REFLECTIVE LISTENING INCLUDES BOTH AN ATTITUDE AND A SKILL

ATTITUDE
- A willingness to temporarily set aside your own perceptions, thoughts, and feelings.
- An attempt to understand the perceptions, thoughts, and feelings of someone else.
- Communicates, "I want to understand your point of view as fully as I can."

SKILL
- Restate the message of your partner in such a way that he/she/they feel understood by you.
- Use the simple formula, "You're feeling _____ because _____."

REFLECTIVE LISTENING RESULTS IN:
- The sender of a message feels safe, heard, and respected.
- The sender more likely is willing to go deeply into his/her/their feelings and inner world.
- The listener gets to fully understand the sender, even if the two don't agree.
- The listener gets to demonstrate his/her/their understanding, helping the sender feel fully heard.
- Creating intimacy, or into-me-see.

Example 1
Sender: She is so loving and affectionate with the children. She really listens to them and takes time to be with them. I don't think I could ever show my affection so openly with the kids.
Receiver: You notice how affectionate and caring she is with the kids, listening to them and taking time to be with them. You recognize that being that affectionate doesn't come as easy for you.
Sender: And in a way I'm almost jealous of her. I guess I see the children going to her in a way I wish they would come to me.
Receiver: You notice the children going to her, and it makes you feel a bit jealous that they don't come to you in the same way.

Example 2
Sender: I'm really angry that you didn't pick up milk on the way home, like I thought we had agreed, because now we have to delay dinner until one of us gets the milk.
Receiver: You're pissed at me because I forgot the milk. And you're angry that we'll have to delay dinner.
Sender: Yeah, I'm real hungry and I've had a lousy day at work and I feel like no one is concerned about helping me out. Everyone expects me to take care of everything.
Receiver: Sounds like you're feeling put upon both at work and at home and you'd like more assistance and concern.

Elsbeth Martindale
CLINICAL PSYCHOLOGIST

Reflective Listening Practice
elsbethmartindale.com/reflective-listening

Practice, practice, practice. Need I say more?

How I use this:
The basic reflective listening formula is at the top of the handout. I suggest that clients practice following this script when they begin and then encourage them to be more creative after they have mastered the basic skill of reflective listening.

I let them hold the handout and follow along as I read a sender statement and ask them to practice reflecting. The sending messages get a bit more difficult as they go along, because the scenarios become more personal. I tend to go in order, sometimes reading every one if a client needs a lot of practice. As they get more skillful, I suggest clients put the handout down and just practice listening without the words. This makes it a bit more challenging but more like real life.

Once they "get it" well enough, I will send a message, not from the script sheet, but from their own current relationship struggle. I will insert it like it's just another script I'm reading. This makes it both playful and a bit more challenging.

Example from practice:
One of the benefits of group therapy is the possibility of practicing basic skills that benefit all participants. In the safe context of group, clients can practice the skills they desire to implement outside of therapy. This handout is helpful for role-playing. I can give each member a chance to reflect one of these practice sentences in order build their skill. Other members can learn the skills of reflective listening just by observing this skill demonstrated.

I offer group therapy clients encouragement to practice reflecting the experiences of other group members. They often benefit by starting with the pre-scripted practice sentences on this handout. When I see a client is able to reflectively listen with these "pretend" situations, I encourage them to practice direct reflection of another group member as this person shares their experience. As a result of reflecting one another in this manner, group members build deep connection and trust. This goes a long way in helping clients not feel alone in their struggles because they feel seen and understood.

Elsbeth Martindale
CLINICAL PSYCHOLOGIST

Reflective Listening Practice

Remember the formula: **You're feeling _____ because _____.**

1 - SENDER: I thought I had that job all lined up. I felt like the interview was a breeze and that the boss really liked me. I can't believe they never called me back.

2 - SENDER: I'm so frustrated about my job. I want a job that is more rewarding, but I feel under qualified for what I really want to do. I'd love to go back to school, but I don't think we could afford that right now.

3 - SENDER: I told the boss that I would have the project ready for him by tomorrow, but there is no way I can put it all together in one night. It's not that I've been lazy. I didn't have all the material until two days ago, and I've been going non-stop on it since then. I'm afraid he'll be disappointed and I'll get the blame.

4 - SENDER: My friend Sue has been calling me every day for the past week. I know she is going through a lot right now, but I'm not feeling very sympathetic anymore. I wish she didn't call so often, but I don't know how to tell her.

5 - SENDER: Your father called and wants to take us out to dinner next week. I really don't feel like being with him for an evening. I can't stand his constant criticism of your ideas. He seems so pessimistic all the time.

6 - SENDER: I really want to get away, just the two of us. We haven't just played together in such a long time. I feel like we're both trying to be successful in our jobs, and I'm afraid of losing touch with each other. I don't want that to happen.

7 - SENDER: I really felt put down by you when you laughed at my new haircut. I wanted to try something new, and I was a bit unsure about it, too. But it really hurt when you just laughed at me.

8 - SENDER: I feel so exhausted when I get home from work. The last thing I feel like doing is cleaning up around here, yet I know it needs to be done. I would really like your help more around the house.

9 - SENDER: You never take the time to listen to me. You seem to listen only so I won't get mad but not because you're really interested in me.

10 - SENDER: I find it hard to tell you this, but I really like it when you do things for me that make me feel special and loved.

Elsbeth Martindale
CLINICAL PSYCHOLOGIST

Who Owns the Problem?

elsbethmartindale.com/who-owns-the-problem

This is another concept I learned while teaching parenting classes early in my career. Problem ownership is important to assess because it directs your next step. If you own the problem, you must speak up. If someone else owns the problem, you only need to use your reflective listening skills. But determining problem ownership can be challenging, and some folks like to jump into solving problems when the problems don't belong to them.

How I use this:

I generally read the top portion of the handout and remind them of the skills they've already been exposed to (ideally): *Reflective Listening* and *Five-Finger Communication*. Those skills need to be in place before I discuss problem ownership.

Then I pick a problem situation and we begin discussing whose problem it is. Once ownership is determined, I ask clients to practice the skillful response to the situation by either using speak-up skills or reflective listening.

Example from practice:

Pauline's eleven-year-old grandson has autism. This concerns her a lot because she knows he doesn't get treated well by other children at school. She worries about him and often feels like her daughter, the boy's mother, is not doing enough to advocate at school for his needs. Pauline can fill her days with worry and fretting over this loved boy's needs. It has been helpful for Pauline to distinguish between her problem and the problems of her grandson and daughter. She has memorized the Serenity Prayer and uses this to help her cope by letting go of things she can't control. Looking at this notion of problem ownership has helped Pauline respond to her concerns with effectiveness. If the problem were hers (e.g., concern her daughter wasn't standing up for her son being bullied), she would use her speak-up skills to share her concern and ask her daughter to take action. If the problem was not hers (e.g., her grandson complaining about being teased), she used her reflection skills to let him know she understood his pain and anger at the injustice. Learning to distinguish problem ownership has helped Pauline feel empowered to do what she can to support her concerns effectively.

Who Owns the Problem?

Identifying problem ownership is necessary before you determine how you might want to respond in a particular situation. In each of the following scenarios, decide who owns the problem. Think of how you would respond depending on to whom the problem belongs. Demonstrate Reflective Listening (if the problem is "theirs") or Five-Finger Communication (if the problem belongs to you).

PROBLEM SITUATIONS

1. Your adult daughter calls to tell you she will not be able to make it to your anniversary dinner this coming weekend. You made reservations to include her and will have to notify the restaurant of changes. You were looking forward to celebrating this event with her.

2. Your coworker tells you she is quitting her job because the boss is mistreating her. You have enjoyed working with her and things won't be the same without her.

3. Your brother wants to visit for the weekend with his family. The last time he came he brought a lot of chaos and drama. He says he really needs a "shoulder to cry on," but you don't know what this means.

4. Your neighbor just bought a motor-home and has been parking it in the street, moving it every other day to avoid city ordinances and tickets. Last week, he stopped you on the street to complain about the "stupid city rules limiting his freedom." You do not share his view.

5. Your child comes home with his/her/their report card showing a D in English. You know he/she/they are afraid to talk about this for fear you will be angry.

6. You win an award for excellence at work, and it comes with a $50 prize. When you look at the check, you realize it was only made out for $40.

7. Your favorite restaurant changed its long-standing menu. Now the dish you favored is no longer offered.

8. Your sister has begun dating someone who is very flashy with his money. He buys her expensive gifts, and you fear they are moving too quickly into commitment.

9. Your sister calls to tell you she is broken-hearted because her new boyfriend turned out to be a real jerk.

Elsbeth Martindale
CLINICAL PSYCHOLOGIST

Five Ways to Say It

elsbethmartindale.com/five-ways-to-say-it

This could be called the Goldilocks method. In this handout, I'm trying to help clients find the voice that is "just right" for them, somewhere between passivity and aggression.

How I use this:

I find it valuable to actually help clients practice the voices they *don't* want to use so they can feel how it doesn't sit well as the sender, to say nothing of the receiver. To feel the wimpiness of a passive tone and the abrasiveness of a harsh or aggressive tone can be instructive, especially when felt at a visceral level.

I explain how it is challenging to find just the right way to say something, and by hearing the options you can hone your style to represent your intentions the best way possible.

My favorite part of this handout is the recommendation to Practice Aloud When Alone (PAWA). This is such a powerful way to feel into finding your voice.

Example from practice:

Jill wanted to begin couples' therapy with her husband. She was worried he would not be willing to accompany her. She stated she didn't know how to bring this up or what to say to get him to go along with her. Jill had learned and practiced effective communication skills but was still intimidated about speaking up. I suggested she consider the five different ways to speak her truth and practice these with me. She loved playfully using an angry and demanding tone to tell her husband, "You need to go to therapy with me or our marriage is over!" We laughed about the ineffectiveness of this approach in winning her husband's cooperation. She then practiced a very timid voice, "I know you probably don't want to do this, but maybe someday we could go to couples' therapy if you thought it would be a good idea." Again, we snickered about how this passive voice would not represent her very well at all. Finally, she worked on finding a voice in the middle, one that spoke clearly of her desire without being demanding. This playful exercise was instructive and helped Jill land on both language and a tone for advocating for her desires. She decided she would practice this "just right" voice several times, without her husband present, so she could hear herself being effective in standing up for herself with confidence.

Elsbeth Martindale
CLINICAL PSYCHOLOGIST

Five Ways to Say It

Whenever you are trying to figure out how to say something that needs to be said, consider the idea that there are five possible ways to say it. Use your hand to identify the five possible ways.

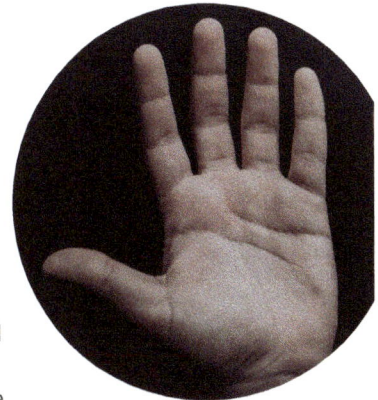

1 The **THUMB** represents the harshest form for saying your truth. If you were mad at your friend for showing up late, you might say, "You are such a jerk. You've totally ruined my day by being late!" It's good to know what this obnoxious voice sounds like and that you have the potency to speak this way if you ever need to. Say this message aloud just to get it out of the way. Feel how it sounds, and ask yourself if this is the voice you want to use. Likely, it is not, and you will need to find another style.

2 The **PINKY** represents the sugary sweet or passive voice. It is excessively nice, accommodating, and very concerned with not making someone else upset. In the example above of a friend being late, you might say, "You came a bit late and I hope you don't mind my saying anything, but I was worried and afraid something happened to you." It's good to know how to be nice and not to hurt others intentionally, but this voice often does not get the job done.

What is left now are three options: a voice that is a little bit harsh, one that is a little bit sweet, and the Goldilocks voice that is "just right." Try finding how each of these voices might sound.

3 The **POINTER FINGER**, closest to the thumb, can sound a bit strong and can be used to convey you mean business. It might sound like, "You were ten minutes late today. It pisses me off to wait. Please don't do that again."

4 The **RING FINGER**, closest to the pinky, might sound gentle and nice, like, "When you come late, I tend to worry that something is wrong. Could you let me know if you are going to be late?"

5 Then there's the **MIDDLE FINGER**, an assertive balance of them all. It might sound like, "I feel annoyed when you are late. I'd like you to be here on time or call me if you are going to be late. Is that something you'd be willing to do?"

Practice all of these voices so you can pick the one that feels most authentic, applicable to the circumstance, and fits your preferred style of communicating.

RECOMMENDATION

PAWA - PRACTICE ALOUD WHEN ALONE
The trick to finding your voice is to practice. It is often best to practice when the person you want to confront is not in the room. PAWA is a way to hear yourself speak in the voice that is most comfortable to you in a given situation. PAWA helps you find your power to communicate your truth in a manner that pleases you the most.

Elsbeth Martindale
CLINICAL PSYCHOLOGIST

Reflective Shield - Front

elsbethmartindale.com/reflective-shield

I made this handout for a retreat I was leading entitled, *Finding Your Superpower*. We used it when talking about owning one's power while simultaneously deflecting unwanted attacks to stay protected. The reflective shield offers a metaphor of the challenge of holding two tasks at once: warding off others' blows while attending to self-care.

How I use this:

When clients tell stories of how they were, or are, fearful of the anger and reactivity of another, this shield can be a helpful handout. The front side of the shield faces the "other"—often someone who is upset, activated, or attacking. The metaphorical mirror coating on the shield, facing outward, is a reminder to use reflective listening with the "attacker," demonstrating understanding of that person's concern, even if you are not in agreement with his/her/their message. People often calm down when they feel they are being heard and taken seriously. So, the front side of the shield offers strategies for calming the "attacker," noting things to do, as well as things to avoid, when the reflective shield is up.

Example from practice:

Steven's mother can be quite harsh and critical. He claims she looks for every opportunity to correct him, even though he is a grown man with a family of his own. Despite this, he loves his mother deeply and wants to spend time with her. As he was planning for her visit over the holidays, Steven talked about his frustration and how he worried she would, once again, be critical of him and his decisions. I took out this image of the *Reflective Shield*, and together we looked at how he could use this in the face of his mother's criticism. He could offer her reflection, without agreement, beaming back her criticism in a manner that would let her know he heard her. I helped him see the challenge of this, in and of itself, but suggested it would also be possible and helpful to offer himself some compassion and validation for his frustration, at the same time. We practiced this, as a role-play, and he was able to see the possibility of being both reflective of his mother as well as protective and kind toward himself.

Elsbeth Martindale
CLINICAL PSYCHOLOGIST

Reflective Shield - Front

CONSIDER:

- Reflecting feelings
- Guessing at needs
- Staying attuned
- Remembering understanding ≠ agreement
- Demonstrating listening through non-verbals (leaning in, eye-contact, etc.)

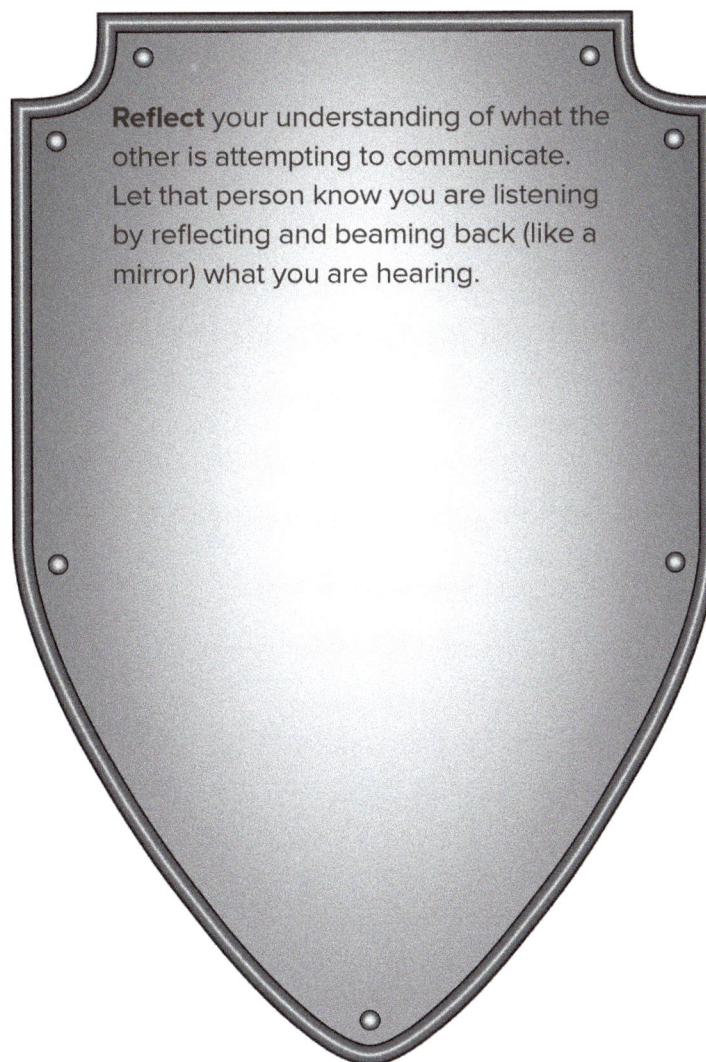

Reflect your understanding of what the other is attempting to communicate. Let that person know you are listening by reflecting and beaming back (like a mirror) what you are hearing.

AVOID THIS:

- Judgment
- Defending
- Explaining
- Solving
- Fixing
- Apologizing
- Talking about you

Reflective Shield - Back

elsbethmartindale.com/reflective-shield

How I use this:

The back side of the reflective shield addresses the various things people need to do for themselves when holding a protective position. This shield shows the challenge of the double duty of reflecting another's concern while comforting self at the same time. Although it is a difficult task, the shield demonstrates the possibility of attending to both self and the other when in the midst of a conflict.

Example from practice:

After reviewing the details of the shield, I try to move into role-play situations from a client's personal life. The goal in acting out these situations is to get this information from the head to the heart. I want my clients to have an embodied experience of using these skills in my office so they feel confident in using the skills outside of therapy. I might pick a conflictual situation from the client's life, demonstrating how I would use the shield if it were my dilemma. Then I would suggest my client take up the shield to practice the skills with me. When clients see themselves successful in the safety of my office, they feel more emboldened to practice the skills at home.

The practice situations on the *Reflective Listening* handout could be used for role-plays, but real-life examples are generally the best.

Elsbeth Martindale
CLINICAL PSYCHOLOGIST

Reflective Shield - Back

The back side of a reflective shield is just as important as the front. From this side, you are using the shield to protect yourself from injury. It's tricky. You'll be doing two things at once: hearing the other person as well as caring for yourself. Practice reflecting the other's concerns, while at the same time noticing, with compassion, your own struggle, feelings, and needs. Doing so will help you to take good care of you in the midst of the storm of another's emotions.

CONSIDER:

- Self-soothing
- Self-compassion
- Self-validation
- Staying differentiated
- Focusing on your body and breath
- Identifying your feelings
- Recognizing your needs
- Holding a meta-awareness perspective

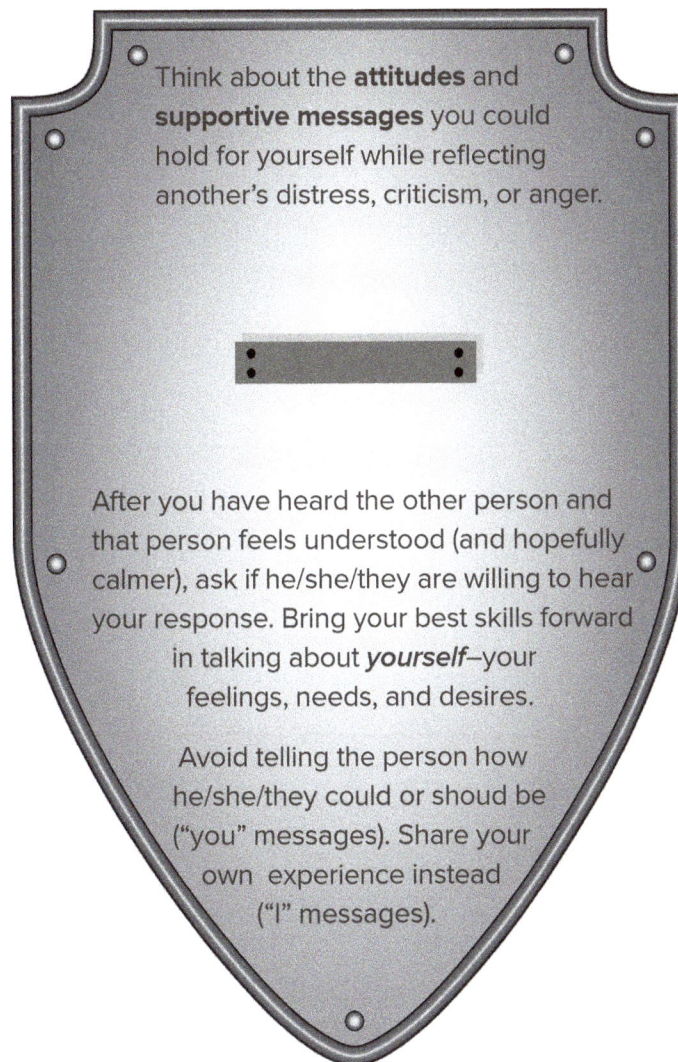

Think about the **attitudes** and **supportive messages** you could hold for yourself while reflecting another's distress, criticism, or anger.

After you have heard the other person and that person feels understood (and hopefully calmer), ask if he/she/they are willing to hear your response. Bring your best skills forward in talking about *yourself*—your feelings, needs, and desires.

Avoid telling the person how he/she/they could or shoud be ("you" messages). Share your own experience instead ("I" messages).

AVOID THIS:

- Self-judgment
- Taking the other's pain personally
- Working on a defense or justification

Elsbeth Martindale
CLINICAL PSYCHOLOGIST

Content-to-Process Shift
elsbethmartindale.com/content-to-process-shift

It is often not **what** is said but **how** it is said that makes a difference in how a message lands. This handout is a simple explanation of this concept. Teaching clients to rise above a conversation's content to observe the dynamics between the individuals and the meta-communication elements of a conversation can make clients more skillful in their interactions. Shifting in the middle of a conflict, from content to process, can allow a change of focus away from the details of the contention to the larger intention behind the struggle.

How I use this:

When clients are struggling in important relationships and claim they don't know why they are so frequently entangled, I often invite them to consider exploring the manner in which they are communicating when fighting. Are they raising their voice, using a belittling tone, name-calling, or taking a position of power over another? These methods of engaging in a conflict will likely lead to conflict escalation.

When clients are the recipients of someone else's condescending tone, it can be helpful to demonstrate how they can change the conversation to a discussion of their experience in the connection, rather than remaining in dialogue about the content of what is being discussed.

Whether a client is the deliverer or recipient of a non-productive communication style, this handout explains how to take a step back by shifting the focus to how a conflict is being managed rather than the specific details of the conflict itself.

Example from practice:

Eric was annoyed with his coworker's lack of productivity. In therapy, he relayed a story of how he had finally spoken up about his frustration to the coworker, who then became enraged with him in response. Eric told the story from a position of his "innocence," stating, "All I said was, 'Are you done with that project yet?'" The story sounded innocent enough until we examined the tone with which the message was communicated. Eric was able to see he had taken an attitude of superiority and effectively scolded his coworker—the outcome of many months of stored and unexpressed anger. Eric learned a lot by examining the process by which he deals with his frustration at work. We then explored a variety of tools and strategies for helping him address his concerns more effectively, attending to the way he said things and not just what was said.

Elsbeth Martindale
CLINICAL PSYCHOLOGIST

Content-to-Process Shift

When we talk with another person, there are at least two levels of communication happening. There is the **content**—what actual information is being shared through words. Along with this is the **process**, which is how the content is being communicated.

- Process can be seen in actions, tone of voice, and non-verbals.
- Process may also be invisible to an outside observer but deeply felt by the sender or receiver of a communication.
- Process is generally fueled by a long-held story, belief, or foregone conclusion. As a result, it can feel reactionary, emotional, and seemingly non-rationally connected to the situation.

PRACTICE EXAMPLES

Read a situation below. Imagine you are Person A. What do you think is going on on the inside of Person A? What might Person A *not* be saying? If Person A were to talk about his/her/their process, what might he/she/they say to Person B? Do the same for Person B.

1
Person A: There's only $750 left in our checking account.
Person B: Don't blame me. I'm not the one buying a latte every day.
Person A: You buy plenty of unnecessary things, like that new power drill! You haven't even started working on the fence yet, and you've had the drill for weeks.
Person B: You're the one who's been complaining about the dog getting out. I'm only trying to help you by fixing the stupid fence. You never appreciate the things I do to try to make your life better. I'm sick of even trying to make you happy.

2
Person A: He said he wanted me to talk with his brother to help him get over his depression. I wouldn't even know where to begin to advise someone about not being depressed.
Person B: Well, someone has to help him! Why not you?

3
Person A: You lost my keys again. I don't know why you have to be so disorganized, especially with MY stuff.
Person B: I'm a wreck, I know.

4
Person A: I want to go to New York again.
Person B: We've already been there for vacation several times. Don't you want a different adventure?

TO GET AT YOUR PROCESS, ASK THESE QUESTIONS

- What is being stirred in me?
- What does this remind me of?
- What feelings are up for me?
- What's this conflict really about?
- How am I being treated here?

- What am I fighting or resisting?
- What am I reacting to?
- What story am I telling myself?
- What beliefs do I have that are driving my reaction?

Elsbeth Martindale
CLINICAL PSYCHOLOGIST

Boundary Fences

elsbethmartindale.com/boundary-fences

It is helpful for clients to understand the many kinds of boundaries. Consideration needs to be given to the type of boundary most beneficial in the situation in which the client is struggling. The metaphor of actual fences is a great way to explore the potency of various boundary options.

How I use this:

When clients are ineffective in setting limits, either by not making their boundaries clear enough or by using a too-restrictive limit, I will pull out this **Boundary Fences** handout. It gives me a chance to help clients assess their boundary setting styles and skills. Exploring boundary options for a current dilemma helps to expand or refine skills in declaring limits. As with most ideas presented in therapy, the actual practice of stating boundaries, through role-play, can help clients embody and experience a skillful expression of their preferences.

Example from practice:

Keith had a very contentious relationship with a colleague. He often felt belittled and judged by this person. It made going to work, to a job he enjoyed, almost unbearable. Keith hasn't know how to make this behavior stop. He's spoken up to his colleague by saying, "I don't appreciate it when you criticize my report in front of others," but this didn't change the behavior. We looked at the **Boundary Fences** to see what kind of boundary might be most effective for him. He decided he needed something strong, not easily dismissed or ignored. A brick wall or barbed-wire fence seemed most appropriate. Keith came up with language to support his boundary—clear, not necessarily friendly— with stated consequences on which he'd be willing to act. His consequence statement sounded something like, "I see you are critical of my work. I ask that you share your concerns with me privately, rather than in front of others. If you are unwilling or unable to do this, I will ask HR to assist you in respecting my request."

Elsbeth Martindale
CLINICAL PSYCHOLOGIST

Boundary Fences

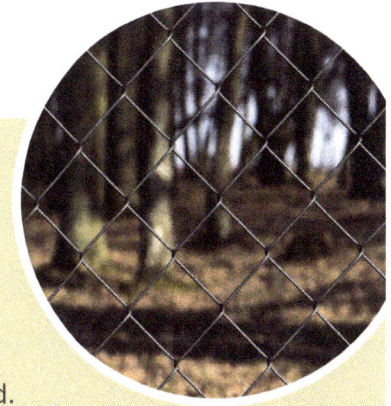

A boundary is a declaration of yourself to the world. It is a statement of your preferences, needs, or desires. It may also take the form of a demand or bottom line. The need for a boundary starts with a recognition of your own discomfort, a sense of dis-ease. Making a clear request, based on your needs, is an early form of setting a boundary. (e.g., "I'm feeling frustrated. Would you be willing to assist me?") You will need a stronger boundary if your initial boundary is unheard or trespassed. Find the appropriate boundary fence necessary for the situation at hand. Setting boundaries can be delicate business. If your boundary lines are too weak, you face the potential of being damaged; if they are too strong, you may injure others. Choose carefully.

TYPES OF BOUNDARIES

1) NO BOUNDARY
Allows others free access, no limits. This is ideal when there is ease and your needs are being met.

2) T.P. BOUNDARY
Looks sort of like a boundary but it's often just full of crap. This boundary has no power and is unsupportable. It's not useful because it doesn't give a clear sense of what you want or expect. (e.g., "Are you late again?")

3) WHITE PICKET FENCE
This fence is friendly and pretty. It often comes with a "please." It's easy to step over. Sometimes this fence comes in the form of an excuse or apology, as if you believe your needs are something for which you must apologize. (e.g., "I don't want to make a big deal about this, but you said you'd be here at 8:00 pm? Could you please be on time?")

4) CHAIN LINK FENCE
Not very pretty, but allows you to see the other side of things. You can't always notice this boundary until you're right on it. It's generally strong and clear once it's visible. (e.g., "It's 8:15 pm. I expected you at 8:00 pm.")

5) GOOD NEIGHBOR FENCE
This fence is generally friendly, and its placement is often negotiated. It offers a little willingness to see another's point of view. It might even have a gate, but it holds a clear edge once placement is agreed upon. (e.g., "Was there a misunderstanding? I expected you at 8:00 pm.")

6) BRICK WALL
Very clearly defined and immovable. No welcomed visibility. Can be cold. Usually has no gates, which limits access. (e.g., "We agreed to 8:00 pm and it's now 8:15 pm. I'm disappointed and annoyed!")

7) BARBED-WIRE
Can hurt if you mess with it. Clearly means business and is not at all welcoming. Boundary crossings come with severe and unfriendly consequences. (e.g., "I don't like waiting around. We had 8:00 pm scheduled, and it's now 8:15 pm. I'm unable to meet with you now, and I won't schedule again unless you can be on time.")

Elsbeth Martindale
CLINICAL PSYCHOLOGIST

Characteristics of Healthy Boundaries

elsbethmartindale.com/characteristics-of-healthy-boundaries

This is a basic how-to handout on limit setting. I developed this handout when teaching a four-week short course on boundary setting for my clients.

How I use this:

Overly passive as well as overly aggressive individuals can often benefit from understanding the characteristics of healthy boundaries. This is a "teach a man to fish" sort of tool. Clients need to grapple with their own preferred ways to speak up for themselves. These general characteristics offer guidelines for what is effective. The key is to give clients a chance to experiment with their own language so they can hear themselves setting boundaries effectively. The therapy office gives them a safe place to experiment with finding their voice and words.

I often use these boundary handouts in group therapy. I take opportunities, when they present themselves, to lead discussions on a topic by which many of the members of the group might benefit. Boundary issues are a common concern, and exploring this issue in a group setting is often very beneficial.

Example from practice:

Rachel's sister relied on her for many things including frequent financial assistance. Rachel was feeling cranky about this but had been helping her sister in this way for many years. She wanted to minimize the build-up of resentment toward her sister. She had little practice in speaking up for herself. I asked Rachel what she might say to her sister to let her know what she was willing and unwilling to do. She said, "I'll just tell her I can't do this anymore." I supported the directness of her message and then looked at this handout with her. We examined each of the characteristics and began honing her message. She realized she needed to clarify the specifics of what she "can't do anymore." She decided she wanted to continue to assist her sister, but in more limited ways, and wanted to figure out how to speak about her boundaries. After playing with what and how to speak her truth, Rachel finally landed on a message she liked. She planned to say, "I want to keep a contented relationship with you. You matter a lot to me. I'm no longer willing to give you money whenever you ask, but I'm willing to give you $200 a month. I trust you will be able to accept and work within this limit." Rachel wasn't able to deliver this message exactly as she practiced in session, but she felt more skillful in her ability to speak with clarity, assertion, and proactivity about her limits.

Elsbeth Martindale
CLINICAL PSYCHOLOGIST

Characteristics of Healthy Boundaries

Boundaries, small or large, are best if set with using the following qualities and characteristics.

CLEAR

Healthy boundaries are clear and specific. Make sure you have the other person's attention and that he/she/they know you mean business. Be specific and clear about what is expected, when it is to happen, and what the desired outcome will look like. (e.g., "I'd like you to call me before you come over. I'd like you to ask if it is a good time for a visit. That way I can be ready and available to spend quality time with you.")

ASSERTIVE

Good boundaries are stated directly and not hesitantly. Eye contact is usually helpful. You may need to check if the intended receiver is in a receptive place before making a statement of a boundary. An assertive stance considers the needs and well-being of the other as well as one's self. When the recipient is attentive, then state your boundary with no apology. (e.g., "Are you willing to hear what I need from you right now? I want you to talk in a calmer voice so that I can stay attentive to your concerns without becoming so scared.")

PROACTIVE NOT REACTIVE

Boundaries are best stated before a problem arises (again). Being proactive allows us to be calmer in our declarations. By being proactive, we let others know what is expected. If we wait until we are pushed to the wall, we may say things we don't mean or threaten consequences we don't intend to follow. Identify potential problem areas and set boundaries to prevent difficulties from arising. (e.g., "I'd be willing to go shopping with you on Tuesday if I can pick you up in front of your house and drop you off before 3:00 pm.")

SOLUTION FOCUSED

Good boundaries focus on solutions to problems or ways to avoid the problem altogether, rather than on what is wrong with a situation or person's behavior. When a boundary is expressed positively, it is easier to hear. (e.g., "I want to have all the laundry to the laundry room by 10:00 am on Saturday. This way you can be assured that your clothes will get cleaned by Monday.")

FOLLOWED THROUGH

Without follow-through, your stated boundaries are useless. Don't ever threaten something you do not intend to follow through on, or your words will lose their power and effectiveness. When your boundaries are respected, it is helpful to recognize and share your appreciation for the gift of cooperation. (e.g., "I appreciate that you didn't ask me to stay later after I told you I needed to leave by nine. Thanks for supporting me getting my project completed.")

NO EXCUSES

You do not have to explain or defend your reasons for setting a particular boundary. Others may try to argue with you and ask you why you need to be so rigid, selfish, or demanding. You can choose to just stand your ground without defense. With some people, the more you explain your reasons, the more you give them opportunities to attempt to talk you out of your position.

Encouragement

elsbethmartindale.com/encouragement

I recall an incident in graduate school when I was called out by a supervisor after giving feedback to a child in a group setting. The supervisor told me never to tell the children in the program that I was "proud" of them. I was shocked, not seeing the harm in my actions. She explained, it is important for the children to take actions based on their own internal motivation, to find the intrinsic value of good behavior, rather than being driven by the praise of adults. This was a new concept to me, and the lesson, albeit harshly delivered, has stayed with me.

The idea of encouraging versus praising people comes from the Adlerian psychologist Rudolf Dreikurs. He believed it important to invite children to evaluate their behavior as a way to build self-esteem. When children are focused on pleasing others to get praise and approval, they build "other-esteem" rather than self-esteem.

How I use this:

I use this notion of encouragement in three important ways. First, encouragement is helpful to clients who are parenting children. Secondly, I find it helpful to teach **Self-Encouragement** to build one's own self-esteem. Finally, clients can use encouragement in their adult relationships. Doing so equalizes relationships, as opposed to being in a one-up position that arises easily when offering praise. When a significant person in a client's life makes a beneficial change, the client can ask this person how it feels to have taken a particular action. The inquiry into the felt experience of change helps with differentiation by inviting the other to explore the personal reasons and rewards of a behavior change, rather than relying solely on the reward of pleasing someone external to themselves.

Example from practice:

Haddie reported her long-time boyfriend recently stopped drinking. This was a great relief to Haddie, who had been speaking of her concerns regarding his drinking for months. Haddie thanked her boyfriend for stopping and told him she was so proud of him for choosing this new path, I suggested she may wish to ask him about this decision to see how he felt about this himself. Maybe, I suggested, she could say, "How do you feel about stopping drinking? What are you hoping to gain for yourself by this decision?" The answers to these questions could help her boyfriend identify his internal motivation and rewards. This would help Haddie know if his behavior change was grounded in his own self-direction or whether it was only an attempt to please her.

Elsbeth Martindale
CLINICAL PSYCHOLOGIST

Encouragement

The best way to build self-esteem is to offer those you love a good dose of encouragement. Many people confuse praise with encouragement, and they are vastly different. Here's what you need to know.

ENCOURAGEMENT AND SELF-ESTEEM

Encouragement is a way to build self-esteem. When you encourage another you give that person an invitation to evaluate if *he/she/they* like what he/she/they are doing. For example, "Do you like that you got an A on the project?" This type of questioning allows people to decide for themselves if they are meeting their own expectations and standards. If they like how they are acting, this is a great boost to their confidence. If they are unhappy with their performance, they have a chance to look at what they wish they would do differently in order to please their own desires. This internal reflection helps to create an inner sense of self-valuing and self-motivation, free from the expectations and evaluations of others.

SELF-ENCOURAGEMENT

You can build your own self-esteem with self-encouragement, asking yourself if *you* like your own performance or actions. For example, "Am I pleased with the way I'm performing?" This kind of questioning is a means of evaluating, for yourself, how you feel about your behaviors and choices.

ENCOURAGEMENT AND PRAISE

Encouragement is different from praise. Praise, which many of us do quite naturally, is a form of external evaluation. Receiving praise lets you know that others are pleased with you. It allows you to look outside yourself to see what others think or feel about you.

Praise is not bad, but in the absence of encouragement you can miss the importance of assessing for yourself whether your actions are acceptable or worthwhile in your own eyes. Praise does not help you stop and listen to your own critique, whether positive or negative. Praise causes a dependence on others' evaluation—which is *other*-esteem not *self*-esteem.

PRACTICE

Below are several situations where you could use praise or encouragement. See if you can respond to the statement in an encouraging manner. To encourage well, focus on assets and strengths. Recognize effort and improvement, as well as accomplishments. How would you respond with encouragement if:

1. Your daughter brings home a report card with straight As.
2. Your employee comments to you that he has successfully completed all the tasks you had assigned him and it only took half the time you had expected.
3. Your single friend confides in you that he believes he will never find a suitable life partner.
4. Your son asks you directly, "What do you think of my drawing? Do you like it?"
5. Your partner tells you about his/her/their promotion at work and asks, "Are you proud of me?"
6. Your friend tells you she is worried she won't do well on her upcoming presentation at work.

Elsbeth Martindale
CLINICAL PSYCHOLOGIST

Twenty-Second Hug

elsbethmartindale.com/twenty-second-hug

Who doesn't need this information?! Touch is so beneficial, and it is a natural (but sort of addictive) antidepressant.

How I use this:

When clients aren't utilizing their partnerships by getting and receiving healthy touch, I might pull out this handout and remind them of what they are missing. Touch, of course, is a tender topic. Many have been injured by unwanted touch. Helping clients know what good touch feels like and the incredible benefits, both psychologically and physiologically, can help them begin to explore this fabulous health enhancer.

Example from practice:

Jess greets their partner with a peck and a hug whenever either of them return home from time away. They claim to enjoy this ritual, but Jess recently stated it was more a habit than an action of deep connection. I suggested they might want to try an occasional full twenty-second hug, hugging until both individuals' shoulders dropped, to see what effect this might have on their sense of connection. Jess went home and introduced this to their partner. Jess returned and reported this longer hug led to a richer experience of connection and appreciation of their partner.

Elsbeth Martindale
CLINICAL PSYCHOLOGIST

Twenty-Second Hug

Hugging is good for you! Stan Tatkin, author of *Wired for Love*, talks about the value of hugging. He says, in safe and connected relationships, that hugging has both emotional and physical benefits. The benefits are caused by the release of the neurotransmitter oxytocin in the body. Oxytocin, known as the "love hormone," generates a feeling of connectedness and counteracts the stress hormone cortisol. This happens for both men and women.

EMOTIONAL BENEFITS

How can something that feels so good also be so good for you? That's the magic of hugs. When we give and receive a full-bodied twenty-second hug, we maximize the benefits of hugging. Within the context of a trustworthy, comfortable, and safe relationship, hugging offers the following benefits:

- increases a sense of bonding and connection
- increases a sense of individual well-being and happiness
- decreases loneliness
- reduces fear
- defuses tension
- increases self-esteem

PHYSIOLOGICAL BENEFITS

In addition to the reciprocal feel-good experience that accompanies a hug, there is lots of research to suggest that hugs have physiological benefits that include:

- boosting the immune system
- lowering blood pressure
- reducing risk of heart disease
- reducing stress
- reducing cravings for drugs, alcohol, and sweets

Twenty seconds is about long enough for three long, deep breaths. Allow your shoulders to drop and your body to lean in. You can move your head with each deep breath as a way to help your body adjust and settle into a relaxed and receptive position.

Psychotherapist Virginia Satir also famously said, "We need four hugs a day for survival. We need eight hugs a day for maintenance. We need twelve hugs a day for growth." So get busy! Here's a coupon to help you offer and claim your daily hugs.

THIS COUPON ENTITLES BEARER TO
ONE FREE HUG
REDEEMABLE ANYTIME

Kudos Catcher

elsbethmartindale.com/kudos-catcher

Remember the Cootie Catchers kids make in grade school? They are sort of origami fortunetellers, designed to predict everything from what kind of day you are going to have to whom you will fall in love with and marry. The *Kudos Catcher* is a twist on that playful activity. In the *Kudos Catcher,* you write positive things about a friend in each section and offer it to the friend, all folded up, so your friend receives a playful message of support and kindness from you.

How I use this:

I've mostly sent this home as a playful homework assignment when clients is interested in showing appreciation to a friend or loved one.

Example from practice:

I've never actually worked on this in an individual therapy session, but it is a wonderful tool for a group therapy activity. I have asked group members to write a positive aspect of another group member on a Kudos Catcher, as directed on the handout, and to pass it around until it is completely filled out. We did this for every group member. Once all the catchers were filled out, the members paired off and played together, revealing the affirming messages others had written about them. They loved this and were able to take home the Kudos Catcher to read again the appreciations of others. Very reaffirming!

Elsbeth Martindale
CLINICAL PSYCHOLOGIST

Kudos Catcher

Giving away compliments and support can enrich both the giver and reciever. Think of a friend who could use some kindness. Make that person a Kudos Catcher with all the compliments, support, and encouragement you can muster. It makes a very simple, heart-felt gift.

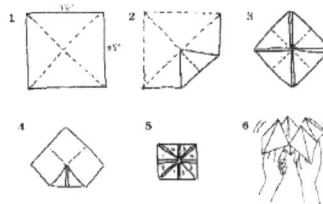

© Elsbeth Martindale, Psy.D., 2015

Instructions:
1. Write your friend's name in each of the blanks.
2. Write a comment for your friend in each of the eight sections.
3. Cut along dotted line and fold the Kudos Catcher as seen on right.
4. Give it to your friend to play with when he/she/they need a kudo.

Elsbeth Martindale
CLINICAL PSYCHOLOGIST

Phone Nap Pad

elsbethmartindale.com/phone-nap-pad

Here's another playful tool for reminding folks to intentionally set their phones down so they can attend to other important aspects of their life without distraction.

How I use this:

I have a laminated version of this on the table next to the couch in my office. Clients often pick it up and a great conversation ensues. If they want their own version of this, I email them a copy. I've had clients put this on their dining table at home to send a message to their teen-aged children—that phones are to be put to bed at mealtime.

Example from practice:

The dinner table was no longer a place for conversation and family connection, according to Mina. Each of her high-school daughters was constantly checking her phone and responding to texts while eating. This bothered Mina greatly, and she found herself nagging her daughters regularly to put down their phones. But, when Mina's husband got a new phone and brought it to the dinner table, so he could keep on top of sports scores, Mina had had enough! As she complained about this in therapy, I reflected her pain of feeling disconnected from her family. I showed Mina the Phone Nap Pad handout and suggested this as a playful way to begin a family discussion about the use of screens during communal time around the table. Mina was delighted. She made copies of the handout—one for each family member—and printed them on paper the color of each person's phone. She cut out the phone image and set each Phone Nap Pad next to each person's place at the table. When her family sat down to eat, they laughed together at the idea of needing a nap pad for a phone. This led to a great discussion around the table, where Mina's concerns and needs were expressed and heard. They understood Mina's desire for more connection and shared the value of making dinner a time to focus on each other in an intentional way. The family kept the nap pads on the table for a time to remind them of their shared commitment to make mealtime a time for family connection, free from the interruption of the outside world.

Elsbeth Martindale
CLINICAL PSYCHOLOGIST

Phone Nap Pad

Phone Nap Pad

PLACE PHONE FACE DOWN HERE

SHOW YOUR DEVICE WHO'S IN CHARGE

Devices can overtake your life and remove you from connection with the people and things that matter to you. It is helpful to intentionally set aside some screen-free time so you can be completely present with the sensual world around you, whether it is the taste of your food, the eyes of your partner, the needs of your body, or the beauty of nature.

Setting your phone to rest sets a boundary around the intrusions of the world, allowing you to choose your own focus for your attention.

Setting your phone down when you're with another person says to that person you want to prioritize your connection with him/her/them. It says you are willing to set aside the needs and requests of others so you can be fully attentive and present in the moment.

You might find the Nap Pad especially helpful at family mealtime, giving you a chance to interact with the people who matter most to you and giving them the gift of your full attention.

You can trust your phone or screen will be ready and able to wake up as soon as its nap time is over.

Elsbeth Martindale
CLINICAL PSYCHOLOGIST

Part V

Enhancement and Growth

The handouts in this section offer tools for both deeper exploration and expanded perspectives in therapy. Since group therapy is a great enhancer of clients' skills and understanding, several group therapy handouts are provided. I've also included handouts for addressing trauma and emotional woundedness. This deeper work is possible after a trusted therapeutic relationship has been established.

DEEPER EXPLORATION

Existential Givens..173
Questions About Existential Givens 175
Contentment Defined..177-179
The Person I Want to Become 181
Playing Angels...183
Qualities of Wisdom..185
Imagine Outrageous Success 187
Values in Action - Strength Inventory..189
Identifying Core Values..191
Common Values...193
Meta-Perspective...195
Meta-Perspective Expanders 197
Trigger Fingers..199-201
    Noticing Automatic Reactions 199
    Managing Automatic Reactions 201

GROUP THERAPY

Group Therapy Invitation... 203-205
Group Therapy Cheat Sheet...207
Group Therapy Contract...209

HEALING WORK

Aggress Energy 211
Making Space for Healing Work 213
Collecting Stories of Injury 215
Healing Old Wounds..217-219

Existential Givens

elsbethmartindale.com/existential-givens

I was a student of James Bugental, PhD, the first president of the American Psychological Association's Division of Humanistic Psychology and one of the leading authors in existential-humanistic psychotherapy. I actually did my dissertation on his work, comparing the journey toward wholeness, through existential psychotherapy, with the path toward union with God in Christian mysticism—a fascinating exploration. The summary of the "givens of existence" suggested in existential theory, as highlighted in my handout, has guided my work and, on rare occasions, led to interesting discussions in therapy with clients. The overarching message is that all humans must face existential challenges, and it is *how* we face them that determines life enhancement or life defeat.

How I use this:

I don't share this concept in therapy very often because it is heady and theoretical. But I do find times when examining these stark existential realities is just what a client needs and wants. I actually painted a set of rocks, each the size of a baseball, with an existential given written on it. I keep these in a basket in the corner of my office. I can show this display to my clients, and then, if I'm daring, I might toss one of the rocks in the client's direction, hoping he/she/they are quick enough to catch it without getting hurt. This lobbing of a rock is a perfect metaphor for existential realities. We all need to be aware of the givens of life and be able to manage them skillfully, so they don't hit us upside the head and cause excessive pain. Fortunately, I haven't yet hurt anyone!

In explaining this exercise, I say something like, *"The existential given of finiteness is real for everyone. Things end—this session, the ink in this pen, and even important relationships. Finiteness comes with the existential anxiety of chance. This anxiety shows up because we can't always predict when things will end. We can run from this anxiety, but running only adds the neurotic anxiety of powerlessness on top of the unavoidable anxiety of chance. It is possible, instead, to face finiteness, accept it, manage the existential anxiety of chance which accompanies it, and move toward trust, hope, and faith. This is often a challenging uphill climb but beats the alternative of feeling neurotically powerless."* I offer this sort of explanation for each of the other four existential givens. In a nutshell, the given is there, and it causes real anxiety. You can run and create additional anxiety, or you can face the given, manage the concurrent anxiety, and get to the possibility of life-enhancing experiences. I love this sort of stuff!

Elsbeth Martindale
CLINICAL PSYCHOLOGIST

Existential Givens

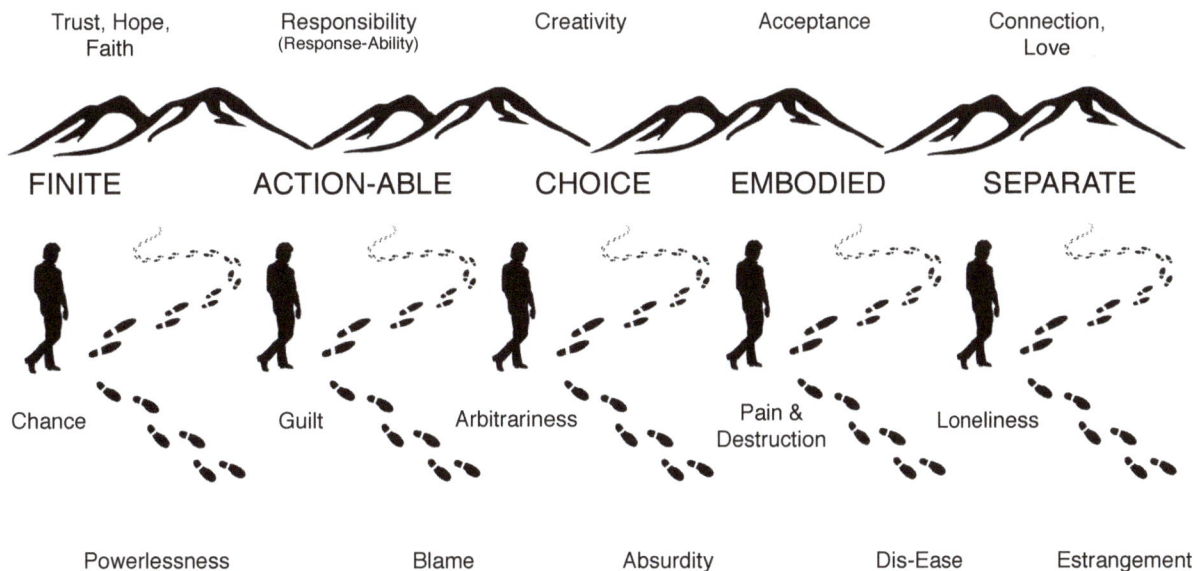

Existential givens are the hard-cold, unavoidable realities of life. They are challenging to face, but running from them only adds more complications. When we face each of the five givens, we are left with an experience of existential anxiety. Should we attempt to avoid these realities and accompanying anxieties, we add neurotic anxiety on top, increasing the emotional load. On the other hand, if we bravely walk toward the existential givens and accept and manage the anxiety that accompanies each given, we make progress toward authenticity.

Existential Givens

Trust, Hope, Faith	Responsibility (Response-Ability)	Creativity	Acceptance	Connection, Love
FINITE	ACTION-ABLE	CHOICE	EMBODIED	SEPARATE
Chance	Guilt	Arbitrariness	Pain & Destruction	Loneliness
Powerlessness	Blame	Absurdity	Dis-Ease	Estrangement

Adapted from Bugental, James. *The Art of the Psychotherapist: How to Develop the Skills that Take Psychotherapy Beyond Science*. New York: W. W. Norton & Company, 1992.

Elsbeth Martindale
CLINICAL PSYCHOLOGIST

Questions About Existential Givens

elsbethmartindale.com/questions-about-existential-givens

This handout is for the existential nerds. Not everyone wants to look this deeply at the givens of life, but, when someone does, I'm prepared! These questions help clients look at each of the five areas of existential reality and ponder their relationship with each.

How I use this:

This is generally a take-home handout. It gives clients a lot to ponder and reflect upon. It can be a useful journaling tool. The clients' reactions to their examination of each of these givens is often where good conversation begins.

Example from practice:

Some clients are curious and want to ask deep existential questions. I've seen this as both a distraction and an enhancer in therapy. Exploring existential questions can be a distraction when clients really need to make changes in basic aspects of their life to function optimally—such as in areas of self-management, relationships, or meaningful activity. Exploring the heady concepts of existential givens can waylay a client from doing necessary skill-building. So I will ask myself if engagement in intellectual conversations are in a client's best interest, based on his/her/their initial self-chosen goals for therapy.

Of course, when clients are functioning well and exploration of existential realities is in the service of their needs and goals, then this sort of conversation is enjoyable and can be fruitful. It is in these circumstances where I will offer this handout to a client—after a discussion of the *Existential Givens*.

Elsbeth Martindale
CLINICAL PSYCHOLOGIST

Questions About Existential Givens

QUESTIONS ABOUT EMBODIMENT
- What sort of body are you living in?
- Do you have a friendly relationship with your body?
- Do you notice, attend, and care willingly for the house of your mind/soul/spirit/emotions?
- When are you in a state of dis-ease?
- In what ways are you experiencing acceptance with your body?

QUESTIONS ABOUT CHOICE
- What choices have led you to be where you are today?
- What choices are currently in front of you, personally and professionally?
- Where do you see yourself dismissing your choices and claiming absurdity?
- What are your creative outlets?
- What do you desire/strive to create?

QUESTIONS ABOUT ACTION-ABILITY
- What actions have you taken that brought you where you are in your life right now?
- What actions have you taken in the last week that have supported your self-care?
- What actions have you taken that have interfered with your best care?
- What are the current circumstances in your life for which you find yourself blaming others?
- When are you most confident about your ability to intentionally respond?

QUESTIONS ABOUT FINITENESS
- What endings are you aware of experiencing in your current life?
- What has been the hardest ending in your life thus far?
- Was there an ending that eased your life?
- What endings are you anticipating or dreading in your near future?
- Where in your life do you feel most powerless?
- In what ways do trust, hope, and faith guide your life?

QUESTIONS ABOUT SEPARATENESS
- In what ways do you push others away because you don't think they'll care or understand?
- What is your relationship with your alone time? Is it too much or too little?
- Do you let others in to support and nurture you?
- When are the times you have relished and celebrated the joy of connection and love?
- Who have you loved most in this life? Who has loved you most?

Elsbeth Martindale
CLINICAL PSYCHOLOGIST

Contentment Defined

elsbethmartindale.com/contentment-defined

What does it mean to be content? How is contentment different from happiness? These are interesting questions to pose to your clients. This handout looks at contentment in seven different areas, inviting clients to look deep at each area to see where greater contentment could be created.

How I use this:

This handout was developed for my workshop, **Self-Care for Professional Therapists**. I have used it with clients as a homework suggestion, encouraging them to journal about their responses. The responses and reactions to these questions are often helpful to discuss in therapy.

I've had clients struggle with describing contentment. It is easy for us to know what makes us discontented, yet doing the opposite and identifying what ease and contentment look like often stops us in our tracks. A turn in focus from the problem to the solution can help everyone, especially our clients, meet the challenge and reach some contentment even if it is just a little. One step at a time!

Example from practice:

Vicki has lots of complaints, and for good reasons. She experiences chronic fatigue and relies on her parents to support her even though she is nearly thirty years old. She sees herself as a victim and, sadly, makes choices which maintain the cycle of victimization. Therapy is slow going, but significant progress has been made. In a recent session, Vicki complained about a variety of annoyances and social injuries. Frustrated, myself, by the unending list of "what's wrong," I suggested we explore what contentment would look like to Vicki. You could almost hear the tires squeal as she turned 180 degrees in her thinking. Vicki was taken aback. She didn't have a clear sense of what contentment might be like for her.

We took each aspect of contentment and began discussing her ideas of goodness for her life. In the first category, physical contentment, she claimed she would be content if she were pain free. We looked at the actions she's taken in the past that have helped her alleviate her pain. She recognized some of these actions weren't being taken today. This got her thinking of things she could do to help herself find more physical contentment. This increased her sense of agency, and she committed to exploring these strategies again. We didn't get all the way through the handout in this session, so I gave her a copy to finish on her own. This was a useful tool in helping Vicki turn from a problem-focus to a solution-focused approach in therapy.

Elsbeth Martindale
CLINICAL PSYCHOLOGIST

Contentment Defined

Contentment is a reasonable goal for which to aspire. It is different from happiness in that it is less focused on pleasure and more concerned with ease and acceptance. Contentment is even possible when external circumstances are challenging. Take some time to reflect on what contentment means to you in each of the seven areas of self-care. Be specific in describing the experience of contentment in each area.

1 PHYSICAL

For me, physical contentment means...

If I were completely content in the physical aspects of my life, I would experience or notice...

The following actions have helped me create or increase physical contentment for myself:
1)
2)
3)
Star any you currently use and find effective.

2 PERSONAL

For me, personal contentment means...

If I were completely content in the personal aspects of my life, I would experience or notice...

The following actions have helped me create and know personal contentment:
1)
2)
3)
Star any you currently use and find effective.

3 EMOTIONAL

For me, emotional contentment means...

If I were completely content in the emotional aspects of my life, I would experience or notice...

The following actions have helped me know emotional contentment in my life:
1)
2)
3)
Star any you currently use and find effective.

Elsbeth Martindale
CLINICAL PSYCHOLOGIST

4 SPIRITUAL

For me, spiritual contentment means...

If I were completely content in the spiritual aspects of my life, I would experience or notice...

The following actions have helped me create or increase spiritual contentment in my life:
1)
2)
3)
Star any you currently use and find effective.

5 RELATIONAL

For me, relational contentment means...

If I were completely content in the relational aspects of my life, I would experience or notice...

The following actions have helped me create or increase relational contentment for myself:
1)
2)
3)
Star any you currently use and find effective.

6 MENTAL/INTELLECTUAL

For me, mental contentment means...

If I were completely content in the mental and intellectual aspects of my life, I would experience or notice...

The following actions have helped me create or increase mental and intellectual contentment for myself:
1)
2)
3)
Star any you currently use and find effective.

7 PROFESSIONAL/WORKPLACE

For me, professional contentment means...

If I were completely content in the professional aspects of my life, I would experience or notice...

The following actions have helped me create or increase professional contentment:
1)
2)
3)
Star any you currently use and find effective.

The Person I Want to Become

elsbethmartindale.com/the-person-i-want-to-become

This concept is both future and goal focused, and it is a key notion in my work. I find it valuable to encourage clients to think about the person they want to be in any given situation, whether it is at their daughter's wedding in the following month or after they retire in twenty years. With a clear vision of their intention, they can begin to step into their agency. This handout takes a time-expanded perspective on the notion of creating life with consciousness.

How I use this:

I often tell my clients about my experience going to the gym, an activity I like more as I *leave* the gym than actually *going*! I tell my clients I go to the gym for my seventy-year-old self. I explain that I don't particularly like the gym, but my future self will be happy if I do this for her. It helps to ask clients to, similarly, take a long-term perspective on their life, to imagine the person they want to be in the future. This vision can call them into taking action today on behalf of the self they want to be tomorrow.

Example from practice:

Charles was entering his middle-age years. No longer able to play basketball at the park on weekends because of recurring knee pain, he had begun to feel the consequences of an aging body. He lamented these changes and feared things would only worsen for himself as he got older. I asked him to describe the image he has of himself at age sixty. It was dreary and depressing. I then asked him to describe his best possible sixty-year-old self. This was a much better version. We talked of what would have to happen to become this more idealized version of himself. It became clear he would have to invest more in physical health. He would need to find ways to work out without damaging his knee. Charles also had relational and professional goals he hoped to achieve, both of which would involve actions today to help set him up for success in both these areas. Taking a long-term perspective on his responsibility and power to steer important aspects of his life made Charles reorganize priorities so he could become the man he wanted to be in the future.

Elsbeth Martindale
CLINICAL PSYCHOLOGIST

The Person I Want to Become

Having a vision of the person you want to become is a powerful way to get clear about the actions that could be taken today to serve the hope of your future self. A vision alone isn't enough to "make it so," but this image, like the North Star, can give you a sense of direction.

Use the questions and suggestions below to clarify your hopes for the person you wish to become. Write your answers on a separate piece of paper, elaborating as desired. Allow an image to form, as clearly as possible, in your mind. Try capturing the important essence of this potential future version of you.

QUESTIONS TO ANSWER

How old will you be in ten years? _____

Name five significant people in your life. How old will they be in ten years?

_____	age _____
_____	age _____
_____	age _____
_____	age _____
_____	age _____

1. Form a vision of this "older you" in your surroundings. What will be important for you to have around yourself?

2. What are the habits, behaviors, and actions of your future self that make you feel content? What do you imagine your future self doing to bring yourself joy?

3. What are the concerns, worries, losses, and sorrows known to your future self? How does this future you self-soothe?

4. What do you hope the "you in ten years" has more of than you currently have? What do you imagine you had to do in order to acquire this?

5. What do you hope this version of you has less of? What did you have to do to release yourself of this?

6. What do you think will be your older self's biggest struggle? How will you support yourself through this?

7. What strengths is your future self exhibiting, utilizing, and enjoying in life?

8. If your future self could make three requests of you today, what would that older self ask you to do on behalf of your future well-being?

a) _____

_____

_____

b) _____

_____

_____

c) _____

_____

_____

Elsbeth Martindale
CLINICAL PSYCHOLOGIST

Playing Angels

elsbethmartindale.com/playing-angels

Over twenty years ago, I did an intensive training with Jean Houston, PhD, on *The Possible Human*, using Homer's *Odyssey* as a template for transformation. This was a life-changing experience. One of the activities presented at the training involved breaking into triads and having people talk about their life from the position of "the gods." Stepping into an elevated spiritual vantage point and speaking about self using the third person voice was enlightening and empowering. I developed this process of *Playing Angels* by adapting my experience with Jean Houston into an activity for therapy. I have used this sort of process successfully for many years. I developed and presented a variation of this concept at the Oregon Psychological Association conference in 1997, calling my presentation, *Strategies for Enhancing the Observing Ego*.

How I use this:

Amazing awarenesses come about when I ask clients to play with this sort of experiment in therapy. Two important factors seem to contribute to the success of this process. The first important factor is stepping outside of the self and into a position of an observer. The second beneficial factor is stepping into a caring position when talking about oneself. This view (also discussed in the handouts *Self-Observation* and *Higher Self Qualities*) seems to have the most powerful impact on clients. It allows for bypassing the negative critic and, instead, invites observing self from the genuine desire of enabling and enhancing potential (just as people often project or expect from their sense of the divine).

I often introduce this activity in the later stages of therapy. I might ask something such as, *"Would you like to take a playful position in talking about yourself today?"* I want to encourage an experimental and spirited tone in beginning this activity. If a client is game, I would then say, *"Let's imagine we are angels. I'm Elsbeth's guardian angel, and you're ____'s angel. Let's pretend we bumped into each other up here in the heavens. So don't be ____, be your angel, and talk about yourself in third person. What's going on with ____ right now? What do you see?).* I like to include the questions, *"Is ____ aware you are watching him/her/them? Would it help ____ to know of your presence?"* I regularly have to remind folks to stay in the third-person voice when talking about themselves in this activity. This is awkward but really helps in maintaining a benevolent and objective perspective. The statements on this handout are some of the questions I like to ask while in this mild trance state. I will then send this handout home with clients and suggest they journal their responses to the statements to get more practice in viewing and talking about themselves from this higher self perspective.

Elsbeth Martindale
CLINICAL PSYCHOLOGIST

Playing Angels

Sometimes we just need a little perspective. Imagining the view of your life from the perspective of a loving guardian angel can be very insightful. Step back and look at your life from this distance. Hold a protective angel's attitude of care, guidance, and compassion and see what this tells you about your current human life. Finish the following statements from the guardian angel's point of view.

As your guardian angel the first thing I notice is...

The strengths and assets I see in you include...

I see you have been brave by doing the following...

I am concerned about the following behaviors in your life...

You may not want to hear this but...

You are walking dangerously close to the edge when you...

One very important thing to remember is...

I would like you to think of me whenever you see...

These are some of my other thoughts and concerns for you...

Elsbeth Martindale
CLINICAL PSYCHOLOGIST

Qualities of Wisdom

elsbethmartindale.com/qualities-of-wisdom

I see wisdom as the ultimate goal of therapy. I want to help my clients have access to as much wisdom as they can get and operate their life from this position as often as possible. I gathered this list of qualities of wisdom so I can talk with clients about these generative attitudes, actions, and awarenesses in order to activate these qualities in them.

How I use this:

I use this handout in the later stages of therapy when clients begin to show improvement in the management of their own challenges. I want them to see which qualities they are using and which ones they may want to practice leaning in to. When clients is successful in responding to a challenge with a new sense of effectiveness, it is often helpful to identify the specific wise actions they took. This handout can be a reinforcement tool for pointing to their skillfulness.

Example from practice:

Cathy had been struggling mightily with self-care. She had a history of self-harm and self-abandonment. We worked hard to explore the notion that she could respond to herself from a place of wisdom and kindness rather than from her familiar negative and abusive patterns. One day, she came into her session and joyfully told of steering herself toward some nourishing videos online instead of her past practice of observing images and stories about injury and abuse. She was proud of herself. I suggested she was responding to herself from wisdom. I took out this handout, and together we identified the attitudes, actions, and awarenesses she employed in the choice to make a conscious decision to filter her entertainment selections. Bravo, Cathy!

Elsbeth Martindale
CLINICAL PSYCHOLOGIST

Qualities of Wisdom

Wisdom is hard to define, but you usually know it when you see it or feel its presence. Wisdom includes attitudes and actions, ways of meeting and engaging with the world. Additionally, there are awarenesses that tend to surround people who demonstrate wisdom.

ATTITUDES
generosity
equanimity
fairness
gratitude
hopefulness
self-acceptance
compassion
positive attitude
empathy
aliveness
curiosity
wonder
humility
joy
kindness
patience
nurturance
peacefulness
reflectiveness
respect
serenity
appreciating significance
acceptance

ACTIONS
responsibility
integrity
caring
attentiveness
commitment
detached concern
cooperation
willingness to risk
desiring the good of the whole
dedication
skillful decision-making
knowledge
experience
deep understanding
discernment
openness
self-investigation
introspection
discipline
humility
fortitude
truthfulness
sound judgment

engaged
trustworthy
steadfast
stability
thoughtfulness
clear boundaries and limits
solution focused
breadth of considerations
undaunted

AWARENESS
self-actualization
self-sufficiency
self-knowledge
adopting multiple perspectives
appreciating ramifications
insight
vision
tolerance of uncertainties
acceptance of ups and downs
long-term perspective
intuitive understanding
open-minded
inclusive

WHAT QUALITIES DO YOU POSSESS?

1. Look over the lists of the characteristics of wisdom.

2. Put stars in front of or behind the qualities of wisdom you believe you possess. Use up to five stars to demonstrate the degree to which each quality is known or practiced in your life.

3. Circle the top ten qualities you are actively engaged in enhancing in your current life. On a separate piece of paper, write about why these qualities are important to you, how you are working to build them, and how you plan to use these qualities in your day-to-day life.

Elsbeth Martindale
CLINICAL PSYCHOLOGIST

Imagine Outrageous Success
elsbethmartindale.com/imagine-outrageous-success

I first came across the concept of "outrageous success" while taking a course on coaching. It is a great strategy for breaking down the visioning process. I often tell the story of how I acquired my office building. My therapist at the time had moved into a beautiful new space and I asked her how she pulled that off. She simply stated, "I visioned it." Then she asked, "You're doing that for your office, too, aren't you?" My visioning began at that moment. By clarifying what was important to me, in full detail, I was able to recognize my ideal office when the opportunity showed up.

Shakti Gawain, the New Age guru and author of *Creative Visualization*, claimed that for visualization to be successful, one must visualize oneself managing the challenges as well as the triumphs. I find this truth really helpful to include when talking with clients about the immense power of visualizing success.

How I use this:
I generally use this handout as homework. I rarely will go through these steps with clients in a session, but I ask them to complete the exercise at home and come prepared for their next session to share what they learned, what was easy, and what brought challenge when they did the steps of imagining themselves being successful.

Example from practice:
Doreen wanted to have more ease in talking about sex with her husband. She was fearful and timid, not because her husband was a threat but because of a history of injury around sexual exploration. We had assessed, with great clarity, that her husband was a safe person with whom she could be more open about her desires. It was helpful for Doreen to start this difficult task with a vision of herself being successful. This handout offered her the important steps to secure her success. She followed this outline, visioning herself capable of addressing her needs and recognizing how her values and strengths fully supported her intentions. She was relieved to recognize that even a minimum level of success would be huge progress. With clarity of vision, Doreen wrote several supportive affirmations to help her act with courage and take the risk. Several weeks later, she reported she had approached her husband and was able to tell him some, if not all, of what she had been longing to share. It all started with a vision of her success.

Elsbeth Martindale
CLINICAL PSYCHOLOGIST

Imagine Outrageous Success

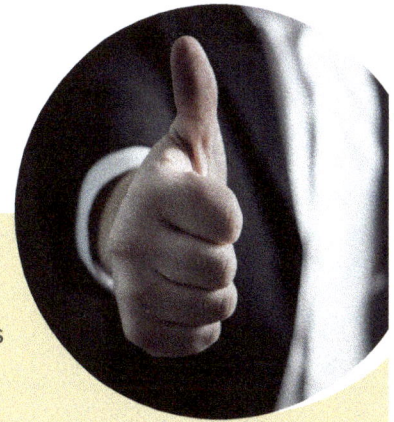

Moving yourself toward success can be challenging in many ways. Having a vision to guide your movement forward can be very helpful. This exercise allows you to play with a vision of complete and outrageous success. This vision can be a focal point to clarify intention, motivate movement, and identify small and achievable steps.

1 **STEP 1**

Set aside time to intentionally focus on your vision of success. The more deliberately you choose this time and free yourself from distractions, the more powerful this activity will be. Start by marking this time in your calendar. Have no other agenda for this time other than to explore your vision. Bring your journal or sheets of paper to this time.

2 **STEP 2**

With journal in hand, identify and connect with your strengths and core values. Essentially, this is about remembering who you really are at your best. Make a list of these in a journal or on a sheet of paper. You might write, "My strengths and my highest values include ..."

3 **STEP 3**

Equipped with your strengths, look at a current challenging situation, perhaps a conflict in partnership, work, family, self-care, finances, or an important decision. Choose a situation in which a successful outcome would bring you joy or relief. Look at this situation with clarity, and honesty. What's really going on? See if you can stir feelings of compassion for all involved in the matter, and most importantly for yourself! Write about this in your journal. You might prompt yourself with the following: "What I see going on is ..." and, "I can feel a sense of compassion for ..."

4 **STEP 4**

Use your imagination to visualize yourself having been completely successful in resolving this situation. What would this situation look like if it were absolutely the way you desire it to be. If you couldn't fail in your efforts, what would be the outcome? Don't worry now about the "how" of getting there. Just envision the results as hugely successful. Hold this vision in your mind and elaborate on the details. Envision the feeling of joy and relief that things worked out the way you desired.

5 **STEP 5**

Now, clarify the minimum level of success you would like to see in this situation. What is the bottom line? Your writing prompt might be: "If nothing else, then at least this..." and "I won't accept less than..."

6 **STEP 6**

Tap into your deepest longing for success. Notice where this hope and desire lives in your body. Stay in this sweet spot for a moment. Allow complete clarity to form. See it, feel it, hear it, and taste it. Let it be fully alive in your mind and body. From this sweet place of knowing, identify one small action step you would be willing to take to help bring your vision forward. Write about this step with the prompt, "The one step I plan to take in the direction of my desire is ..."

Elsbeth Martindale
CLINICAL PSYCHOLOGIST

Values in Action - Strength Inventory

elsbethmartindale.com/values-in-action-strength-inventory

What a gift this is—a free online survey to rank values! Martin Seligman, the father of Positive Psychology, has made this available online.

How I use this:

I ask clients to take this test and bring me a list of their signature strengths, their top five values. I write their strengths on sticky notes and keep them in their charts. I refer to these notes over and over as a way to help clients approach their challenges from a position of strength and values, whenever possible.

Example from practice:

Tami discovered she was pregnant with her second child. She shared a mix of joy and overwhelm at the prospect of parenting another child, as her first child was quite a handful for her. She was a stay-at-home mom with a husband who worked long hours and was frequently out of town on business. Referring to the sticky note in her chart that identified her top five signature strengths from her Values in Action test, I asked, *"Do you remember what you told me are your top strengths?"* With some prompting, she recalled them as honesty, humor, love, fairness, and gratitude. I encouraged her by saying something like, *"You have some pretty decent strengths you can pull from to help you manage this situation."* We looked at each strength as it pertained to her unexpected pregnancy. *"Your value of honesty will help you speak up to your husband about how he can support and assist you so you don't get overwhelmed. Your sense of humor will help you find playful and joyous times, even in the midst of this added stress. Your value of love will be exercised in an even larger way by having another child to care for. Your value of fairness might be more difficult to utilize, but we can think about this some more. And your gratitude value will be of great assistance to you, finding appreciation and goodness even in the midst of all the stress."* This strength-focused feedback is not a way to sugarcoat the challenges clients face, but a way to help them see they have much of what they need to be successful in managing the challenges they face.

Elsbeth Martindale
CLINICAL PSYCHOLOGIST

Values in Action
- Strength Inventory

Knowing what you value and what matters most to you will help you make decisions that support your vision of the person you want to be. Our values influence or decisions. Values are seen as strengths—something you are unlikely to compromise or dismiss when making choices.

HOW TO TAKE THE FREE ONLINE TEST

VIA (Values in Action) is a free strength survey available online at https://www.viacharacter.org. After answering the questions, you will recieve a ranked list of all twenty-four unique human strengths. Your top five are called your Signature Strengths. These strengths can be guiding lights in your life. They can help you manage life's challenges from a place of solidness and deep intention. Write them down and share them with those helping you grow and advance, so they can support you in using your strengths in day-to-day life.

WHAT TO DO WITH YOUR SCORES

Here are some ways to use the scores you obtained in doing the Values in Action survey.

1) Look at your Signature Strengths and examine how you use these strengths in your daily living with family, work, and relationships. Think of an example of each Signature Strength in these areas.

2) Notice where on your list of twenty-four strengths the following key strengths are located.
- Gratitude
- Curiosity
- Hope
- Zest
- Love

These five strengths are directly associated with happiness. By living from these strengths in work, love, play, and parenting, you will likely increase your happiness in these areas of life.

3) Think about a past conflict in your life. How did your strengths support you in managing or resolving the conflict? In regard to a current challenge, which strength would be the most helpful in facing and dealing with the situation? Approaching conflicts from a place of strength can give you the courage to move forward with confidence.

4) Choose one of your five Signature Strengths. Respond to each of the questions below while thinking of this particular strength.
- When, and in what circumstances, do I most live from this strength?
- Am I aware I am living from this strength when I participate in the above activity?
- What do I feel in my body when I am living from this strength?
- How is living from this strength related to feeling "most alive?"

Identifying Core Values

elsbethmartindale.com/identifying-core-values

Value-driven action is key to contented living. It is helpful to have a variety of ways to explore values with your clients. This handout lists several methods for helping clients become clear about their motivators and values.

How I use this:

I often offer this handout as a homework assignment with encouragement to discuss what is discovered in therapy. Clients who enjoy self-exploration will find this sort of exercise interesting and helpful. Accurate language for values can be challenging, especially to those unfamiliar with this concept. The **Common Values** handout list is useful to pair with this handout because it provides the words for various values.

Once clients have explored and identified core values, your showing interest in and reinforcing their discovery is crucial. Values and needs underlie all intentional actions. Helping clients see and appreciate these inner drivers is a way to honor their uniqueness. As stated in the **Values in Action** handout, I keep a sticky note of my clients' strengths and values in their file folders, allowing me to easily refer to those strengths and values during therapy. Recalling and reminding clients of their strengths and values as they face their challenges is paramount to effective client-driven psychotherapy.

Example from practice:

Fay was looking for new employment. She wanted something more rewarding than her current position. She clarified that by "rewarding" she wasn't necessarily looking for greater financial gain but wanted work that felt as if she were contributing to a worthy cause. I used the handout **Identifying Core Values** to help Fay explore the actions and experiences which had given her meaning in the past. It became immediately clear to Fay that she valued being of service, working cooperatively, and helping others advance and grow. This awareness guided Fay's work exploration, steering her toward employment opportunities where she could work as a team member and contribute to the success of others.

Elsbeth Martindale
CLINICAL PSYCHOLOGIST

Identifying Core Values

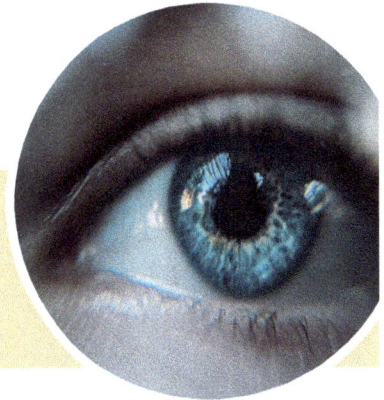

When we live from our values, our lives feel rich, meaningful, and authentic. Get to know your values as a way to help clarify the actions and decisions you may want to take in your future. Grab a journal and complete this writing and reflection exercise.

PEAK EXPERIENCE
Think about a personal peak experience, a time when you felt "on top of the world." What were you doing at the time? What got you to this place? What was so exceptional about this experience? Take ten minutes to write about this experience, addressing each of the questions above.

CHALLENGING EXPERIENCE
Think about a very challenging time in your life, a time when you felt as though you were walking close to a precarious edge. How did you make it through this time? What did you do to stay balanced or centered? How was this situation resolved? How would you describe the best in you during this challenge? Take ten minutes to write about this experience, again, answering the questions presented.

FANTASY EXPERIENCE
Finally, think about the fantasy of the way you would live your life if there were plenty of money in the bank and your physical needs were completely satisfied. What would you be doing with your time and energy? How would you spend your days? Who and what would you have in your life? Again, write for ten minutes about this fantasy, addressing the questions.

INDENTIFY VALUES
After writing about each of the scenarios above, reread them, one at a time, with an eye for identifying the values exhibited in each situation. Use the list on the "Common Values" handout to find words to match your experience. List these top values under the scenarios below.

Peak Experience Values

1) _____
2) _____
3) _____
4) _____
5) _____

Challenging Time Values

1) _____
2) _____
3) _____
4) _____
5) _____

Fantasy Values

1) _____
2) _____
3) _____
4) _____
5) _____

COMMON VALUES
What common values do you see across these three situations? What have you learned about the things that matter most to you? Write about this in your journal.

Common Values

elsbethmartindale.com/identifying-core-values

This handout offers a good, but not comprehensive list of common human values.

How I use this:

This list can accompany the *Identifying Core Values* handout. This list also can be used as a stand-alone tool for discussing values and how values are expressed in action.

Example from practice:

I have used this list, several times, in creating a Values Auction. During this activity, each person, in a group of six to fifteen participants, is given one hundred points to be used to bid on values. They must first identify the values that matter most to them. A total of 148 values are listed here, so, if the group is small, it will be necessary to reduce the number of values used in the auction. This can be a playful group activity, one that helps people see which values they rank highest and what they are most willing to fight for.

Elsbeth Martindale
CLINICAL PSYCHOLOGIST

Common Values

Abundance	Efficiency	Modesty	Self-esteem
Acceptance	Equality	Money	Seriousness
Accuracy	Empathy	Non-violence	Service
Accountability	Excellence	Openness	Simplicity
Accomplishment	Fairness	Opportunity	Sincerity
Achievement	Faith	Optimism	Skill
Adventure	Family	Order	Speed
Agility	Flexibility	Organization	Spirit
Awareness	Forgiveness	Outcome	Stability
Balance	Freedom	Orientation	Strength
Beauty	Friendship	Outstanding Service	Style
Boldness	Fun	Passion	Systemization
Bravery	Generosity	Peace	Teamwork
Calm	Going the Extra Mile	Perseverance	Timeliness
Caring	Goodness	Persistence	Tolerance
Challenge	Gratitude	Personal Growth	Tradition
Change	Happiness	Pleasure	Tranquility
Cleanliness	Hard Work	Poise	Trust
Collaboration	Health	Positive Attitude	Truth
Comfort	Holiness	Power	Unity
Commitment	Honor	Practicality	Variety
Communication	Humility	Preservation	Well-Being
Community	Humor	Privacy	Wisdom
Compassion	Improvement	Productivity	
Competence	Independence	Progress	
Competition	Influence	Prosperity	
Confidence	Inner Peace	Punctuality	
Connection	Innovation	Quality	
Content Over Fluff	Integrity	Quiet	
Continuous	Intelligence	Rationality	
Convincing	Investing	Recognition	
Cooperation	Joy	Reliability	
Courage	Justice	Religion	
Creativity	Kindness	Resourcefulness	
Decisiveness	Knowledge	Respect	
Determination	Learning	Responsibility	
Dignity	Leadership	Righteousness	
Discipline	Loyalty	Risk-Taking	
Discovery	Love	Romance	
Diversity	Meaning	Safety	
Education	Merit	Security	
Effectiveness	Mindfulness	Selflessness	

Meta-Perspective

elsbethmartindale.com/meta-perspective

Meta-awareness is another way to talk about consciousness. It is a way to take an observing perspective on one's desires, choices, and reactions to life. Awareness expansion is a common result of effective therapy, but the invitation can be met with lots of resistance. Not all clients express a desire to be more open and aware; they may just want their problems to go away. Expanding awareness, however, may help clients manage their challenges more effectively. The best way to help clients take an observing perspective will vary from person to person. This handout offers one method, designed to help clients look at and reflect upon three aspects of themselves. The **Meta-Perspective Expanders** handout can accompany this, if deeper exploration is desired.

How I use this:

This handout is best offered as homework, something to do outside the therapy office and brought back to discuss.

Example from practice:

I designed this handout around the winter holidays to help my clients gain perspective on the new year. I gave it to clients in January, inviting them to take a step back and view their lives from a distance. I left several of these in my waiting room so clients had something to consider while waiting for their appointment. I had several interesting conversations with clients who filled out the handout. I haven't used this as much as I had hoped. Some handouts are like that. They seem like a great idea at the time, but they don't get used in day-to-day practice. C'est la vie!

Meta-Perspective

Building a meta awareness is important in giving you the capacity to observe yourself and your choices. Stepping back and looking at your life from a distance can bring you clarity, understanding, and the power to purposefully direct your actions. Ponder the following questions as a way to see your life from a distance. Further broaden your understanding by considering the questions listed on the Meta-Perspective Expanders handout.

1   WHAT BRINGS ME JOY?

What do I love? What excites and expands me?

_____
_____
_____
_____
_____
_____

2   WHAT DO I NEED TO ACCEPT?

What are my current limits and immovables? What is it that I just have to come to terms with because it cannot be changed today?

_____
_____
_____
_____
_____
_____

3   WHAT DO I WANT TO INFLUENCE?

What am I willing to put energy behind in an attempt to bring about change?

_____
_____
_____
_____
_____

Meta-Perspective Expanders

elsbethmartindale.com/meta-perspective

This handout deepens the exploration of these three areas of human experience: what I love, what I have to accept, and what I can change. The *Serenity Prayer* addresses some of these aspects of life. That simple prayer really summarizes most of what we need to know in order to live contentedly. So simple, yet so hard to do!

How I use this:

This can be added to the *Meta-Perspective* handout for further exploration of the concept.

Elsbeth Martindale
CLINICAL PSYCHOLOGIST

Meta-Perspective Expanders

1 **WHAT BRINGS ME JOY?**

What happens in my body when I am participating in activities which bring me joy? Where is this joy felt inside me?

How often am I participating in the activities which delight me?

Do I do the things I love with full awareness of my participation?

How does my conscious participation in joyous activity affect my experience of life?

RECOMMENDATION

Take time every day to do or appreciate something joyful with full awareness of participating in it in each moment. What happens as a result?

2 **WHAT DO I NEED TO ACCEPT?**

What does it feel like in my body when I recognize and accept my limits?

In identifying a limiting factor, am I telling myself a "story" or personal fable that may not actually be true?

Where and how do I notice resistance to accepting my limits?

What is the hope that lives in the resistance to acceptance?

What is the loss I have to face in honestly accepting my limits?

RECOMMENDATION

When facing an undesired limit of your ability to have things be different, you will encounter a loss. Name this loss and allow yourself to grieve it. This grief is part of the difference between acceptance and denial.

3 **WHAT DO I WANT TO INFLUENCE?**

What do I have power to influence in my life?

What small nudges would I like to make to exercise this power?

What does it feel like in my body to recognize and utilize my authority to bring about change?

RECOMMENDATION

Superman said, "Use your power for good." Recognize the small and large ways you can use your power to incline yourself toward the person you aspire to be. Own your personal authority to influence your life in the directions you want to go.

Elsbeth Martindale
CLINICAL PSYCHOLOGIST

Trigger Fingers: Noticing Automatic Reactions

elsbethmartindale.com/trigger-fingers

This complicated-looking handout is actually designed to simplify the process of what to do when one is triggered emotionally. It gives a five-step process, with each step easily identified as a separate finger, for how to recognize a triggering event. The goal of this awareness is to bring consciousness to an often unconscious reactivity. Teaching clients to listen to the various components of a reactive response can slow things down enough for them to choicefully respond and manage the reaction skillfully. Also see the handout, *Trigger Fingers: Managing Automatic Reactions*.

How I use this:

When clients have automatic reactions based on survival strategies developed around trauma, it is difficult to undo or slow down the progression from trigger to automatic reaction. I teach clients to identify their triggers, so they can be aware of the things that throw them into a primitive reactive pattern. Following the notion that, "If you can see it, you can steer it," clients can learn the steps to responding to triggers differently and more mindfully. After noticing, the five areas, specified on this handout, to which clients can bring their attention to slow the process of reactivity.

Example from practice:

Rochelle is a mildly schizophrenic client in therapy with one of my psychologist residents. My resident was working with Rochelle to help her notice her reactivity to being approached by strangers. Rochelle often became angry and combative when someone spoke to her unsolicited, even in a gesture of goodwill. My resident wanted to give Rochelle an easy tool for helping her slow her reactivity, allowing her time to act with more intention. This handout gave Rochelle an in-the-moment tool that was easy for her to remember.

Elsbeth Martindale
CLINICAL PSYCHOLOGIST

Trigger Fingers:
Noticing Automatic Reactions

Automatic responses are triggered when you experience a perceived threat. The threat may be physical (danger, potential injury, and such) or emotional (sense of rejection, judgment, loss, and such). Your reactions to triggers are attempts to protect itself. Very often the strategies of protection were developed as the 'best available solution' in the midst of a trauma. Updating your body system about new options of responding, especially if the trauma has passed, is often greatly beneficial.

3 FEELINGS

Pay attention to your feelings.

When triggered, you may feel flooded, overwhelmed, and unable to think clearly. This is a natural response to an activated physiological system. When you're physiologically activated, your neocortex goes off-line, yet the amygdala (emotional center of the brain) remains engaged. Primary emotions such as shock, fear, anger, and sadness come up quickly. Secondary emotions may follow. These are often judgments about your reaction or its cause. Secondary emotions result from mixing thoughts with the feelings. Common secondary responses to a trigger can include feeling abandoned, rejected, humiliated, unloved, dirty, or inadequate.

2 THOUGHTS

Pay attention to your thoughts/ conclusions.

You're probably scrambling to make mental sense of the situation and your reactivity. Automatic thoughts arise in response to past trauma and injury (often conclusions designed by a very young person) and are not always applicable to the current situation. Pay attention to your habitual patterns of thinking and the conclusions you draw. They may need to be reviewed and updated.

4 NEEDS/WANTS

Notice your immediate needs and wants.

The effect of a trigger is to disturb your sense of balance, and you will have a natural inclination to fix or mend the turmoil. It is common to want someone else to act in order for you to feel better. You may attempt to get others to repair things for you by saying, "I need you to... hold me, apologize, go away, promise, etc., believing someone else has the power or responsibility to solve your distress.

1 SENSES

Notice your body.

How is the activation showing up in your physical system? Is your heart racing, head hurting, throat dry, hands shaking, stomach tight, breath short? These are common physiological responses to stress or threat.

TRIGGER

5 ACTIONS

Notice your reactions to being triggered.

If you believe you are unsafe or threatened, you will strive to protect yourself. Defensive/protective patterns tend to be some version of fighting, fleeing, or freezing. Some patterns get set early in life and then are repeated automatically. Do you know your typical protective patterns?

START - TRIGGER

Get to know your triggers.

Make a list of the events, actions, experiences that are likely to trigger you. Typical triggers for me include:

_____
_____
_____

_____
_____
_____

Elsbeth Martindale
CLINICAL PSYCHOLOGIST

Trigger Fingers: Managing Automatic Reactions
elsbethmartindale.com/trigger-fingers

This handout offers strategies for how to hold a trigger in awareness in a new way, in contrast to habitual reactive patterns. It can serve as a map of a rather long and challenging process.

How I use this:
Once clients are aware of their triggers and their typical automatic responses, I can help them hold the trigger in a new way. The five areas of awareness around triggers can now be used for soothing and comforting the reactiveness. This, of course, is a slow process of practice and integration.

Example from practice:
Terry is a survivor of sexual abuse and trauma. After years of reparative therapy, Terry began exploring the healing of her sexuality, something she had never considered possible to resolve. She began to look at how she found herself triggered by her own sexual arousal. Her reactive response was to immediately judge herself as dirty, disgusting, and unlovable. This put a significant dent in her sexual connection with her current, very loving partner. Even though she could clearly assess her partner as "safe and caring," her mind and body were stuck in a long-standing pattern of self-denigration. She used the concepts on this handout to respond to her trigger (arousal) in new ways. She began to notice her body sensations as "just sensations," with no judgment necessarily attached. She could observe her thoughts as "just thoughts," not necessarily true or the only option for her conclusions. She began to accept her feelings as "just feelings," recognizing they are temporary and without full authority over her. Slowly, she began to listen to her wants and needs. She identified as her highest priority that she wanted to stay connected to her partner. She could then choose to ask her partner to just remain present with her, to listen as she shared her observation of her reactivity and told of her skills for managing it. These steps eventually allowed Terry to ask her partner to simply hold her tenderly and remind her of his love. This shift in response didn't happen after just one look at the handout. (I wish!) This handout, however, summarizes the practice she committed to, which is responding more kindly to a natural response she had once condemned. Terry's work isn't finished, but she has made great progress in the direction of her desire to not shut down and disengage from a partner she deeply loves.

Elsbeth Martindale
CLINICAL PSYCHOLOGIST

Trigger Fingers:
Managing Automatic Reactions

The good news is that automatic reactions can be updated and new, more effective, patterns and pathways can be formed. The tool for shifting your reactivity is Mindful Awareness. By observing yourself and your trigger reactions, you can begin to neutralize the triggers and increase your freedom for responding. Consistent and frequent mindfulness practice will allow you to watch and observe the sensations, thoughts, and feelings as they ride their way through your body.

2 THOUGHTS

Notice thoughts as "just thoughts."
Identify your familiar thought patterns and conclusions. Don't scold yourself for these, just practice curiosity. Automatic thoughts have long roots. You can get curious about their origins. "Don't believe everything you think," may prove a helpful motto. You can recognize your capacity to **filter your thoughts**, and even **inject new, self-supportive thoughts** into your inner experience. You could say things such as, "This too shall pass," "My conclusions may not be 100% accurate," or "I can tolerate my discomfort in this moment."

1 SENSES

Notice sensations as "just sensations."
Practice accepting the sensory signals as information. Respond with curiosity and marvel at how the body works to alert, support, and protect you. **Soften** your body, especially where there is tension, and allow yourself to just be present with your sensations.

START - AWARENESS

Practice Mindful Awareness.
Calm and center your body, mind, and spirit. From this place, observe what happens in your body, mind, and emotional world. As an observer, you can disidentify with your sensations, thoughts, and feelings. This objectivity allows you the opportunity to choose how to respond to your experiences.

3 FEELINGS

Notice feelings as "just feelings."
Feelings, just like thoughts, pass like weather in the vast blue sky. You can invite yourself to just step back and watch feelings run through you. You can practice the skills of **allowing, tolerating, and accepting.** This practice leads to a sense of equanimity, where you can stay centered even when circumstances are difficult.

4 NEEDS/WANTS

Identify your core needs.
What need is currently disturbed in you? You wouldn't be upset if your needs were all being met. Find language for your needs so you can be a good spokesperson for them. You can **soothe** your discomfort by validating your distress and pain, giving a name to your disturbed needs and taking action on behalf of your needs. To do this skillfully, it's important to distinguish strategies from needs. A strategy is a way to get a need met. Saying, "I need *you* to ___," is likely a strategy for getting a need met. It's best to start with, "I have a need for ___," naming the need, and following this with a clear request in the service of your need. You might say, "Would you be willing to ..."

5 ACTIONS

Choose value-driven action.
Recognize that being triggered is an opportunity to be observant and aware of your body, mind, and emotions. It's also a chance to stand as an ally to yourself, make your needs clear, and to **take action with intention.** You can incline your actions toward soothing, self-compassion, and kindness. You can begin to see each reactive moment as an opportunity to practice rewiring your brain.

AWARENESS

Group Therapy Invitation

elsbethmartindale.com/group-therapy-invitation

I LOVE group therapy. I find it the most powerful way to integrate the learning that happens in individual work. I typically have two or three groups running at any one time. We meet for ninety minutes, if six or less members are present, and 120 minutes if seven or eight members are in attendance. I max my groups at eight members. I do a lot of training in group, giving clients a chance to learn together the important skills needed for healthy connection such as presence, attunement, empathy, and reflective listening. I also give them a chance to practice many of these skills with each other.

How I use this:

When someone is considering group therapy, I often will send them this handout. It explains the process and benefits of group therapy and lets clients know what to expect if they decide to join.

Example from practice:

After much progress in individual therapy, Ricki was feeling solid in her skills of self-management. She turned her focus in therapy to her relationships, both with girlfriends and in partnership. She longed for more meaningful connection—something she had experienced in therapy but couldn't replicate in her life outside of the therapy office. I suggested she consider group therapy. Participation in group could help her develop a different set of skills, skills that would allow her to build more connection and intimacy with others. I gave her the *Group Therapy Invitation* and suggested she read it over and consider joining my evening group.

Group therapy was a perfect fit for Ricki's needs. She observed and practiced empathic resonance with others. She watched others articulate their needs with clarity and was encouraged by group members to practice her own speak-up skills. Ricki blossomed in group. She felt a sense of belonging and connection that had previously not been known to her. She began seeing who in her life, outside of group therapy, was interested and capable of deep and meaningful contact and, as a result, built a strong network of support. Many of the skills she acquired in group therapy would have been much more difficult to establish and practice in individual sessions. This is why I love group.

Elsbeth Martindale
CLINICAL PSYCHOLOGIST

Group Therapy Invitation

INVITATION

I would like to invite you to consider group therapy. It is one of my favorite ways to work with clients. This suggestion may seem exciting or a bit frightening, but there are some reasons you have been asked to think about working in this way. There are a variety of powerful things you can gain from this kind of therapeutic experience. Group therapy can be very transformative, but it isn't for everyone. Make sure you make a clear choice about involving yourself in group work. This handout will help you understand what group therapy is all about, what to expect when you come, and it will offer you some suggestions on how to get the most out of your group experience.

WHAT IS GROUP THERAPY?

Group therapy is a gathering of people who desire to bring growth and change into their lives. Sometimes groups are formed around specific themes (e.g., depression management, relationship skill-building, developing better boundaries, and the like). Other groups are less theme-based with people gathering for the sake of building general support for personal change and growth. Both types of groups give you the opportunity to get the support of others and offer others support in return.

Many therapy groups are ongoing and continuous; that is, some clients are just starting, while others, whose purposes for group have been met, are finishing. Other groups are closed and meet for a fixed period of time. Make sure to ask if the group you are considering is ongoing or time limited and closed. This handout will focus on what to expect in an open-ended, ongoing group.

The purposes for group involvement differ from person to person. Not everyone in your group will have the same concerns or interests. The value of group can be quite broad, so the individuals in the group may be quite different from you. Groups will provide you with an opportunity to give feedback to and receive feedback from others. In groups, you can gain a great deal just by observing the work of others. Groups also offer the opportunity to try new behavior and hold yourself accountable for positive change. These differing purposes and benefits are all part of what makes group powerful and enlightening. Come with an open mind and heart, and you will gain the most from your experience.

WHEN YOU COME TO GROUP

When you arrive for your first group session, you probably will feel a bit apprehensive. This is a normal response. You will find a circle of a half dozen other individuals. I will do my best to help you feel at home and welcomed in the group. Group members will also offer you reassurance and support right away, so your anxiety will be lessened by the time the first meeting ends. At your first group session, I will explain the rules and structure of the group, have you sign a copy of the Group Contract form, and ask the other group members to introduce themselves to you.

Elsbeth Martindale
CLINICAL PSYCHOLOGIST

At the outset, others will want to know some things about you and perhaps why you have joined the group. You may feel timid to say much in the beginning. Share only what feels comfortable to you. Take your time in allowing the group members to prove themselves trustworthy to you. In time, confidence will form and you can begin risking more openly about who you are and what you are wanting to add or change in your life. It won't take long for an authentic caring and trusting support to develop. You can allow yourself several sessions to observe, without sharing much, in order to build your comfort and trust.

Group therapy will assist you in knowing yourself and identifying the direction of change you may wish to make in your life. The group will give you the experience of unconditional acceptance. It is such a rewarding experience to be seen, supported, and encouraged to become your fullest self. Group members will help hold you accountable to achieving the goals you set for yourself. In addition, group will help you learn to identify your needs and communicate these directly and confidently.

A chief value of group therapy lies in the fact that you, as a participant, can come to perceive yourself through the reactions of others. You will get feedback on how you function as a member of a group. You may wish to use the group as a crucible in which to test out news way of behaving, following which you may receive feedback on how others perceived the new you. A successful group therapy results in a close-knit, interdependent group where members affirm one another and assist each another in achieving their individual growth goals.

GROUP WILL OFFER YOU:

- an experience of unconditional acceptance
- heightened awareness of your inner feelings toward yourself and others
- feedback about how others see and react to you
- clarity about directions for behavioral change
- an experience of a trustworthy environment in which change can successfully occur
- an opportunity for support, empathy, and compassion from others
- a safe place to practice new and constructive behavior
- accountability for taking steps toward your desired goals

HOW TO GET THE MOST OUT OF GROUP THERAPY

The following guidelines are set forth to assist you in making group therapy a meaningful growth experience:

1. Know why you are in the group. Keep your focus on your personal goals.

2. Be a participant, not just an observer. Growth comes from risking, and the group offers a safe place where risks are encouraged and supported.

3. Communicate with the whole group. Keep in mind that any communication about other group members that occurs outside the group setting, as during a break, should be communicated back to the group.

4. Information gained in group is confidential. Group experiences are not for sharing with family and friends outside the group. You are encouraged to share with others how you are growing, as this tends to strengthen you, but group information is to be kept in trust.

5. Every member is responsible for the interaction and the success of the group.

6. As much as possible, keep the experience in the here and now. Deal with conscious feelings, perceptions, and behaviors with a focus on what is alive in the room.

Elsbeth Martindale
CLINICAL PSYCHOLOGIST

7. Speak directly from your honest feelings and thoughts, whether it be anger, affection, or indifference. The kindest thing you can do for fellow group members is to communicate to them your honest perceptions of them.

8. Be as spontaneous and authentic as possible. Do not filter yourself for the sake of pleasing others.

9. Avoid advice giving. It may seem as though you are trying to help another, but allow others the freedom to ask for support or guidance if they desire it. Be aware of the tendency to rush in to fix others out of your own anxiety. Speak about your anxiety instead of advising others on how they can change.

10. Be aware of your changing feelings toward others and happenings within the group, both positive and negative.

11. Group is a place to watch yourself. A basic principle is, "As you are in the group, so you are in the world." Group therapy is a perfect place to increase your self-awareness and growth.

CONCLUSION

Small-group gatherings in themselves are not new. Through the centuries, they have been an integral part of spiritual traditions, learning processes, work task-forces, and general emotional support. Group therapy is designed as an instrument by which you can achieve your goals of self-realization. The group will provide for you an atmosphere in which you can gain self-understanding and find motivation to become the person you want to be.

Welcome to group!

Elsbeth Martindale
CLINICAL PSYCHOLOGIST

Group Therapy Cheat Sheet

elsbethmartindale.com/group-therapy-cheat-sheet-short

I use group therapy as a way to teach clients the powerful tools of connection and relational presence. I basically teach the stuff we were taught in our Counseling 101 courses. Remember how good it felt to master the skills of reflective listening and empathic resonance? This stuff is gold in relationships. I want my clients to know how to effectively communicate in all their important relationships. Group therapy offers a perfect environment for this kind of teaching. It gives clients the capacity to meet others in their lives in a deep and meaningful way. This handout has been useful in teaching both clients, as well as future therapists in supervision, about what to do and what to avoid in group therapy. The cheat sheet is reviewed in group therapy whenever I see the need to help participants know how to work supportively and deeply. I keep laminated copies of these sheets in my group room, along with the noted *Feelings List* and *Needs List* handouts, laminated, for clients to access anytime.

I offer a group therapy apprenticeship to psychology and counseling students. This cheat sheet is a handy tool when someone is new in leading groups. It helps newbies see what is useful to emphasize and avoid when running an effective group.

How I use this:
When new members join a group, I give a copy of this handout to everyone to review. Together we go through the do's and don'ts and discuss what each of these actions looks like and what language might be used to portray each quality. With these expectations made explicit, I can speak up and challenge clients when they are doing something disruptive in group.

Example from practice:
Michael is a fabulous storyteller. He likes to launch into detailed descriptions of events from his life in a manner which can be quite compelling. Knowing this will keep him engaging with others at a superficial level, I said to him, *"I hear you telling a story of what happened to you. I'm wondering if you'd be willing to describe for the group your experience rather than relaying just the details of what happened? It might take things to a deeper level. Want to see what happens? I can help."* I invited Michael to experiment with a new way of being seen and connecting. I posed it as an experiment so he could stay curious about what might be different if he approached things in a new (and awkward for him) manner. We then examined the effect of this more personal way of talking and asked others to give him feedback.

Elsbeth Martindale
CLINICAL PSYCHOLOGIST

Group Therapy Cheat Sheet

Group therapy is a fabulous way to learn about yourself and others. These simple suggestions will help you get the most out of your experience.

DO FOR YOURSELF

- **Assess if you are safe** - Start here, stay here, until you can create safety and keep yourself protected.

- **Speak up** for what you want and need

- **Allow yourself to be seen**, supported, and reflected.

- **Run experiments** to test your perceptions, conclusions, and limits.

- **Be honest**, real, and brave.

- **Take risks** and be vulnerable.

- **Talk about your experience** - struggles, desires, hopes, fears, doubts, pain, growing edge, how you hide, how you pretend/fake it, your judgments, your anxieties, and your injuries.

- **Be receptive** - Allow yourself to be moved and affected by others.

- **Absorb feedback** - Discover how you impact others.

DO FOR OTHERS

- **Listen deeply -** Identify feelings, core needs, beliefs, and conclusions.

- **Allow silence** - Remain present while holding connection. Don't rush.

- **Be curious** - Ask questions.

- **Reflect** what you hear, see, and feel. Show others they are seen, heard, and understood. Understanding does not mean agreement.

- **Share your experience of being impacted**.

- **Share your relatedness** - How is their experience known to you? What in you resonates with their experience? This helps undo aloneness.

- **Hold up others** - Recognize their efforts, vulnerability, honesty, courage, and strength.

- **Allow others to stay with emotion** - Help expand their capacity to stay in the present moment in a deeper way.

- Invite a **meta-perspective -** Tell others what you observe in their responses.

AVOID DOING

- **Advising, fixing, solving, educating,** or taking the expert role over someone else's experience.

- **Blaming, judging, or criticizing** yourself or others.

- **Comparing**, ranking yourself or others.

- **Defending** or trying to manage the thoughts of others.

- **Explaining** and telling others how it is. Talk about your experience instead.

- **Storytelling** about your life. Especially don't tell stories about the lives of others.

Elsbeth Martindale
CLINICAL PSYCHOLOGIST

Group Therapy Contract

elsbethmartindale.com/group-therapy-contract

This is a simple and clear contract outlining the important aspects of committing to group therapy.

How I use this:
Before clients attend group therapy, I ask them to sign this contract. When they come to the first group meeting, I will often review the contract with the whole group so all are reminded of the important aspects of their commitment to group therapy.

Example from practice:
When Donnell missed a second group session within four months, I charged her the full fee for her absence. She had gone on vacation and had given me plenty of notice. However, the group policy states that clients can miss only one session every four months without charge. Although I was sorry she had to incur this cost, I did not feel as though I was being harsh or uncaring. Donnell was aware of the policy. She had been reminded of it several times when new members joined the group. Donnell didn't fuss about the charge; she expected it. This policy relieves me from having to consider each client's special circumstance every time a client has an absence. Participants understand the value of having a cohesive group of committed members. They are willing to pay the cost if their circumstances prevent them from being present.

By the way, this is also good modeling for clients. Demonstrating clear boundaries and consequences upfront helps clients see how they, too, can set expectations in order to get the respect they want for their values.

Elsbeth Martindale
CLINICAL PSYCHOLOGIST

Group Therapy Contract

Group therapy involves several important aspects, which are listed below. Please review these and discuss any concerns with your therapist before joining the group.

BOUNDARIES

Others may ask you to reveal things about yourself in the group. It is up to you to share as much as you feel safe to share. As your trust grows in the group, you will likely feel more comfortable with disclosing. Likewise, respect the boundaries of others. Feel free to ask whatever you wish, as long as you allow others to decline to reveal. Time boundaries are also important. Be conscious of the fact that you are sharing the group time with others.

CONFIDENTIALITY

The issues that come up in group stay in the group. Feel free to share as much as you feel comfortable revealing within the group. Conversations about any group member should only take place when that group member is present. Discussions outside of group, between group members, should also be considered confidential. Breaking confidentiality will lead to automatic dismissal from the group.

COMMITMENT

You are asked to give the group a two-week notice if you plan to discontinue. This allows the group to finish any issues that may have come up with you and gives the group a chance to say good-bye.

COST

Group therapy costs $____ per 90-minute session. You are expected to attend each session. Because your insurance will not pay for missed sessions, payment of a missed group will be your responsibility. You are allowed one holiday or absence every four months without charge. Any additional absences will be charged.

I have read and can abide by these group standards.

_____   _____

Name   Date

Aggress Energy

elsbethmartindale.com/aggress-energy

"Aggress energy" is the name for the powerful life-force energy which allows humans to assert themselves and make their needs known. For example, it is the energy that leads to anger when needs are disrespected or ignored. While a necessary quality, aggress energy can be misused and turn destructive. Because I want my clients to understand how to use aggress energy constructively, I developed this handout as a tool to help them identify safe and instructive ways to explore its power.

How I use this:

This handout explains the necessity and power of aggress energy. It offers a variety of safe methods for letting the powerful emotion of anger be expressed and witnessed. I want my clients to not fear their potency but learn how to use their power for good. I might say something like the following to clients who seem to be suppressing their anger, *"It is clear you have a great deal of pent-up energy in your system. I wonder what it would be like to explore this and let this impulse be big so we can understand more about it. Would you like to try an experiment of finding a safe way to let this energy be expressed through you?"* Then I would direct them to try one of the activities on the handout in a boundaried way, either at home or in my office (for boundary information see, *Making Space for Healing Work*). In the office, I like the ripping-magazine option because it is messy but super easy to clean up.

I always encourage clients to find words that go along with the feelings in their body or the thoughts in their head. I want to encourage them to use language, if possible, as this gives some clear handles on the experience so it can be discussed or shared with others.

Example from practice:

Dawn is a frustrated mother of twin ten-year-old boys as well as a working professional. She was often overwhelmed by the demands but had been raised to be really "nice" and to put others' needs above her own. She experienced frequent migraines which were interfering with her work and parenting. She wanted more assistance at home but also wanted to support her husband's career, so she tried to "manage things on her own." It was clear Dawn was holding a lot of pain and anger. I suggested she give herself permission to demonstrate her pent-up inner feelings by tearing up some magazines. Dawn dove into this, no convincing needed. My office was full of small scraps of paper everywhere. Dawn marveled, "Wow, this is what the inside of me feels like most of the time!" We began to work on a plan for identifying and expressing her needs more clearly to get more support from her husband.

Elsbeth Martindale
CLINICAL PSYCHOLOGIST

Aggress Energy

We all know the experience of having our needs discounted or neglected. This is usually a frustrating and often painful experience. When you hold the feelings of pain and anger inside for long periods of time, these feelings often intensify and are compounded with new hurts. Releasing these feelings indiscriminately can be dangerous and damaging. Sometimes the feelings are so jumbled and confusing that it is hard to differentiate them and understand their sources. Expressing these complex feelings with aggress energy can help.

WHAT IS AGGRESS ENERGY?

Aggress energy is the life-force energy that mobilizes you to step forward on behalf of yourself, to insist your needs get the attention they deserve. Infants and children use their aggress energy quite easily. They kick and scream to let the adults around them know that they are in need of assistance. As you grew up, you may have learned to suppress your feelings and needs because of the negative consequences you received when expressing them. You may have learned to hide or disregard your feelings, causing a build-up of repressed emotions. Playing with aggress energy is a way to "make big" your inner emotions, as a way to examine and understand them more fully. Aggress energy is both passionate and assertive. It allows you to say, "I will be seen."

WAYS TO MOBILIZE AGGRESS ENERGY

There are many ways to get your aggress energy moving within your body. Be creative and thoughtful as you consider the ways that feel right to you. Look at this list and identify the actions you imagine might feel like useful ways to mobilize your own aggress energy.

- Grunt, stomp, shout - essentially, act like an animal!
- Lie on a soft surface (e.g., bed or carpeted floor) then kick and scream - give yourself permission to throw a tantrum
- Hit your bed with an object (e.g., rolling pin, tennis racket, plastic bat, etc.)
- Scream into a pillow

- Pound a pillow, mat, or bed with your hands or fists
- Rip up magazines (avoid magazines with staples) - make a big mess that is easy to clean
- Scream while driving
- Bite a towel or pillow
- Twist and wring a towel
- Kick a foam pad or pillow
- Throw old dishes in a safe place
- Write an angry letter - send it or destroy it
- Dig a hole or claw at the ground with garden tools

THEN WHAT?

When you are finished with your expression, spend some time reflecting on your experience. Write about it or talk about it with another person. Remember, the purpose in these exercises is to examine the underlying feelings and honor them by giving them form. After the feelings are expressed and visible, examine new methods for speaking up for the needs underlying the feelings so you can prevent a backlog of emotion in the future.

FOLLOW THESE RULES

1. Agree not to hurt yourself, others, or property.
2. Put time boundaries on your expression. Usually 2 - 3 minutes is sufficient.
3. Clean up what you mess up.
4. Process your experience afterward.

Elsbeth Martindale
CLINICAL PSYCHOLOGIST

Making Space for Healing Work

elsbethmartindale.com/making-space-for-healing-work

As clients get more and more invested in their emotional healing work, it can be helpful for them to create time, outside the therapy office, to continue the process they've practiced in their therapy sessions. The boundaried space of therapy, a private office with clear time limits, can be replicated by clients at home. For this to be effective, both time and space boundaries are necessary. This boundaried space gives a structure to the unconscious mind, saying this is a special time and place for healing work, and requesting the unconscious mind respect the limits of that structure. The unconscious material, which longs to be brought to resolution, is asked to hold its concerns until the boundaried time is made available. This structure provides an effective means for doing emotional work, safely, outside the therapist's office. It is not unlike the therapeutic strategy of "Worry Time" employed for worry management.

How I use this:

I will suggest clients make boundaried space outside of therapy when I see they understand and have practice at skillful empathic resonance toward the wounded parts of themselves, as demonstrated in therapy. Assessment of their ability to self-soothe and manage distressful emotions is also a prerequisite to this suggestion. I might say something such as, ***"You are making great progress at bringing a healing presence toward the wounded parts of yourself. It seems you've developed a sense of inner trust and respect toward the various aspects of yourself. Do you think you are ready to continue with this kind of work at home? Let me show you a safe and structured way to do the same sort of work you're doing in therapy in the comfort of your own home."*** I would explain the details outlined in the handout and suggest they give it a try. If they find themselves greatly uncomfortable or dis-regulated, I would insist they tuck things away and leave the work until they come back to therapy. Of course, minor emotional disturbances allow clients to practice distress tolerance and self-soothing. If clients can regulate themselves and use this boundaried structure effectively, I find this can quicken the healing work of repairing old wounds.

Example from practice:

Don was building a relationship with his wounded twelve-year-old self. His younger self had been severely neglected. I suggested Don use this handout as a guideline for how he might continue to engage with his wounded self within the limits of time and space boundaries. This structure provided the freedom, within safe limits, that Don needed.

Elsbeth Martindale
CLINICAL PSYCHOLOGIST

Making Space for Healing Work

Working on issues of healing and personal growth takes intention and commitment. Change requires action, not just reflection and contemplation. To help set a pattern of taking action, it is helpful to create a space in which you can do the work of deep listening, visioning, and inner healing. Creating this intentional space puts you in an action mode. You demonstrate to yourself your commitment to begin making things better.

Making a healing space can be enjoyable, creative, and playful. It need not be elaborate. Below are several ways to make this space with intention, investment, and action.

CREATE A SPACE BOUNDARY TO CONTAIN YOUR WORK

Use a scarf, blanket, mat, towel, or piece of fabric as your place to work. Lay this down where you desire, maybe on the couch, the floor, your bed, or the grass in the backyard. By defining a specific space, you symbolically contain the work to this area (just like a therapist's office provides a safe, contained space). You will do your work here, and when you are finished you can put the work away. Do this by carefully folding the material and setting it aside until your next work time. It often helps to name when you plan to return. Doing this keeps your emotional work safe and contained, not spilling into other parts of your life.

SET TIME BOUNDARIES FOR YOUR WORK

Usually twenty to thirty minutes is enough to get a good chunk of work accomplished. Knowing the time is limited allows you to fully invest without fear that the work will take over the rest of the day. Set a timer so you don't have to watch the clock. You can always add more boundaried time, if you need it to finish up your session.

DEFINE YOUR INTENTION

Be clear about what you wish to address as you enter your space. You may want to light a candle, burn herbs (e.g., sage, cedar, lavender, etc.), or ring a bell as a way to mark your intention to go within. You can mark your exit from your work by blowing out the candle or ringing the bell again. Remove any distractions from the space in which you are working and request that others not interrupt your time. These actions help you make your intention clear and defined.

BRING SUPPORT TO YOUR WORK

You may find that saying a prayer or invocation helps you feel guided and supported in your work. You also can bring images of loved ones, inspirational figures, totem animals, or spiritual guides to assist you as you dive into your inner world. Consider making your space beautiful by adding flowers, gentle music, scents, or other sensually pleasing objects. Actively engage in designing this part of your world to be exactly as you wish it to be. From the success of creating a safe and comfortable space in which to heal and grow, you build trust in your ability to craft a more contented world in and around you.

EXPLORE YOUR INNER WORLD

Very likely you have been talking with your therapist about the work you wish to explore or continue at home. Gently remind yourself of your intention and then dive in to the writing, talking, or feeling work you have chosen for this time. Allow yourself to go only as fast and as deep as the slowest part of you feels safe to go. When you are finished, put your blanket away and name a time (if desired) when you will return. Ask this inner world to wait patiently and nondisruptively for your return.

Collecting Stories of Injury

elsbethmartindale.com/collecting-stories-of-injury

This handout explains to clients how we can begin to address the emotional wounds in need of healing. To begin, I ask clients to write individual stories of injury on 3x5" index cards or pieces of paper. Then I request that clients let me hold these cards as we work in therapy to address these wounds.

The cards do several important things: a) they let clients know we are taking their injuries seriously; b) they break the injuries into small bites, specific stories which can be worked with separately; c) they put boundaries on the wounds that are often anxious for attention, asking this material to wait until it can be held by skillful hands; and d) they allow clients to keep adding stories as they recall them, so nothing will be overlooked. I like the metaphor of healing wounds in a prepared environment much like an operating room with clean instruments and a trained surgeon. I really want to help my clients with a history of trauma to learn a skillful approach to healing, so they can do an effective job in bringing themselves to wholeness.

How I use this:

When it is clear a client has a backlog of childhood pain, I talk about the value in bringing a healing presence to the wounds. See *Healing Old Wounds* for a full sense of the process. I might say, *"I can see you have a lot of unresolved pain and injury in your history. It will be important in our work together to address these wounds. I want to help you build the skills necessary to do an effective and thorough job in this healing process. Would you be interested and willing to collect some of these stories of injury so we have them cataloged for when we are ready to go in and heal them?"* Clients are generally very willing to do this. I will keep the stack of cards, in a client's chart, so we can work through these wounds in an organized fashion in therapy when the time is right.

Example from practice:

In the beginning of my work with Kathy, she wanted to unload the burden of her history of trauma and injury. I wanted to offer her relief but realized she would only re-traumatize herself if she were unable to meet the wounded parts of herself with full presence and skillfulness. I assessed she lacked these necessary competencies. I asked her to make cards outlining the injuries, assuring her we would eventually give the wounds the full attention they needed. Kathy seemed to appreciate the respect this approach demonstrated toward the very hurt parts of herself.

Elsbeth Martindale
CLINICAL PSYCHOLOGIST

Collecting Stories of Injury

You, like all others, probably have painful experiences from your childhood. These injuries were likely not caused with intent to harm you, yet they may have been impacting you for a long time. There is great value in identifying these stories of wounding while in therapy. A supportive therapist can validate your suffering as real and consequential. But acknowledgment from a caring witness is only the tip of what is possible by re-viewing your stories of injury. If you listen deeply to your stories of woundin, you can build the capacity to bring healing to yourself. A skillful therapist can teach you how to bring a healing presence to your wounds. Healing from the inside out is absolutely possible.

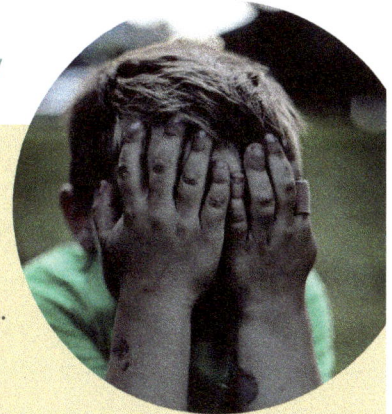

1 **COLLECT THE STORIES**

Write down several stories of wounding in an outline form (e.g., Playground, third grade, mean boy, teasing). Write each abbreviated story on a small piece of paper. These stories will become portals through which you can access your injured self in order to offer healing. Give these cards to your therapist to keep, or bring them with you to your sessions.

2 **MASTER EMPATHIC RESONANCE**

Learn the skill of empathic listening, basically reflecting the feelings of the speaker. Practice this in therapy until you are confident in your skills. You will need this skill when you encounter the wounded parts of yourself. Empathy is the salve that softens and allows emotional access. You can, of course, use this skill in your relationships with others as well as toward yourself. You must know how to hold an empathic presence before you begin encountering your past injuries.

3 **ENSURE YOUR SELF-MANAGEMENT AND SELF-SOOTHING SKILLS ARE STRONG**

Identify a variety of self-soothing strategies in case you find yourself disregulated by reviewing your history. It is not good for you to bring up traumatic injuries if you don't have practice at soothing and comforting yourself. Talk with your therapist about these practices and become skillful at rebalancing yourself when you get triggered. Only after you have practice at doing this should you attempt to do any internal work which might throw you off balance. Your therapist will help you assess if your skills for self-management are strong enough. Do not go to the wounded parts of yourself if you are not equipped. The last thing the hurting parts of you need is someone fumbling around in there without the right skills and tools. It would only cause more wounding.

4 **WITH GENTLENESS, DO THE WORK**

With your therapist's guidance, pick a story of wounding and begin the work of healing your old wounds. You'll practice empathic resonance and validation of emotions. You'll learn to stay identified with the healer aspect of yourself rather than the wounded parts. You'll learn how to find the beliefs which attached themselves to your wounds. You'll learn to filter the conclusions developed by the injured parts and challenge these. You will update your internal operating system by correcting and repairing outdated beliefs, conclusions, and judgments. Basically, you'll practice being the kind of parent you wish you had had, a protective force who can prevent and, if not prevent, help you repair emotional pain.

Yes, it's a lot of work but it is life-changing work. Life will likely continue to bump and bruise, but having done this sort of healing work will give you the confidence that you can care well for yourself no matter what comes your way. And that's a great reward.

Elsbeth Martindale
CLINICAL PSYCHOLOGIST

Healing Old Wounds

elsbethmartindale.com/healing-old-wounds

This is a summary of the kind of healing work I offer many of my clients. It is an amalgamation of the many therapeutic approaches which have been meaningful to me such as Internal Family Systems, Accelerated Experiential Dynamic Psychotherapy, Emotionally Focused Therapy, Gestalt Therapy, Voice Dialogue, Psychosynthesis, and Psychodynamic psychotherapy. It is what works for me and my clients in building a positive, supportive, and healing relationship with self. I have been following this self-designed structure for over ten years with clients, and it is hugely successful. I've organized it into a workshop and taught this to colleagues as continuing education. It has been very well received.

How I use this:

I probably do this sort of healing work with 25% of my clients. I use the approach with clients who have unresolved childhood trauma and need to come to peace with past injuries as well as with clients who have a negative relationship with themselves, those who haven't learned to be compassionate and attentive to their own needs. This process allows the practice of empathy at the very core of self, where emotional injury is held until a healing presence is available.

I would introduce this process to clients by saying something like, *"I see you have a lot of hurt and pain in you which doesn't appear to have been resolved. I would like to teach you a process for attending to the wounds of your past in a manner that heals and soothes these injuries. Are you interested in learning how to bring these wounded parts into wholeness?"* I might add the caveat that it is a process they can use over and over again, should new injuries happen or old wounds become revealed, so they can always know how to heal and set things right within themselves.

Example from practice:

Eva's history of injury was long and painful. She had tried therapy several times but found no relief from her anxious recollections. After several months of grounding work and skill building in therapy, I invited Eva to experiment with visiting the wounded girl inside. We followed the steps of *Healing Old Wounds* and Eva learned to comfort and soothe herself in a new and sustainable way. She was amazed at the relief found after meeting the injured parts of herself with tenderness and consolation. The wounded parts of herself now had companionship and support like never before.

Elsbeth Martindale
CLINICAL PSYCHOLOGIST

Healing Old Wounds

Healing yourself from your old injuries is a necessary step in self-growth and wholeness. Although you can often "survive" with your wounds still infected, you likely won't thrive unless the roots of your pain are treated.

Healing old wounds does not mean dredging up the pain of the past or re-experiencing the emotions of the wounded parts of yourself. On the contrary, this process will help you learn to explore and engage your old wounds from a place of strength and wisdom. Healing old wounds is an invitation to comfort and strengthen the wounded parts of yourself in order to live healthier and more whole.

There are some basic and essential steps in the process of healing old emotional wounds. The steps are sequential, one building on the other.

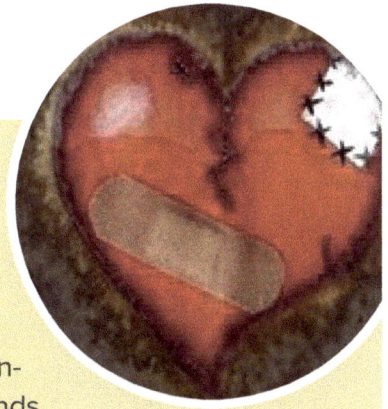

1. FIND A COMPASSIONATE WITNESS
This is often a therapist who understands the healing process. The witness must not try to fix or solve the situation but rather guide you to your own inner resources to heal and resolve the pain.

2. TELL A STORY OF WOUNDING
Tell this story as a narrative of what happened. For example, tell about who was involved, what was the setting/context, and how things turned out. Any story of wounding will serve as an entrance point. It need not be your "most painful" story in order for this work to be effective.

3. TELL ABOUT THE FEELINGS YOU FELT DURING THE INJURY
Name the variety of feelings you experienced. Often this is quite a broad range. Feelings become the portals through which your current wise self will travel to make contact with your injured self for the purpose of healing. An empathic bond between the injured self and the wise self/healer is necessary in order for the wound to be fully examined, cleaned, and brought into wholeness.

4. MAKE A CONNECTION WITH THIS WOUNDED PART
Intentional and skillful dialogue provides the means for building a healthy healing relationship with the wounded parts of yourself. Imagine your wisest self, willing to engage in conversation with this injured part. Envision the wisest and most compassionate aspects of yourself reaching in to make contact with the wounded part. Pay attention to how this injured part prefers to be met. This ability to revisit the injury and offer the presence of comfort and wisdom is the key to healing.

A simple structure is to imagine your own wise man or woman knocking on the door of the bedroom of the hurt boy or girl the night the injury occurred. Maybe the injured self will allow the wise adult to come in the room, sit on the bed, possibly even hold the child in his/her/their arms. Maybe, instead, the wounded child doesn't want to open the door to let the wise self enter. Whatever the child's response, allow his/her/their needs/desires to lead. A good rule of thumb is: "Go only as fast as the slowest part of you is willing to go."

Elsbeth Martindale
CLINICAL PSYCHOLOGIST

If the wounded child is resistant, so be it. Show respect for the injured parts of self by not imposing your agenda, being patient instead, and trust that healing is desired and will eventually be welcomed. Make a gesture of good-will if you want. You may want to slip a note under the door telling of your hope and intention. Come back again and again and wait patiently for the child to see you are trustworthy.

5. NOTICE THE EXPERIENCE AND REACTION OF THE WOUNDED PART

After a connection is made, notice if this part is open and receptive or cautious and closed. Use your imagination to see if eye contact is made. This is often a strong indication of the trust in the relationship. Remember to go slow. Trust that emotional wounds desire repair just as physical wounds naturally work toward a state of healing.

6. ESTABLISH AN EMPATHIC BOND

This bond is created when the wounded self feels seen and understood by the healer. By emotionally attuning, the wounded part begins to see that the healer "gets it," trust is established, and the wounded heart can be fully exposed. Naming the feelings experienced in the injury, asking if they are accurate, and checking if there is more to share are all important steps in establishing an empathic connection.

7. EXPLORE AND EXPOSE THE BELIEFS

Look at what beliefs formed around the wounding, once the relationship bond is clearly in place. These be-liefs are part of the coping strategies used by the wounded self to survive and protect from further injury. The problem with these beliefs is that they are often primitive, unchecked, and developed by a child. And because they provide a long-standing sense of protection, they are often carried forward and clung to without conscious regard for their usefulness in effective living. Identifying unhealthy and unhelpful beliefs is a vital step in healing the roots of the pain.

8. OFFER REPLACEMENT BELIEFS TO THE WOUNDED SELF

Healing the wound involves clearing unhealthy belief structures and replacing them with life-affirming and self-supporting constructs. These replacement beliefs must be realistic, chosen, life-enhancing, and flexible in or-der to support and sustain growth. Up until this point, the wounded part of the self may not have considered any alternative beliefs. This is an educational process only possible once the wounded self is engaged in a trusting relationship with the healer.

The wise healer may now tell the wounded part how it would have prevented the injury from occurring had he/she/they been the parent in charge at that time. The healer may also say what he/she/they would have done to soothe and comfort the injured child if the injury were not preventable. Essentially, the wise man or woman is modeling a new option; through imagination, a new experience of hope is offered to the injured self, full of possi-bility and potential. The injured aspects of the self begin to develop trust and hope that the adult in charge today (the wise man or woman) has the intentions and means to protect, prevent, and assuage pain. Presented with this alternative perspective, the wounded self is given a choice of internal drivers: to be driven by the old belief structures set up in childhood or by the new narrative of the wise healer.

9. TRANSLATE THIS HEALING INTO DAY-TO-DAY LIFE

You can begin to identify current self-defeating patterns, behaviors, and thoughts that may have developed around your woundings. You can examine the health of these patterns, the underlying assumptions and beliefs that sustain these patterns, and explore alternative perspectives, allowing for growth beyond survival.

Elsbeth Martindale
CLINICAL PSYCHOLOGIST

Part VI

Professional Advancement

The handouts in this section are for you as a professional therapist. Here you will find assessments to evaluate your own levels of stress and self-care. I've also featured tools for keeping yourself restored and invested in the hard work of providing services to those who suffer.

Stress Symptoms for Therapists...223
Trauma Exposure Response...2135
Professional Self-Care Assessment..227-231
Professional Self-Care Solutions...233-235
Buoyancy Factors for Therapists...237
Super Hard Questions..239-241
Healing Salves...243-247
Creating Handouts and Tools..249

Elsbeth Martindale
CLINICAL PSYCHOLOGIST

Stress Symptoms of Therapists

elsbethmartindale.com/stress-symptoms-of-therapists

I developed this handout listing of signs of stress for a professional self-care training I offer for therapists. Of course, these symptoms aren't unique to therapists but common signs of stress for which all therapists should be watching. Stress symptoms are early warning signs. If we ignore the messenger of stress, the symptoms often will get louder so as to be heard, often resulting in illness or emotional burn-out.

How I use this:

I encourage participants in my professional trainings to mark up this handout by identifying their symptoms. Then I suggest they check in with the list often to gauge their functioning. We want to be able to hear stress whispering before it starts screaming in our face. Remember, you are your primary tool in your work. Keep your tool sharp if you want to be most effective.

Stress Symptoms of Therapists

Stress shows up in many ways in our bodies, minds, feelings, and behaviors. Take a look at the list below. Mark the symptoms you experience in your life as a professional therapist working to heal the wounds of others.

PHYSICAL

- Headaches, migraines
- Jaw clenching or pain, gritting, grinding teeth
- Tremors, trembling of lips, hands
- Heaviness in limbs
- Neck ache, back pain, muscle spasms
- Light headedness, faintness, dizziness
- Cold or sweaty hands, feet
- Dry mouth, problems swallowing
- Frequent colds, infections, or sores
- Rashes, itching, hives, "goose bumps"
- Heartburn, stomach pain, nausea
- Constipation, diarrhea
- Difficulty breathing, sighing
- Panic, chest pain, palpitations
- Racing heart, arrhythmia
- Poor sexual desire or performance
- Constant tiredness, weakness, fatigue, exhaustion
- Impaired sleep, insomnia, nightmares, disturbing dreams

_____
_____
_____
_____

EMOTIONAL

- Anxiety, worry, guilt, nervousness
- Rumination
- Anger, frustration, hostility
- Depression, mood swings, crying, suicidal thoughts, feeling worthless
- Boredom, daydreaming, wishing you were somewhere else
- Wishing clients/patients wouldn't show up
- Loss of enjoyment, low motivation
- Frustration, irritability, edginess
- Overreaction to petty annoyances
- Loss of objectivity, over identification with clients' problems
- Distancing from clients
- Victim blaming, resistance to work with traumatic material
- Negative feelings toward clients
- Negative feelings about work, accomplishments
- Dreading opening email

_____
_____
_____

BEHAVIORAL

- Ending sessions early or arriving late
- Missing or canceling appointments
- Not returning calls for new patient inquiries
- Not taking breaks at work
- Nervous habits, fidgeting, feet tapping
- Increased number of minor accidents, increased errors
- Obsessive or compulsive behavior
- Reduced work efficiency or productivity
- Social withdrawal and isolation
- Self-medicating, overuse of street or over-the-counter drugs
- Increased or decreased appetite
- Weight gain or loss without diet
- Excessive use of caffeine
- Increased smoking, alcohol or drug use
- Excessive gambling or impulse buying
- Violating boundaries with clients
- Neglecting the needs of those you love
- Arguing, fighting, conflict with others

_____
_____
_____
_____

COGNITIVE

- Trouble learning new information, difficulty making decisions, poor concentration
- Forgetfulness, disorganization, confusion
- Feeling overloaded or overwhelmed
- Little interest in appearance, punctuality
- Intrusive thoughts
- Difficulty concentrating, racing thoughts
- Revisiting sessions after they've ended
- Images related to clients' disclosures
- "Shoulding" on yourself or others

_____
_____
_____
_____

"Symptoms are an invitation to deeper awakening." - Scott Peck

Elsbeth Martindale
CLINICAL PSYCHOLOGIST

Trauma Exposure Response

elsbethmartindale.com/trauma-exposure-response

Laura van Dernoot Lipsky has researched the effect of dealing with secondary trauma. If you work with clients who have experienced trauma, you need to know about her work. This handout, used in my professional self-care training, summarizes her work and offers recommendations for self-care.

How I use this:

We need to take this stuff seriously. None of us is immune to the effect of dealing with the trauma of others. It gets to us because it's really hard to look at over and over again. We need to know when we have had too much. Hopefully, that happens before we ourselves have a breakdown.

Elsbeth Martindale
CLINICAL PSYCHOLOGIST

Trauma Exposure Response

Laura van Dernoot Lipsky, in her book, *Trauma Stewardship: An Everyday Guide to Caring for Self While Caring for Others,* says, "A trauma exposure response occurs when external trauma becomes internal reality." To limit the negative impact of trauma in your life, it is important to recognize the following signs of trauma exposure. Put a check mark in front of those symptoms plaguing you.

___ 1) **Feeling Helpless and Hopeless** - A sense of no escape from the challenges and the challenges are too big

___ 2) **A Sense that You Can Never Do Enough** - Feeling as though no matter what you do it will never be enough

___ 3) **Hyper-Vigilance** - Finding it hard to turn off the information, get away from work, and relax and be present in your life

___ 4) **Diminished Creativity** - Loss of ideas, innovation, and creative problem-solving, like the well is dry

___ 5) **Inability to Embrace Complexity** - Black-and-white thinking, short-sighted solutions, snap judgments, and internalization of binary structures

___ 6) **Minimizing** - Thinking your struggle is "not that bad"; comparing your challenges with others who have much more, as a way to tell yourself to "buck up"

___ 7) **Chronic Exhaustion/Physical Ailments** - Hard-earned exhaustion that wears on the body, mind, and spirit

___ 8) **Inability to Listen/Deliberate Avoidance** - Hiding out, hoping not to be asked to act or do more; happens in personal life as well as at work

___ 9) **Dissociative Moments** - Spacing off, being absent from a conversation or action; the body's self-protective strategy to manage trauma

___ 10) **Sense of Persecution** - Feeling a profound lack of efficacy and that others are responsible for your well-being; lack of personal agency to effect change

___ 11) **Guilt** - You may diminish your own radiance and wellness because it is in such contrast to others' struggles; feeling bad about feeling good

___ 12) **Fear** - Fear of intense feelings, vulnerability, or potential victimization

___ 13) **Anger and Cynicism** - Directed at sources of injustice, treatment from organizations, or clients themselves; can be both cold and slow or heated and reactive

___ 14) **Inability to Empathize/Numbing** - Often as result of overwhelming incoming stimuli; like a sponge that is completely saturated and has never been wrung out

___ 15) **Addictions** - Attachment to something so strong it persists despite understanding its destructive nature; abuse or overuse of drugs, food, sex, alcohol, adrenaline

___ 16) **Grandiosity** - An inflated sense of importance related to your work; work is the center of your identity; often difficult to notice and challenging from which to step back

RECOMMENDATION

If you find yourself having a number of responses to trauma, Laura van Dernoot Lipsky suggests asking the following questions:

To **manage the effects of trauma exposure** ask: "Why am I doing what I'm doing?" and, "Is it working for me?"

Ask questions about a **value-driven life**: "Where am I putting my focus?" and "What is my plan B?"

Ask these questions to **keep daily activity intentional and choiceful:** "Am I creating a micro-culture for encouragement and account-ability? "Am I practicing compassion for self and others?" and "What can I do for large-scale systemic change?"

To **build a supportive structure** in and around yourself, she says you must:

- Move energy through - Don't hold it and allow it to freeze.
- Practice gratitude -These practices help to create balance.
- Create a daily practice of centering - Set intention for action, release, and reflection.

Elsbeth Martindale
CLINICAL PSYCHOLOGIST

Professional Self-Care Assessment

elsbethmartindale.com/professional-self-care-assessment

This assessment will help you look at seven aspects of professional self-care. Use it to evaluate your areas of strength and weakness. Fill out the pie chart at the end to get a visual representation of your self-care domains. You may be happy to know that, following this assessment, is a handout highlighting *Professional Self-Care Solutions*!

How I use this:

During professional trainings and workshops, I have participants take the test to see where they are strong and weak. Then I have them use the *Professional Self-Care Solutions* to build strength in needed areas. Remember, we are THE tool in our work! Good crafts-people take good care of their tools!

Elsbeth Martindale
CLINICAL PSYCHOLOGIST

Professional Self-Care Assessment

This assessment tool provides an overview of a variety of effective strategies to maintain self-care. Using the scale below, rate the following areas in terms of frequency.

5 = Consistently   4 = Frequently   3 = Sometimes   2 = Rarely   1 = Tried it once   0 = Never

PHYSICAL SELF-CARE

TODAY'S DATE _____

1. _____ Eat regularly (e.g., breakfast, lunch, and dinner)
2. _____ Eat healthy
3. _____ Drink enough water
4. _____ Exercise regularly
5. _____ Stretch your body
6. _____ Release body tension regularly
7. _____ Get regular medical care for prevention
8. _____ Get medical care when needed
9. _____ Take time off when needed
10. _____ Dance, swim, walk, run, play sports, or other physical activity that is aerobic and fun
11. _____ Weigh-training exercise
12. _____ Take time to be sexual—with yourself, with a partner
13. _____ Get enough sleep
14. _____ Wear clothes you like
15. _____ Take vacations
16. _____ Take day trips or mini-vacations
17. _____ Live, work, and play where you are safe
18. _____ Nurture physical comfort through massage, soaking, or other physical pampering
19. _____ Manage alcohol and substances effectively
20. _____ Take consistent time away from screens

TOTAL _____ ÷ 2 X 10 = _____%

PERSONAL SELF-CARE

1. _____ Make time for self-reflection
2. _____ Read literature unrelated to work
3. _____ Allow yourself times when you are not the expert or in charge
4. _____ Manage life stress effectively
5. _____ Invite others to know different aspects of you
6. _____ Notice your inner experience—listen to your thoughts, judgments, beliefs, attitudes, and feelings
7. _____ Attend to your needs, longings, and desires by speaking up or taking actions
8. _____ Know your values and take actions in support of them
9. _____ Seek new experiences and new learning
10. _____ Strive to reach your personal potential
11. _____ Engage in personal growth opportunities
12. _____ Practice receiving from others
13. _____ Be curious
14. _____ Know your strengths and utilize them in daily living

15. _____ Retreat from caring for others when you are depleted so you can invest in personal restoration
16. _____ Create time for relaxation and play
17. _____ Sing, dance, play, be exuberant
18. _____ Engage in a non-work hobby
19. _____ Live within your means
20. _____ Save for the future

TOTAL _____ ÷ 2 X 10 = _____%

EMOTIONAL SELF-CARE

1. _____ Be mindful of your thoughts and feelings
2. _____ Say "no" when necessary to set boundaries
3. _____ Affirm yourself and notice your successes
4. _____ Be loving with yourself and demonstrate self-compassion
5. _____ Talk kindly to yourself
6. _____ Express feelings effectively
7. _____ Manage emotions and reactions with skillfulness
8. _____ Identify comforting activities, objects, people, relationships, and places, then seek them out
9. _____ Allow yourself to cry
10. _____ Allow yourself to laugh
11. _____ Engage in activities that bring you joy
12. _____ Stay optimistic and hold a positive attitude
13. _____ Express your outrage in social action, letters and donations, marches, and protests
14. _____ Keep a reflective journal
15. _____ Reach out for help and support when needed
16. _____ Participate in psychotherapy as a client
17. _____ Communicate your needs clearly and effectively
18. _____ Speak the truth
19. _____ Practice non-attachment
20. _____ Forgive yourself and accept your imperfections

TOTAL _____ ÷ 2 X 10 = _____%

SPIRITUAL SELF-CARE

1. _____ Make time for contemplation and reflection
2. _____ Spend time with nature
3. _____ Find a spiritual connection or community
4. _____ Be open to inspiration
5. _____ Cherish your optimism and hope
6. _____ Be aware of non-material aspects of life
7. _____ Examine personal values and beliefs
8. _____ Be open to not knowing
9. _____ Identify what in meaningful to you and notice its place in your life
10. _____ Meditate, pray, practice mindfulness
11. _____ Notice and share gratitude regularly
12. _____ Contribute to causes in which you believe
13. _____ Seek inspiration (lectures, talks, music, pod-casts, etc.)
14. _____ Find comfort in the sweet territory of silence
15. _____ Learn and grow from experiences
16. _____ Adjust to change with acceptance and grace

Elsbeth Martindale
CLINICAL PSYCHOLOGIST

17. _____ Relinquish and let go of things no longer needed
18. _____ Ponder your beliefs about the afterlife
19. _____ Practice good goodbyes, facing death, and loss
20. _____ Manage guilt and regret with skillfulness

TOTAL _____ ÷ 2 X 10 = _____%

RELATIONAL SELF-CARE

1. _____ Prioritize close relationships with partner, family, children
2. _____ Create time for romance
3. _____ Maintain good boundaries so the best of you is available for those you love
4. _____ Spend time with others whose company you enjoy
5. _____ Stay in contact with important people in your life
6. _____ Attend special events of family and friends
7. _____ Share meals with friends regularly
8. _____ Reach out for connection and support
9. _____ Allow yourself to receive care and nurturing
10. _____ Allow yourself to receive affection and touch
11. _____ Be picky about the people with whom you surround yourself
12. _____ Express boundaries and expectations with skillfulness
13. _____ Resist pressure to conform, stand strong in yourself
14. _____ Play with children
15. _____ Show generosity
16. _____ Demonstrate compassion
17. _____ Forgive others and accept their imperfections
18. _____ Know your needs and be an advocate for them
19. _____ Practice clear and honest communication
20. _____ Accept others' differences without taking these personally

TOTAL _____ ÷ 2 X 10 = _____%

MENTAL/INTELLECTUAL SELF-CARE

1. _____ Read stimulating material
2. _____ Learn something new (language, skill, craft, etc.)
3. _____ Take a class or course on a topic of interest
4. _____ Travel or visit someplace new
5. _____ Strive for competence and mastery
. _____ Listen to the telling of stories
7. _____ Go to cultural events (lectures, theatre, performances)
8. _____ Allow yourself to be awe-inspired
9. _____ Play with your own ideas and write them down
10. _____ Engage in intellectually challenging connections
11. _____ Allow your mind to wander and rest
12. _____ Be creative
13. _____ Solve puzzles
14. _____ Play games
15. _____ Research a topic of interest
16. _____ Delve into current events
17. _____ Teach someone something you know
18. _____ Participate in group dialogue about important topics (book or movie group, political group, etc.)

19. _____ Listen to stimulating music
20. _____ Play a musical instrument

TOTAL _____ ÷ 2 X 10 = _____%

WORKPLACE/PROFESSIONAL SELF-CARE

1. _____ Take a break during the workday (e.g., lunch)
2. _____ Take time to chat with co-workers
3. _____ Make quiet time to complete tasks
4. _____ Identify projects or tasks that are exciting and rewarding
5. _____ Set clear limits and boundaries with your clients and colleagues
6. _____ Have clear policies and declared expectations for your clients
7. _____ Balance your caseload so that no one day, or part of a day, is "too much"
8. _____ Arrange your work space so it is comfortable and comforting
9. _____ Get regular supervision or consultation
10. _____ Negotiate for your needs (benefits, pay raise, hours)
11. _____ Take regular time away from work demands (phone, pager, email, texts)
12. _____ Have a peer support group
13. _____ Develop a non-trauma area of professional interest
14. _____ Cultivate hope and optimism for your work
15. _____ Bring creativity and joy into your work
16. _____ Move your body during breaks (stretch, walk, climb stairs, etc.)
17. _____ Refrain from owning responsibility for your clients' growth and change
18. _____ Involve yourself in your professional community (conferences, workshops)
19. _____ Participate in professional development through studying your interests
20. _____ Give back to your community and profession

TOTAL _____ ÷ 2 X 10 = _____%

SOURCE

Modified from the Self-Care Assessment in *Transforming the Pain: A Workbook on Vicarious Traumatization*. Saakvitne, Pearlman and Staff of TSI/CAAP (Norton, 1996) and the University of California, Davis, *Mind Body Wellness Challenge* http://wellnesschallenge.ucdavis.edu/index.html.

Elsbeth Martindale
CLINICAL PSYCHOLOGIST

Professional Self-Care Pie Chart

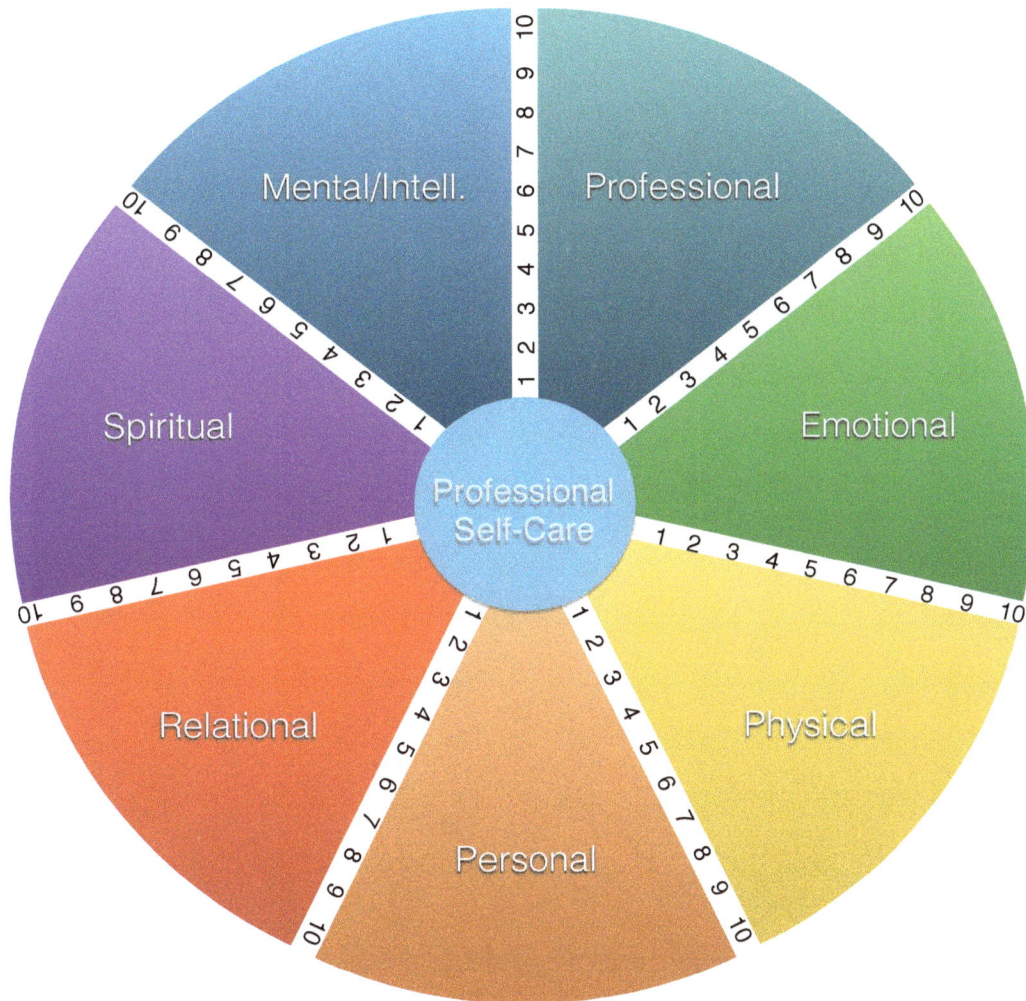

Using your scores from this assessment, make a pie-graph representation of your self-care. Notice your strengths and where you could use improvement.

Elsbeth Martindale
CLINICAL PSYCHOLOGIST

Professional Self-Care Solutions

elsbethmartindale.com/professional-self-care-solutions

Good to know the things you can do to make things better in each of the seven areas of self-care, right?

How I use this:

After participants in my professional trainings and workshops identify the areas in which they would like to improve their self-care, I have them read each of the ideas in this handout and journal about how they might incorporate new strategies for both personal and professional self-care.

Elsbeth Martindale
CLINICAL PSYCHOLOGIST

Professional Self-Care Solutions

What can you do, specifically, to make healthy changes in self-care? The possibilities are endless. Don't shoot for perfection. As in parenting, go for good enough. Find actions that will bring you joy and enhance your life. Highlight several ideas in each of the seven aspects of self-care you would be interested in adding to your life for the sake of increasing your overall sense of well-being.

PROFESSIONAL SELF-CARE

- Outsource parts of your work, e.g., billing, scheduling, office assistance, banking
- Give your practice a professional make-over, e.g., new logo, new furniture, artwork, more comfortable chair, improved privacy, better music, standing desk, wheel-chair access
- Change practice setting, e.g., new location, group practice, better view, access to outdoor space with clients
- Get natural light into your office
- Shift your practice, e.g., more variety in your day, more breaks, different start or stop time, offering walkie-talkie sessions, hire an assistant, rearrange your furniture
- Get help with practice management by hiring a business consultant, coach, financial consultant, scheduling service, answering service, office assistant
- Establish a mentor relationship
- Seek new or expanded training in theoretical orientation, practice management, or skill expansion
- Get professional support through mentoring, supervision, consultation group, peer support group, colleague assistance programs
- Set boundaries about solving others' emotional problems outside work
- If you're having a hard session, visualize a support person in the therapy room with you
- Imagine a loved one reminding you of life beyond your work

Diversify Your Practice
- Research suggests diversification is a protective factor against professional burnout (Skovholt and Jennings, 2004)
- Teach what you know to the general public through workshops, community outreach, in churches or medical clinics
- Teach to professionals - college classes (adjunct or as an academic); offer consultation or supervision
- Add multiple forms of therapy, e.g., individual therapy, couples therapy, group therapy, hypnosis, bio-feedback, pain management
- Expand your professional practice, e.g., mediation, assessment, research
- Expand your client diversity, e.g., various ages, ethnicities, diagnoses/disorders, genders, SES
- Distribute the level of distress of cases; mix struggling clients with healthier ones
- End the day with a positive activity or client
- Write professional blogs, books, handouts, research summaries
- Arrange for a job exchange for a period of time

MENTAL/INTELLECTUAL SELF-CARE

- Read a classic or intellectually stimulating books
- Attend a lecture or watch/listen to an educational show
- Build cognitive reserve (delay Alzheimer's disease) by learning a new language, learn to play a musical instrument, juggle, play chess
- Conduct periodic distress and impairment self-assessments
- Focus on prevention
- Know your limits and be realistic
- Keep realistic expectations about work
- Strive for balance
- Maintain awareness of stressors
- Take mental breaks in your day, e.g., intentionally shift focus to something good, connect with someone positive/supportive, helpful to do every ninety minutes to avoid brain fog

SPIRITUAL SELF-CARE

- Give more attention to spiritual matters through reading and discussions
- Spend more time in nature
- Participate in religious/spiritual communities
- Volunteer for service work
- Explore your values and contrast these with your time and energy investments
- Begin meditation, journaling, or other reflective practice

RELATIONAL SELF-CARE

- Deepen investment in romance and partnership
- Invest in your own psychotherapy, e.g., individual, couples, family
- Get consultation or supervision, individual or group
- Maintain connections with colleagues, e.g., mentoring, consultation or peer study group
- Organize a professional brown bag lunch
- Become active in a club, group, choir, politics, or organization
- Cultivate new friendships outside of your work and family; make a new friend every year
- Nurture meaningful relationships
- Create a celebration of life without waiting for someone to die
- Make dinner for friends

PERSONAL SELF-CARE

- Develop a creative outlet outside of your work
- Build a better relationship with yourself, e.g., engage in more positive self-talk, listen deeply to your own needs, prioritize your care
- Create more space for personal growth
- Give priority to your own mental and physical needs by developing and working toward specific goals
- Seek fresh or more emotional support
- Set limits, boundaries, by saying "no" when already saturated
- Adopt a pet—they love unconditionally
- Pamper yourself, e.g., take a walk, soak in a bath, get a massage, daydream
- Explore your world in new ways, e.g., ride your bike, walk or take public transportation instead of driving, travel
- Practice curiosity by staying engaged and amazed (increases longevity)
- Laugh more, e.g., watch or read comedies, go to see a stand-up comedy show, learn a few new jokes
- Name your gratitudes daily

Elsbeth Martindale
CLINICAL PSYCHOLOGIST

- Garden or plant a tree
- Declutter and organize your home or workplace
- Schedule a time weekly, and write it in your calendar, that is just for you and your restoration
- Turn off the TV/computer/screens and interact with people
- Limit negative media input

PHYSICAL SELF-CARE

- Attend to your health, e.g., talk with a medical professional, personal trainer, dietician
- Find fun or engaging exercise
- Get minimum of twenty minutes of physical activity at least three times each week, including aerobic, balance training, and weight-bearing exercise
- Hire a personal trainer
- Eat five to ten servings of fruits and vegetables each day or try one new vegetable each month
- Eat foods as close to their natural state as possible
- Increase whole grains (pasta, rice, flour, etc.) to replace refined grain options
- Drink plenty of water (at least two liters/day)
- Don't skip meals; eat at regular intervals
- Maintain a healthy weight—if overweight, reduce caloric intake and/or increase physical activity
- Get adequate rest—try to get seven to eight hours of sleep per night
- Take a nap during the day; best time for naps is twenty minutes between 2:00 pm and 4:00 pm
- Curb addictions and excesses; limit caffeine, sugar, nicotine, and alcohol
- Get twenty minutes of sunlight each day
- Get a standing desk or desk adjuster
- Stretch between sessions
- Take a five-minute walking break
- Relax your body regularly
- Mini-meditate by taking ten deep breaths; practice short meditations available on apps
- Hand on heart in a gesture of self-compassion
- Rub the back of your neck to stimulate the release of oxytocin at the base of your brain stem

EMOTIONAL SELF-CARE

- Accept that you're human, in need of assistance, and a work in progress
- Don't try to be perfect, to have it all, or to do it all
- Create time for play and fun
- Focus on creating rather than consuming, e.g., take an art class, cooking class, writing class; make a blog, find a new craft, build something with your hands
- Take a sabbatical for several months
- Confront the source of your negative attitudes
- Take a self-compassion break when feeling stressed, triggered, or overwhelmed
- Eat one meal each day without doing anything else

Buoyancy Factors for Therapists

elsbethmartindale.com/buoyancy-factors-for-therapists

Focusing on the rewards of practicing therapy enables us to reduce our work-related distress. This handout asks therapy practitioners to recall the reasons they entered into this work. Much like reminding ourselves why we fell in love with our partners, this act of recalling our attraction to this field can renew our sense of calling.

How I use this:

In my professional trainings and workshops, I have participants share what drew them to becoming psychotherapists. Then they journal about their journey, using this handout for inspiration.

Elsbeth Martindale
CLINICAL PSYCHOLOGIST

Buoyancy Factors for Therapists

Identify several of the things that drew you to the decision to be a therapist. Use the list of common benefits to generate your own ideas about what influenced your choice of profession. Research shows that remembering these reasons can help you reduce work-related stress. There is great value in reviewing these benefits from time to time.

- freedom
- independence
- variety of experiences
- engagement in the lives of others
- intellectual stimulation
- emotional growth
- fit with your personality

- enhanced relational skills
- personal effectiveness
- meaningful work
- public recognition
- variety of employment opportunities
- control over work environment
- comfortable income

- variety of human engagement options
- experimentation and research
- increased self-knowledge
- connection and interdependence
- autonomy
- personal healing

I chose to become a therapist for the following reasons:

_____

_____

_____

_____

_____

_____

_____

_____

_____

_____

Super Hard Questions

elsbethmartindale.com/super-hard-questions

As part of my training on professional self-care, I offer this set of questions from Jeffrey Kottler's book, *The Therapist's Workbook*. He poses some challenging questions to consider about your work as a psychotherapist. If you want a deep dive into looking at the effect of your work as a therapist on your own psyche, these questions will assist you.

How I use this:

I challenge my professional training participants to have an honest look at themselves as therapists by exploring the questions on this handout. There are many ways to play with this. Individually, you could write about the ideas in a journal, share them in discussion with a colleague, or discuss them in consultation or supervision.

I recently took on this challenge with my consultation group. Exploring these concepts together led to some deep and vulnerable conversations. Given that my consultation group has been meeting for over twenty years, we were comfortable with this level of honesty and vulnerability.

Elsbeth Martindale
CLINICAL PSYCHOLOGIST

Super Hard Questions

The following questions were borrowed directly from Jeffrey A. Kottler's *The Therapist's Workbook* and are used with his permission. Kottler defines *impairment* as, "any quality, behavior, or attitude that somehow compromises your maximum effectiveness." To get at your truths, he suggests you respond to the following questions without filtering your thoughts.

1 WHAT HAUNTS YOU?

Example: "I'm plagued by the feeling of not being good enough, that no matter how hard I try and how much I learn and grow, it still isn't enough for me to overcome my essential mediocrity."

2 IN WHAT WAYS ARE YOU NOT FULLY FUNCTIONING?

Example: "I worry too much about things I can't control. I don't sleep well some nights, while my brain runs over all the things I have to do, what to do, or should do."

3 WHAT ARE SOME ASPECTS OF YOUR LIFESTYLE THAT ARE UNHEALTHY?

Example: "I try to pack too much into each day, so I don't get as much time as I need to relax, to reflect on things, to enjoy more fully what I'm doing."

4 HOW DO YOU "MEDICATE" YOURSELF?

Example: "That's an easy one: ice cream, or when I'm 'good,' frozen yogurt. That's my comfort food, the indulgence I use instead of alcohol or drugs. I also exercise a bit too frantically to work off excess nervous energy."

5 **WHAT LIES DO YOU TELL YOURSELF?**

Example: "I say things in sessions I convince myself are to help the client, but they are really to meet my own needs or satisfy my curiosity. I tell myself that I'm in this field primarily to help people, but I acknowledge I'm also in it for the fame and glory."

6 **WHAT ARE YOU HIDING FROM?**

Example: "From stillness. If I stopped moving, stopped working so hard, stopped achieving, ceased all the distractions in my life, I'd face that person that is me, stripped from all adornments."

7 **HOW DOES YOUR NARCISSISM REVEAL ITSELF?**

Example: "In my desire to be the center of attention. In the credit I seek for being the impetus, if not the motivation, for other people's growth."

8 **WHO "GETS TO YOU" MOST, AND WHY?**

Example: "Any one from whom I can sense judgment or disapproval of me. People who are bullies. People who talk during movies. People who talk loudly on their cell phones or text in the middle of a conversation. As for the why, I think it's about feeling not in control or not valued."

9 **WHAT IS IT ABOUT THESE QUESTIONS THAT YOU FIND MOST THREATENING?**

Example: "That I'll have to face the fact that I don't know myself nearly as well as I pretend to, or think I do."

Healing Salves

elsbethmartindale.com/healing-salves

As a synthesizer and organizer, I find great joy in identifying the essential healing concepts. These salves are twenty-four common concepts discussed in therapy that bring soothing and comfort. Not every client will want to utilize each of these healing agents, but every therapist should have the ability to reach for one of these tools when needed. These concepts should be familiar to therapists and be at-the-ready to offer as a prompt for discussion or practice which will ease clients' suffering.

These salves were developed for my training I call, *"The Psychotherapy Toolkit."* The handouts can be printed, front and back, on card stock and then cut out as little jars, imitating an apothecary of healing salves. If aligned correctly, a brief description of the salve will appear on the back of each jar. I also include several blank jars upon which you can add additional soothing concepts, if you desire.

How I use this:

I use these salve "jars" in trainings, helping therapists gain clarity about key concepts that, when applied properly, can alleviate suffering and pain. When these ideas are fully understood by the therapist, they can be presented with ease to clients, over and over again. The wisdom held within each of the healing salves is invaluable in the process of effective therapy.

Elsbeth Martindale
CLINICAL PSYCHOLOGIST

Healing Salves - Front 1

These therapeutic treatment concepts can be invaluable in helping clients reach optimal soothing, healing, and wholeness. Print two-sided copies of the front and back of this handout onto card stock, lining up jars (front) with descriptions (back). Cut out the jars to create an apothecary of therapeutic healing salves. Use empty jars for your own healing concepts.

Self-Observation

Faith

Breath

Gratitude

Mindfulness

Non-Attachment

Highest Self Qualities

Truth Telling

Attend to Heart & Meaning

Be Present

Self-Compassion

Empathy

Forgiveness & Grace

Strength Awareness

Celebration

Support

Elsbeth Martindale
CLINICAL PSYCHOLOGIST

Healing Salves - Back 1

Bring your mind's focus to the things for which you feel grateful and blessed. Name these things aloud. Allow yourself to feel this appreciation in your body.

Pay attention to your breathing. Inhaling, take in what you need and desire in your life. Exhaling, release what is no longer serving you. Let your body relax.

Allow your understanding and beliefs about the way the world is organized show you how to be your best in your current circumstances. Ask for guidance.

Watch yourself with curiosity. Notice what happens inside yourself as circumstances outside you change. Gather data. Once you see yourself, you can begin to guide yourself.

Speak the truth without blame or judgement. Keep the stories you tell yourself, and others, grounded in realty without adding emotional drama.

Look at yourself with an attitude of; connection, curiosity, compassion, calm, confidence, clarity, courage and creativity. See others through this same lens.

Take action because it fits your values or calling. Do it because it's right for you, not because of the reward or outcome that may, or may not, come.

Notice where your thoughts go. Let them float by without clinging to them. Notice with curiosity the various things upon which your mind likes to land.

When facing challenges in life, always start with empathy. Show openness to the feelings and needs of those involved in the struggle, including yourself.

Demonstrate warmth and caring toward yourself, especially in times of doubt, fear, and suffering. Offer understanding, gentleness, and kindness to yourself.

Show up and be present in your life circumstances. Listen deeply to yourself, your relationships, and your environment. Sit in receptivity and openness.

Learn about your values and what matters most to you. Make decisions that resonate with and promote your values.

Reach out for connection. Ask for contact and support. Struggles are lighter when shared with others who care about you. You don't need to be alone.

Find ways to soak in the joy and goodness of life when joy is present. Feel it in your body, tell others about it, make it a big deal! Dance, sing, laugh.

Get to know your top strengths. Find ways to exercise these strengths in your day-to-day life as much as possible. Living from strengths will make you feel powerful.

Decide what kind of person you want to be when injustice, pain, and judgment are inflicted upon you (especially when self-inflicted). Choose to forgive and be gracious.

Elsbeth Martindale
CLINICAL PSYCHOLOGIST

Healing Salves - Front 2

Receptivity

Relax

Need Awareness

Relinquish-ment

Intention Setting

Reinforce Success

Nature

Pause

Elsbeth Martindale
CLINICAL PSYCHOLOGIST

Healing Salves - Back 2

Get to know the language of needs so you can identify and express your needs clearly and be a good spokesperson for yourself. Know the difference between a need & a strategy.

Notice where tension is being held in your body. Intentionally allow the muscles in this area to ease, soften, & relax. Visit your body, one area at a time, & relax.

Put yourself in a place of openness. Invite the goodness & success you desire. Be open to hearing another's perspective. Practice openhearted listening. Be porous.

Pay attention & honor your accomplishments toward your goals with a small reinforcer (e.g., smiley face or gold star, on calendar, marble in a jar, etc.). Reinforced behavior repeats.

Get clear about the direction you are heading & make a declaration of this to self & others. State your intention aloud & ground it with symbol or ritual.

Choicefully let go. Recognize natural life cycles & accept the passing or ending of things. Say your good-byes while accepting & feeling the loss.

Take time before you respond so you can act & not react. Remind yourself of your goals & intentions. Allow yourself to feel calm, clear, and directed before taking action.

Take time to be outdoors. Watch how nature allows, endured, repairs, & grows to the light. Use your animal nature to allow all your senses to absorb and be present in the natural world.

Elsbeth Martindale
CLINICAL PSYCHOLOGIST

Creating Handouts and Tools

elsbethmartindale.com/creating-handouts-and-tools

Here's a handout about making handouts! I want to encourage you to try your hand at taking your often-shared ideas and putting them into a form that can remind your clients of important concepts explored in therapy. Making this book of *Handouts for Psychotherapy* has been a way of making my work meaningful and purposeful. I want to equip my clients, and doing so brings me great joy.

How I use this:

I wrote this handout to encourage you to do something similar. Use your knowledge to teach others. Find your own creative way to pass along your wisdom.

Elsbeth Martindale
CLINICAL PSYCHOLOGIST

Creating Handouts and Tools

Doing your day-to-day work with a sense of intention, based on what you value—embues your work with purpose and meaning. You will be more invested, enthusiastic, and engaged when you have a chance to talk about issues you believe are important. What's important to you?

You are an incredible resource in the world. That's why clients come and pay you, to talk things out and discover solutions for making life more manage-able. They come to you because you have the knowledge they need. Take a moment to think about the lessons you find your-self teaching in therapy on a regular and repeated basis.

Your recurring messages, your retold illustrative stories, and your favorite theoretical chunks of wisdom speak of your professional values and your knowledge. Start noticing the themes. This is your juice, your wisdom, your best offerings to your clients. Capture these. Then make the lesson concrete by creating a handout or a kinesthetic tool that helps to convey this message. Your clients will benefit receiving your lessons with clarity, creativity, and precision. With a tool in hand, you can look for opportunities to share your honed wisdom so your clients can get the very best of your wisdom. After all, that's what they are paying you for!

When you teach your clients from a place of your known values, your message will be clear and purposeful. This gives you, as a therapist, the opportunity to be working from a place of personal passion and strongly held values, which in turn adds meaning and purpose to your work. It is one of the great blessings of being a therapist, this ability to do work which is deeply grounded in meaning.

Think about your current case load and the individuals whose lives you touch. What are the things you wish your clients knew about that would help them run their lives more successfully? Do they need to know how to stand strong in them-selves? Do they need more skills in communicating with their loved ones? Do they need to set limits on harmful relationships? There are dozens of topics we return to over and over again with our clients. Each client struggles with some common issues in a unique way, but the underlying concepts are often applicable to many.

Frequently discussed topics include:

- Boundaries
- Assertion/Self-Advocacy
- Communication Skills
- Symptom (depression, anxiety, etc.) Management
- Mindfulness
- Stress Reduction

See if you can come up with a list for yourself.

ASK YOURSELF

- What do I know to be true that many of my clients have not yet understood?
- What skills do my clients need to learn and practice in order for their lives to run more effectively?
- What lessons do I find myself repeating over and over in my sessions with clients?
- If I saw my work as a mission, what would be the goal of my investment?
- Can I create tools or handouts that summarize the important points of common lessons? A good tool will identify a problem, speak of the solution, offer clear steps to move toward the solution, and give the reader some practice options. If this can be summarized, with bullet points, on one page, with nice fonts and graphics, all the better!

Elsbeth Martindale
CLINICAL PSYCHOLOGIST

Index

HANDOUT TITLE

Aggress Energy 211

Anger Balloon 61

Assess Your Support 79

Boundary Fences..159

Buoyancy Factors for Therapists...237

Caregiving Assessment 115-123

Characteristics of Healthy Boundaries 161

Collecting Stories of Injury 215

Commitments to Better Self-Care...125

Common Values..193

Conflict in Relationships..137

Content-to-Process Shift...157

Contentment Defined...177-179

Creating Handouts and Tools...249

Crisis Management.. 53

Critic Catcher 57

Depression Pit.. 55

Differentiation vs. Fusion 131

Distress Tolerance Activities..65-67

Encouragement..163

Existential Givens...173

Feelings List.. 15

Five-Finger Communication..143

Five States of Being 43

Five Ways to Say It..151

Four Versions of Self.. 45

Gems of Wisdom..127

Getting Needs Met... 19

Give Yourself a Hand 95

Goals for Therapy - Client's View...3

Goals for Therapy - Therapist's View...5

Goodbye Letter 75

Gratitude Homework 97

Grief and Loss..71

Elsbeth Martindale
CLINICAL PSYCHOLOGIST

Grief and Loss Ritual 73

Group Therapy Cheat Sheet...207

Group Therapy Contract...209

Group Therapy Invitation 203-205

Healing Old Wounds...217-219

Healing Salves 243-247

Hidden Feelings and Needs..141

Higher Self Practice..25

Higher Self Qualities 23

Holding Yourself in a Positive Light...59

I'm Sorry vs. What I Wish I Would Have Done Differently 139

Identifying Core Values..191

Imagine Outrageous Success 187

Journal Protector 111-113

Kudos Catcher 167

Ladder of Differentiation...133

Landing Pads.. 109

Letters to Myself When I'm Depressed...69

Making Life Sweeter 99

Making Space for Healing Work...213

Managing Automatic Reactions 201

Managing Self in Conflicts...135

Meta-Perspective 195

Meta-Perspective Expanders 197

Mood Chart... 13

Motivation to Change 105

Need List 17

Noticing Automatic Reactions 199

Phone Nap Pad... 169

Playing Angels 183

Professional Self-Care Assessment...227-231

Professional Self-Care Solutions 233-235

Qualities of Wisdom 185

Questions About Existential Givens 175

Reflective Listening 145

Reflective Listening Practice...147

Reflective Shield...153-155

Resilience Building 83

Resiliency Factors 85

Restoration and Rejuvenation 81

Retroactive Learning 39

Elsbeth Martindale
CLINICAL PSYCHOLOGIST

ROLF Filter 37
Savoring the Moment 101
Self-Care 101 89
Self-Compassion Break 27
Self-Compassion Exercises 29-31
Self-Empathy Practice 35
Self-Encouragement 87
Self-Observation 11
Self-Soothing Statements 33
Self-Reinforcement 107
Selfishness Defined 91-94
Session Goals 7
Session Summary 9
Stages of Change 103
Strengths List 21
Stress Boulders 51
Stress Symptoms for Therapists 223
Super Hard Questions 239-241
The Person I Want to Become 181
Therapy Summary Sheet 47
Trauma Exposure Response 225
Trigger Fingers 199-201
Twenty-Second Hug 165
Values in Action - Strength Inventory 189
Who Owns the Problem? 149
Why Questions 41

Elsbeth Martindale
CLINICAL PSYCHOLOGIST

www.ingramcontent.com/pod-product-compliance
Lightning Source LLC
Chambersburg PA
CBHW042355030426
42336CB00030B/3492